WOMEN AND ALCOHOL
Social perspectives

Edited by Patsy Staddon

PP

First published in Great Britain in 2015 by

Policy Press
University of Bristol
1-9 Old Park Hill
Bristol
BS2 8BB
UK
t: +44 (0)117 954 5940
pp-info@bristol.ac.uk
www.policypress.co.uk

North America office:
Policy Press
c/o The University of Chicago Press
1427 East 60th Street
Chicago, IL 60637, USA
t: +1 773 702 7700
f: +1 773-702-9756
sales@press.uchicago.edu
www.press.uchicago.edu

British Library Cataloguing in Publication Data
A catalogue record for this book is available from the British Library

Library of Congress Cataloging-in-Publication Data
A catalog record for this book has been requested

ISBN 978-1-4473-1889-7 paperback
ISBN 978-1-4473-1888-0 hardcover

Cover design by Qube Design Associates, Bristol
Front cover image: istock
Printed and bound in Great Britain by by CPI Group (UK) Ltd, Croydon, CR0 4YY
Policy Press uses environmentally responsible print partners

Contents

List of figures and boxes

Figures

Box

Foreword

Elizabeth Ettorre

Women and alcohol: Social perspectives sets into motion a debate about how gendering works in the alcohol field and demonstrates that gender-sensitive knowledge production allows us to move forward effectively. Contributors choose deliberately to show how we are able to transform our epistemologies, knowledge, paradigms, discourses, notions and practices which are capable of being transformed. Contributors demonstrate that we need 'to revision' which means 'letting go of how we have seen in order to construct new perceptions' (Clarke and Olesen, 1999, p 3). *Women and alcohol: Social perspectives* underlines the need to let go of any damaging, prejudicial, unjust, outdated images and ideas about women who use or 'misuse' alcohol, in order to construct new insights and theories about women's alcohol using, gendered experiences.

Given the book's focus on a social model, it takes a revisioning stance which makes the book quite distinctive. A great effort is made to politicise the issue of women and alcohol as well as to detach this issue from a rigid, medical model. An unstated assumption embedded in all chapters is that helping to create a society which is *difference centred* and which acknowledges the marginality of women alcohol 'misusers' is needed. The consequence of this assumption is that these authors are able to cast doubt on normative beliefs and practices that are shaped in both marginalised and privileged spaces. They want to make those who hold these normative beliefs feel uncomfortable as well as to affect changes that are structural, relational and cultural.

Related to this discussion, the disease regimes of addiction and their related knowledge making practices in research and treatment have made the field resistant to gendered, classed and racialised power differentials that structure the lives of drug and alcohol using women (Campbell and Ettorre, 2011). Without knowledge of these power differentials what we need to know about women's specific needs will continue not to be known. Here, feminist or gender sensitive knowledge production is a promising route for overcoming pervasive 'epistemologies of ignorance' (Tuana, 2006) that prevails in these particular disease regimes of addiction. In the context of examining the women's health movement, Tuana (2006) contends that this resistance movement was concerned not only with the circulation of knowledge but also ignorance. Simply, behind the complex factors which account for why something is known are the practices which account for not knowing. Tuana (2006, p 2) argues that we need to have an account of the practices that resulted in a group *unlearning* what was once a realm of knowledge. These ideas helps us to confirm not only how ignorance is embedded in the realm of addiction science but also how crucial ingredients in the development of social movements are constructed and produced by both knowing and not knowing practices. Indeed, multiple 'epistemologies of ignorance' work along gendered, sexualised, classed and racialised lines to make knowing what women alcohol users and 'misusers' need difficult to discern.

In a gender-sensitive analysis of women alcohol misusers, the notion of power differentials must be placed at the core of our political struggles. *Women and alcohol: Social perspectives* does that by placing women's alcohol use, whether or not it is problematic, within the particular culture and circumstances in which these women are living. Additionally, the logic of arguing for a social model which draws initially from the social model of disability is innovative and politically sensible. It is about time that there is a solid, UK contribution to the women and alcohol field that is interdisciplinary, theoretically sound and empirically based. *Women and alcohol: Social perspectives* is just that book.

References

Campbell, N.D. and Ettorre, E. (2011) *Gendering addiction: The politics of drug treatment in a neurochemical world*, Basingstoke: Palgrave Macmillan.

Clarke, A.E. and Olesen, (1999) 'Revising, diffracting, acting', in A.E. Clarke and V.L. Olesen (eds) *Revisioning women, health and healing: Feminist, cultural and technoscience perspectives*, New York, NY: Routledge, pp 3-48.

Tuana, N. (2006) 'The speculum of ignorance: the women's health movement and epistemologies of ignorance', *Hypatia*, vol 21, no 3, pp 1-19.

Elizabeth Ettorre
Professor of Sociology (Emerita)
University of Liverpool

Notes on contributors

Marian Barnes is Emeritus Professor of Social Policy at the University of Brighton, England. She previously held a Chair in Social Research at the University of Birmingham and has also worked at the Universities of Leeds and Sheffield. She is well known for her research in user involvement and user movements, public participation, citizenship and new forms of democratic practice. In the last few years her work has focused on the ethics of care, ageing and wellbeing. Her many publications include: *Power, Participation and Political Renewal* (Policy Press, 2007, with J. Newman and H. Sullivan); *Caring and Social Justice* (Palgrave, 2005); and *Care in Everyday Life* (Policy Press, 2012).

Peter Beresford OBE is Professor of Social Policy and Director of the Centre for Citizen Participation at Brunel University London, a long-term user of mental health services and Chair of Shaping Our Lives, the national disabled people's and service users' organisation and network. He is author of *A Straight Talking Introduction To Being A Mental Health Service User* (PCCS Books, 2010).

Shane Blackman is Professor of Cultural Studies at Canterbury Christ Church University, UK. He received his PhD at the Institute of Education, University of London as an ESRC scholarship student. His publications include *Youth: Positions and Oppositions: Style, Sexuality and Schooling* (Avebury Press, 1995); *Drugs education and the National Curriculum* (Home Office, 1996); *Chilling Out: The Cultural Politics of Substance Consumption, Youth and Drug Policy* (Open University Press, 2004) and *Young People, Class and Place* (ed, with T. Shildrick and R. MacDonald (Routledge, 2010). He is an editor of the *Journal of Youth Studies* and *YOUNG: Nordic Journal of Youth Research.*

Daisy Bogg is Director of the Daisy Bogg Consultancy. She has worked within mental health and addiction services for 18 years, both for the NHS and the voluntary sector. She is a qualified social worker registered with the Health Care Professions Council and has spent a large part of her career working within integrated health and social care environments, providing and developing professional leadership and integrated service improvement.

Terry Bogg is Director of the Daisy Bogg Consultancy. Terry is a counsellor by background and has worked within voluntary sector substance misuse services in community, residential rehabilitation and prison rehabilitation contexts for the last 15 years, most recently as Director of Adult Services for a county-wide substance misuse charity/ NHS trust partnership where he was responsible for a county-wide service redesign programme.

Laura Doherty is a PhD research student in the Faculty of Arts and Humanities at Canterbury Christ Church University, UK. She was awarded a scholarship by the Department of Media, Art and Design to undertake her PhD research, which is a qualitative sociological study exploring youth drinking cultures in a London community. Her research specialisms and interests include: alcohol and drug studies, media and cultural theory, ethnography, youth studies and gender. Laura is also a co-convenor for the British Sociological Association Alcohol Study Group.

Jeff Fernandez is Nurse Consultant for alcohol and drug service provision in the London Borough of Islington. This involves audit and research on treatment systems and also providing expert advice and clinical work for the borough. He has over 20 years' experience in delivering treatment in the clinical field of substance misuse and primary care and has been prominent in the formation of the Primary Care Drug and Alcohol team established in Islington since 2007. He has a special interest in treatment pathways for women in the area of substance misuse.

Sarah Galvani is currently Professor of Social Care at Manchester Metropolitan University, UK, following six years as Assistant Director of the Tilda Goldberg Centre for Social Work and Social Care at The University of Bedfordshire. She is a registered social worker, with a background in mental health, homelessness, and substance use in both the UK and the US. She has also worked for the Probation Service and with women experiencing domestic abuse.

Lydia Lewis is a post-doctoral research fellow in the Institute of Education at the University of Wolverhampton, UK. Her academic work has involved critical, applied sociological research across the areas of mental health and education. She has previously held research posts in Sociology and Education at the Universities of Birmingham, Leicester and Warwick and a lecturing post in Education Studies (Sociology and Inclusion) at Bath Spa University. She founded, and for

10 years (until September 2014) co-convened, the British Sociological Association Mental Health Study Group.

Alison Mackiewicz is a teaching fellow in the Psychology Department at Aberystwyth University. Alison's research interests are in the areas of identity, such as gender, embodiment and culture; consumerism, including marketing and consumer cultures; alcohol (and drug) use; and qualitative research methodology. As part of her PhD research she explored how femininities are taken up, reworked and resisted within the dominant discourses of agency and consumer-oriented subjectivity; intersecting with issues of sexuality, gender, power and class, her research documented the lived-experience of women's negotiations of sexiness and alcohol consumption in the twenty-first century.

Rachel McErlain is a research assistant and part-time lecturer in Social Policy at Anglia Ruskin University, Cambridge, UK. Her doctoral studies explore the regulation of women's drinking through alcohol regulation campaigns in the mid-19th century, with a comparative analysis of 21st-century campaign materials. The work explores themes of moral regulation, post-structuralist feminism and social history.

Robert McPherson is a PhD research student in the Department of Media, Art and Design at Canterbury Christ Church University, UK. He teaches Sociology, Media and Cultural Studies, Youth Studies, Popular Music and Alcohol Studies. His doctoral research is an ethnographic study on a city-centre pub, studying young people's alcohol consumption within the Canterbury night-time economy.

Lyndsey Moon is a Chartered Psychologist (Counselling) who worked for over 20 years in the NHS and voluntary sector with people who have alcohol and drug-related issues. She is an Associate Fellow at the University of Warwick, UK.

Laura Serrant is Professor of Community and Public Health Nursing and currently Director of Research and Enterprise in the Centre for Health and Social Care Improvement (CHSCI), School of Health and Wellbeing at the University of Wolverhampton, UK. She is Visiting Professor at the University of the West Indies and the Faculty of Health Sciences at Dominica State College. Her research interests relate to disparities in community and public health, specifically health of Caribbean communities. She was editor of *Nurse Researcher Journal* for four years and in 2010 was appointed as member of the Prime Minister's Commission for the Review of Nursing and Midwifery by the Department of Health.

Patsy Staddon is founder and Chair of Women's Independent Alcohol Support in Bristol, UK, which runs small women's groups and offers consultancy and strategy pathways. She is an Honorary Research Fellow at the University of Wolverhampton and a Visiting Fellow at Plymouth University. She also founded and convened the British Sociological Society's Alcohol Study Group and is a Trustee for the Social Perspectives Network of Mental Health. Her personal experience of severe alcohol dependence over many years of her life has informed her approach to the sociology of women's alcohol use.

Christine Toft has worked in social care for over 15 years, starting her career at the NSPCC working with families affected by alcohol problems, then as a county domestic abuse lead, giving her the opportunity to work at a strategic level to develop partnerships with alcohol domestic abuse and families. She went on to work for Alcohol Concern on the Embrace project aimed at developing practice in alcohol services nationally. On a personal level, nine years ago Christine developed a drinking problem to cope with her own struggle with an abusive relationship from which she successfully recovered. In the past four years she has worked as a private psychotherapist specialising in women, alcohol and domestic abuse. She has continued to train and supervise other professionals to improve practice in these key areas.

Lizzie Ward is a senior research fellow in the School of Applied Social Science, University of Brighton, UK. Prior to returning to higher education, she worked for over 12 years in the voluntary sector.

Introduction

Patsy Staddon

Why this book is needed

The central theme of this book is that issues relating to alcohol 'misuse' can only properly be understood within their social and environmental context. Such an understanding, often termed a 'social model' (Beresford, 2002; Beresford, Chapter One, this volume), will inevitably include a political perspective, since looking sociologically involves looking critically at the connections between the social and personal elements in our lives (Mills, 1959) rather than allowing a narrower understanding, such as a purely medical interpretation, to predominate (Oakley, 2007). Applying these perspectives will have implications for how alcohol issues are perceived and consequently dealt with, both socially and medically. In particular, the central significance of gender needs to be addressed urgently.

The main aims of the book

One of the aims of the book is to illustrate the ways in which women's alcohol use has been depicted and sometimes distorted by the media, so that something of a moral panic (Cohen, 1972) has been generated (Plant and Plant, 2006). In contrast, the writers of the following chapters each in different ways show that women's alcohol use, whether or not it is problematic, is related to the particular culture and circumstances in which they are living. The book as a whole demonstrates the many ways in which women cope with varying drinking cultures. In other words, alcohol has a different significance, and is often used in different ways and for different purposes, among for example Black Caribbean women and among many lesbian women. It also often appears to offer a way of coping with living with domestic violence, and may help women in dealing with the aftermath of past abuse and other traumas.

The book also considers barriers to the development of a social model, particularly in relation to alcohol treatment. Such barriers include public (mis)understanding of 'alcoholism' as both immorality and illness. Such an understanding serves a social function in that 'wrongdoers' may be labelled and marginalised so that society as a whole may feel it is 'not like that' itself (Becker, 1963; Goffman, 1963; Staddon, 2005; Ettorre, 2007). This approach is, however, ultimately self-defeating, emphasising deviance (Merton, 1968) and resulting in alienation (Staddon, 2005; Ettorre, 2007) and social dissonance (Wearing et al, 1994). Also, most of the resultant sanctions fall more heavily on women than on men, whose behaviour is more heavily monitored and criticised while carrying high moral expectations (Ettorre, 1992, 1997; Waterson, 2000).

Third, the book aims to demonstrate that as well as there being many ways in which women use alcohol, there are also many ways in which they recover from its problematic use.

Background to the book

In the United Kingdom (UK), gender has not until recently been seen as a relevant factor either in research into alcohol issues, or in treatment, whether in respect of why people drink, what sometimes makes it a problem or how such a problem should be addressed (Ettorre, 1997; Waterson, 2000; Raine, 2001). This omission may have been partially due to women having been reluctant to admit that they had a problem, for fear of disgrace. One of the earliest texts about women's drinking is the collection of essays entitled *Alcohol problems in women* (Wilsnack and Beckman, 1984) where attention was drawn to such gendered factors as women's iconic role (Fillmore, 1984) and the difficulties experienced (although not always recorded) by early researchers in the field in finding enough women who acknowledged that they drank enough to be included in their configurations. More than a decade later, the history of women's alcohol use was well documented by Plant (1997), showing important differences in the way that women use and have used alcohol, the different consequences for them physically and psychologically, the different construction put upon that use by the rest of society, and their different experiences in treatment and in Alcoholics Anonymous (AA).

Sociological understandings of women's alcohol use were markedly increased by Ettorre's two publications, *Women and substance use* (1992) and *Women and alcohol: A private pleasure or a public problem?* (1997). Measham and Brain (2005) were to acknowledge the pressure on women of social factors, making it more likely that they would drink heavily, a finding confirmed by Van Wersh and Walker (2009) and by Staddon (2009, 2011a, 2011b, 2012, 2013a, 2013b). At the same time, the right to pleasure, to being free, at least briefly, from social pressures, was being discussed by Ettorre (1997, 2007), as was alcohol's role in being the key to various spheres of adulthood and competence (Staddon, 2005; Sulkunen, 2007).

This background has led in the UK to an increasing awareness of the relevance of gender when looking at a policy of alcohol 'treatment', and of considering potentially discriminatory characteristics such as race, ethnicity, faith and disability in relation to alcohol use. This kind of understanding, focusing on the effects of social organisations and structures upon women (and men), illuminates many of the reasons for ill-health and addiction to substances. In other words, a social model of alcohol use (Staddon, 2013b) involves looking differently at sources of distress; seeking them not so much in the individual psyche as in the very fabric of our society itself (Wilkinson and Pickett, 2009).

The politics of women and alcohol

As I have noted elsewhere (Staddon, 2012, 2013a), survivors of alcohol misuse and of the public and the medical response, have yet to develop their critical voice in the way that other mental health survivors have done. It is crucial that they become able to challenge the view of themselves, even when they no longer use alcohol, as being a form of social outcast, untrustworthy, immoral and ill (Staddon, 2013b). This social injustice and oppression is an important theme within the book and leads writers to express the need to create a different environment for recovery from alcohol problems, whereby women may recover self-respect and establish social capital.

Clearly '[t]he questions drink poses are about much more than drink alone' (Nicholls, 2009, p 261). A social model of alcohol use and misuse quickly connects with the politics of inequality. The book's contributors refer to a form of structural violence, engendered by inequality and lack of opportunity. I have written elsewhere of the political significance of such a model to women's alcohol issues, how they are perceived and how they are 'treated' (Staddon, 2013b).

Areas of women's alcohol use that the book has not been able to include, for reasons of length, are those of pregnancy and of disability, although they are areas that the editor would like to explore in the future. The sociology of women's 'wellbeing' will find there some interesting debates around freedom of choice and the nature of health.

The recovery approach and treatment

There has previously been little solid evidence as to how people recover, how successfully they recover or what recovery means for them (White,

2008). 'The recovery approach originated within the US Civil Rights Movement (Chamberlin, 1978; Davidson et al, 2010). It focuses on maintaining quality of life with or without ongoing symptoms, and is defined by the person experiencing a mental health problem' (National Involvement Policy, 2014, p 4). Rather than just treating or managing symptoms, this model emphasises building the resilience of people with mental health problems through hope, acceptance, control, basic needs and meaningful activity[1] (National Involvement Partnership, 2014, p 1).

Concepts of recovery, or even of wellness, may, however, run the risk of material inequalities being ignored (Friedli, 2009; Beresford, Chapter One, this volume) and both terms have perhaps become overloaded with meaning and significance. A further danger that is present in this wellbeing agenda is that of de-politicisation – the acceptance that alcoholism is an individual problem, rather than a condition largely produced by social factors and exacerbated by a range of inequalities. The concept could support such ideas as the deserving and non-deserving sick (Shaw, 2004) and the blaming of people for their own disadvantage. Nonetheless, they support, at least in theory, a holistic way of seeing life's journey, learning from each other while making our own decisions and running our own lives (Wright, 2012). They may also challenge traditional ways of understanding addiction (White, 2008) and could promote social change.

In this book, as well as elsewhere (Women's Health Council of Ireland, 2005; Neville and Henrickson, 2005; Eliason, 2006; Niv and Hser, 2007; Women's Resource Centre, 2007), women using alcohol are shown to have different treatment needs from those of men. These differences may not be understood by doctors, who are frequently described as lacking in the skills they need to listen to patients talking about alcohol issues, and also lacking information about appropriate and holistic sources of help (Beresford, Chapter One, this volume). General practitioners may try to avoid treating patients for whom they have some sort of distaste based on 'moral grounds' and whom they experience as 'difficult' or 'dirty work', that is, work that doctors have to do, but find unpleasant and demeaning (Shaw, 2004). Another term in use is 'heart-sink patients'. For example, it has been suggested that medical training is inadequate in preparing doctors to be the moral arbiters that both doctors and patients frequently expect (Crome, 1999; Abbasi, 2004; International Centre for Drug Policy, 2007). Doctors face a dilemma of training versus experience; enculturation in a sexist and pejorative ethos, versus lived experience of human distress and injustice (as quoted in Staddon, 2009, p 213).

Commissioned treatment is meant to be based on good practice and satisfactory outcomes, but there is disagreement about the nature of both. Alcohol treatment has been criticised by some experts for some time; for example:

> There is a mismatch in the United Kingdom between the available evidence and the evidence selected to inform policy. The health-care agenda has been largely replaced by a public order agenda as has happened for illicit drugs. The current preoccupation with binge drinking and its companion responsible drinking release the government and the industry from imposing limits on the availability of alcohol: treatment will be directed at binge drinking individuals. (Raistrick, 2005, p 1213)

Treatment effectiveness is hard to measure, since patients and clients often do not return to report 'success' or 'failure'. Safe care implies provision which accepts that mutual aid messages reinforce notions of powerlessness. However, a call for change in addiction treatment is beginning to be heard (White, 2008), as the chapters of this book demonstrate.

Summary of the book

The book opens with an explanation of a 'social model', and its applicability to issues of women's alcohol use, written by Professor Peter Beresford.

The chapters in this book fall into three main sections:

- **Part One: The social construction of women's alcohol use** shows the ways that women's alcohol use and misuse are currently misunderstood and misrepresented. It centres the public perception of women's use and misuse of alcohol, and the inferences which might be drawn, before developing policy and practice.
- **Part Two: Different women, different perspectives**, explores the social factors affecting women within different cultures. It considers the different meaning that alcohol may have for, respectively, older women, women suffering domestic abuse, women with a different ethnic and cultural background, and lesbian women.
- **Part Three: A social approach to women's alcohol treatment**, considers ways in which a social model may inform service provision

offered to women who see themselves as having an alcohol problem and might lead to different kinds of treatment.

Finally, the book concludes with a summing up of what the application of a social model may mean for women with alcohol issues

Part One: The social construction of women's alcohol use

Beresford's opening chapter explains that the 'social model' could be seen to have begun with the disability movement, which showed the concept of 'disability' to lie in a society that is constructed for the convenience and benefit of non-disabled people. He points out that humans keep order by moralising and telling special stories that keep people in their 'proper place'.

Discriminatory attitudes to conditions that are seen as 'difficult', ugly or shaming are themselves disabling. This understanding illuminates how mental health issues are seen. Stigma may affect wellbeing and recovery. It may be difficult to achieve a sense of self-worth or, often, to obtain employment. These responses to, for example, personality disorders, an inability to respond 'normally' (for example in those affected by autism), facial deformity, obesity and so on make it difficult for the person to make changes or to move forward in any way at all. There are similarities in many people's response to drunkenness (especially when evidenced by women and/or older people).

The following four chapters, by McErlain, Blackman et al, Mackiewicz and Galvani with Toft, show the ways in which women's alcohol use and misuse are currently misunderstood and misrepresented, and the inferences that should be drawn before developing considerations of policy and practice.

McErlain (Chapter Two) demonstrates that a focus on women's alcohol use, and panicked responses to 'binge drinking' (Plant, 1997), has historical roots, and is not a new phenomenon. Is this the latest 'moral panic'? (Nicholls, 2009, p 251; Blackman et al, Chapter Three; Mackiewicz, Chapter Four). Women are seen to be controlled by moral regulation, well documented in public responses to their using alcohol, in media representations of failing to behave 'properly' and in treatment. McErlain suggests that the effect, and perhaps the purpose, of the message of 'relapse is always possible' is 'the use of shame as a device for promoting normative feminine drinking'. She concludes that 'Victorian gender values endure in the moral regulation of women's drinking'.

The simplistic picture of women's drinking portrayed in the press is challenged by both Blackman et al (Chapter Three) and Mackiewicz (Chapter Four) while they show the many ways in which women – frequently young women – have succeeded in negotiating and managing the difficulties presented by an alcohol-focused culture (Mackiewicz, Chapter Four). These ideas are taken up again later in the book, particularly by Moon.

The chapter by Galvani with Toft (Chapter Five) provides a disturbing account of the role of domestic violence as a further agent of women's social control, and its links with their alcohol use, and confirms that women who get drunk are seen as deserving of abuse, in a way very similar to that described by McErlain (Chapter Two). Domestic abuse is gendered and shrouded in shame, and is one of the major factors operating when women develop drinking problems. Abused women often feel shame and hence have a need to recover self-respect and establish social capital, which may or may not involve abstention from alcohol. An additional complication is that domestic violence services may often respond ambivalently to women with drinking problems, and in particular might be unable to offer them space in refuge accommodation, due to safety concerns.

Part Two: Different women, different perspectives

The social factors underlying women's drinking continue to be explored in the four chapters in Part Two, which consider the way that alcohol has different meanings for particular individuals as well as within different communities. Women's narratives strongly inform these chapters.

Barnes and Ward (Chapter Six) explore issues emerging from their research on older people. They confirm that for this group, too, there appears to be a greater awareness among the women themselves of the pleasures and the risks of alcohol, and a more nuanced understanding of how they are using it, than is shown by the media and by public coverage in general (see also Serrant, Chapter Seven; Moon and Staddon, Chapter Eight; Moon, Chapter Nine). This chapter does, however, speak clearly of the negative effects of, for example, loneliness, although for most of those interviewed their alcohol use was not seen as problematic.

Serrant presents a political, feminist approach in her chapter on the drinking of Black Caribbean women in the UK. She notes that professionals are affected by public fears and misunderstandings about women's alcohol use, and looks at how the 'shared assumptions of groups of professionals can become enshrined in academia and training'. There are issues of inequality, but also of confusion: inaccurate information often leads to bad recommendations. Preconceptions as to the meaning of alcohol use in different ethnic communities have often detracted from an understanding of its use overall. In addition, as Galvani with Toft also observe, alcohol treatment is a male domain.

Moon and Staddon (Chapter Eight), writing about lesbian women's drinking, see alcohol as having the potential to have a positive role in some circumstances. For example, it can be a celebration of independence. 'Rebellion may be crucial for women growing up in a social straitjacket.' The support and friendship of peers is seen as crucial to life with or without alcohol.

Part Two concludes with Chapter Nine, a powerful auto-ethnographic account from Moon with a critical humanist perspective. Moon, like Staddon, has experienced severe alcohol issues, and she successfully demonstrates the effects of the 'structural violence' cited earlier in the Introduction and later referred to by Lewis in Chapter Eleven. She attempts to disentangle the underlying historical scripts and issues that influence decisions to use alcohol and inserts an auto-ethnographic account of her life and relationship to using and 'misusing' alcohol. Others too have cited women's alcohol 'abuse' as a logical response to social structures that are disabling and unjust (Smart, 1976; Jacobson, 1986; Hendry, 1994; Raine, 2001; Ettorre, 2007).

In all cases these four writers note the relevance and meaning of alcohol use within the social environment, friendship networks and family relationships. Where these are lacking, alcohol frequently fills the gap no longer filled by family and friends (also see Staddon, Chapter Twelve). These chapters emphasise the inadequacy of stereotyped and outdated public 'knowledge' about alcohol issues, and of many treatment systems, and suggest new ways of understanding why and how different 'groups' of women drink.

Part Three: A social approach to women's alcohol treatment

In Part Three, the authors each consider ways in which a social model can inform service provision and support for women who see themselves as having an alcohol problem. Ways in which these changes might be effected, whether within or outside existing National Health Service (NHS) structures, are considered, with the focus being on the impact of social context and gendered experiences.

Fernandez (Chapter Ten), while working within the NHS as a nurse consultant for substance misuse, has developed ways of providing a safe environment for women to deal with their substance use issues, primarily with a focus on abstinence, but in an environment they are used to, and within easy access of their homes.

Lewis (Chapter Eleven), like Galvani with Toft in Chapter Five, notes the relevance of domestic abuse in gendered experiences of mental health and alcohol use. Her focus group work has implications for policy and provisioning in the areas of mental health and adult community learning. She describes how feminist models of adult learning may promote the accumulation of social and emotional capital, perhaps 'of a less tangible nature residing in the cultural or symbolic realm – the relational dimension of social justice (Gewirtz, 2001) encompassing matters of identity and social recognition'.

Staddon (Chapter Twelve) goes on to report on service user controlled research, aimed at finding out from women themselves what kind of alcohol provision they would like and would support. From this, it seems that the priorities might be peer support, women-only provision and in particular a helpline where women who had themselves experienced issues with alcohol would provide non-judgemental support and – when requested – information about appropriate services.

Finally, Bogg with Bogg (Chapter Thirteen) consider the importance of building recovery capital, so that any gains made in the treatment process may be sustained. They refer to the unfortunate predominance in treatment of medical approaches that inadequately or totally fail to deal with 'issues of self-esteem, identity and the impact of role expectations'. They do see a development in treatment services of a more holistic approach, but conclude that medical approaches in women's alcohol treatment remain predominant and are not effective in the longer term. Drawing on evidence both within and outside the UK, they too see the development of social approaches to be crucial to an improved, successful treatment policy for women.

Conclusion

The book concludes with a summary of the most important lessons to be learnt from its chapters as to how a social model of women's alcohol use may lead to an increased understanding, an informed policy and a practice that includes a heightened awareness of domestic abuse, of the different needs of women and other marginalised groups and the need to build self-esteem and recovery skills, both within the treatment services and within the community as a whole. It also considers the extent to which the political and social factors described may assist in the development of new understandings and new approaches

The book is concerned to emphasise meaningful and sustained interpretations of recovery, involving 'an empathic and informed response' (Galvani, Chapter Five), social learning (Moon, Chapter Nine), openness to a wide variety of 'solutions' (Moon and Staddon, Chapter Eight), a suitable and safe environment (Fernandez, Chapter Ten), education (Lewis, Chapter Eleven), service user controlled independent support (Staddon, Chapter Twelve) and a process of building recovery capital (Bogg with Bogg, Chapter Thirteen). The likelihood of the methods described here is that they will promote social change, and in that sense, the book is both practical and political.

Note

[1] http://rethink.org/living-with-mental-illness/recovery/what-is-recovery

References

Abbasi, K. (2004) 'The four pillars of global academic medicine', *British Medical Journal*, 329 (7469) pp 752-53, http://www.bmj.com/cgi/content/full/329/7469/0-g [Accessed 19 February 2009]

Becker, H.S. (1963) *Outsiders: Studies in the sociology of deviance*, New York, NY: The Free Press, 1966.

Beresford, P. (2002) 'Thinking about "mental health": towards a social model', *Journal of Mental Health*, vol 11, no 6, pp 581-584.

Chamberlin, J. (1978) *On our own: Patient-controlled alternatives to the mental health system*, New York: Haworth Press.

Cohen, S. (1972) *Folk devils and moral panics*, Abingdon: Routledge, 2002.

Crome, I.B. (1999) 'The trouble with training: Substance misuse education in British medical schools revisited. What are the issues?', *Drugs: education, prevention and policy*, vol 6, no 1, pp 111-13.

Davidson, L., Rakfeldt, J. and Strauss, J. (2010) *The roots of the recovery movement in psychiatry: Lessons learned*, Chichester: John Wiley & Sons Ltd.

Eliason, M.J. (2006) 'Are therapeutic communities therapeutic for women?', *Substance Abuse Treatment, Prevention, and Policy*, vol 1, no 3, www.substanceabusepolicy.com/content/1/1/3

Ettorre, E. (1992) *Women and substance use*, New Brunswick, NJ: Rutgers University Press.

Ettorre, E. (1997) *Women and alcohol: A private pleasure or a public problem?*, London: The Women's Press.
Ettorre, E. (2007) *Revisioning women and drug use: Gender, power and the body*, Basingstoke: Palgrave MacMillan.
Fillmore, K.M. (1984) 'When angels fall: women's drinking as cultural preoccupation and as reality', in Wilsnack, S.C. and Beckman, L.J. (ed) *Alcohol problems in women*, The Guilford Alcohol Studies Series, New York, NY: Guilford Press.
Friedli, L. (2009) *Mental health, resilience and inequalities*, www.euro.who.int/__data/assets/pdf_ file/0012/100821/E92227.pdf
Gewirtz, S. (2001) 'Rethinking social justice: A conceptual analysis', in J. Demaine (ed), *Sociology of education today*, Basingstoke: Palgrave, pp 49-64.
Goffman, E. (1963) *Stigma: Notes on the management of spoiled identity*, Harmondsworth: Penguin Books, 1968.
Hendry, J. (1994) 'Drinking and gender in Japan,' in McDonald, M. (ed) *Gender, drink and drugs: Cross-cultural perspectives on women*, vol 10, Oxford: Berg, 1997.
International Centre for Drug Policy (2007) *Substance misuse in the Undergraduate Medical Curriculum. A United Kingdom Medical Schools' collaborative programme*, The International Centre for Drug Policy (ICDP), www.sgul.ac.uk/depts/icdp/our-programmes/substance-misuse-in-the-undergraduate-medical-curriculum/substance-misuse-in-the-undergraduate-medical-curriculum_home.cfm (accessed 18 March 2009).
Jacobson, B. (1986) *Beating the ladykillers: Women and smoking*, London: Pluto Press, 1988.
Measham, F. and Brain, K. (2005) 'Binge drinking, British alcohol policy and the new culture of intoxication', *Crime, Media, Culture*, vol 1, no 3, pp 262-283.
Merton, R.K. (1968) *Social theory and social structure*, New York, NY: Free Press.
Mills, C.W. (1959) *The sociological imagination*. New York, NY: Oxford University Press.
National Involvement Partnership (2014) *The language of mental wellbeing*, www.nsun.org.uk/assets/downloadableFiles/networkspringsummer2014FORWEB2.pdf
Neville, S. and Henrickson, M. (2005) 'Perceptions of lesbian, gay and bisexual people of primary healthcare services', *Journal of Advanced Nursing*, vol 55, no 4, pp 407-415.
Nicholls, J. (2009) *The politics of alcohol: A history of the drink question in England*, Manchester: Manchester University Press.

Niv, N. and Hser, Y. (2007) 'Women-only and mixed-sex treatment programmes: service needs, utilizations and outcomes', *Drug and Alcohol Dependence*, vol 87, no 2-3, pp 194-201.

Oakley, A. (2007) *Fracture: Adventures of a broken body*, Bristol: Policy Press.

Plant, M.L. (1997) *Women and alcohol: Contemporary and historical perspectives*, London: Free Association Books.

Plant, M.L. and Plant, M. (2006) *Binge Britain: Alcohol and the national response*, Oxford: Oxford University Press.

Raine, P. (2001) *Women's perspectives on drugs and alcohol: The vicious circle*, Aldershot: Ashgate.

Raistrick, D. (2005) 'The United Kingdom: alcohol today', *Addiction* vol 100, no 9, pp 1212-14.

Shaw, I. (2004) 'Doctors, "dirty work" patients and "revolving doors"', *Qualitative Health Research*, vol 14, no 8, pp 1032-1045.

Smart, C. (1976) *Women, crime and criminology*, London: Routledge & Kegan Paul.

Staddon, P. (2005) 'Labelling out: the personal account of an ex-alcoholic lesbian feminist', in Ettorre, E. (ed) *Making lesbians visible in the substance use field*, New York, NY: The Haworth Press.

Staddon, P. (2009) '"Making whoopee"? An exploration of understandings and responses around women's alcohol use', PhD thesis, Plymouth University, http://hdl.handle.net/10026.1/415.

Staddon, P. (2011a) 'Service user led research in the NHS: wasting our time?' in Barnes, M. and Cotterell, P. (eds) *Critical perspectives on user involvement*, Cambridge: Polity Press.

Staddon, P. (2011b) 'Many roads to recovery', *The Big Issue*, 10 January.

Staddon, P. (2012) 'No blame, no shame: towards a social model of alcohol dependency – a story from emancipatory research', in Carr, S. and Beresford, P. (eds) *Social care, service users and user involvement: Building on research*, London: Jessica Kingsley Publishers.

Staddon, P. (2013a) Report for Folk.us: *Improving support for women with alcohol issues*, www.wiaswomen.org.uk

Staddon, P. (2013b) 'Theorising a social model of "alcoholism": service users who misbehave', in Staddon, P. (ed) *Mental health service users in research: A critical sociological perspective*, Bristol: Policy Press.

Sulkunen, P. (2007) 'Images of addiction: representations of addictions in films', *Addiction Research and Theory*, vol 15, no 6, pp 543-559.

Van Wersch, A. and Walker, W. (2009) 'Binge-drinking in Britain as a social and cultural phenomenon: the development of a grounded theoretical model', *Journal of Health Psychology*, vol 14, no 1, pp 124-134.

Waterson, J. (2000) *Women and alcohol in social context: Mother's ruin revisited*, Basingstoke: Palgrave.

Wearing, B., Wearing, S. and Kelly, K. (1994) 'Adolescent women, identity and smoking: leisure as resistance', *Sociology of Health and Illness*, vol 16, no 5, pp 626-643.

White, W.L. (2008) *Recovery management and recovery-oriented systems of care: Scientific rationale and promising practices*, Northeast Addiction Technology Transfer Center, Great Lakes Addiction Technology Transfer Center, Philadelphia Department of Behavioral Health/Mental Retardation Services.

Wilkinson, R. and Pickett, K. (2009) *The spirit level: Why more equal societies almost always do better*, London: Allen Lane.

Wilsnack, S.C. and Beckman, L.J. (ed) (1984) *Alcohol problems in women*, New York, NY: Guilford Press.

Women's Health Council of Ireland (2005) *Women's mental health: Promoting a gendered approach to policy and service provision*, Conference Proceedings 2005, Dublin: Desire Publications.

Women's Resource Centre (2007) *Why women-only? The value and benefits of by women, for women services*, London: Women's Resource Centre.

Wright, N. (2012) 'The politics of recovery in mental health: a left libertarian policy analysis', *The Institute of Mental Health Blog*, http://imhblog.wordpress.com/2012/05/06/dr-nicola-wright-the-politics-of-recovery-in-mental-health-a-left-libertarian-policy-analysis/

Part One
The social construction of women's alcohol use

ONE

The context for a social model of alcohol use

Peter Beresford

Introduction

We know that dependence on, and inappropriate use of, alcohol is now widely seen as a global *social* problem. It is closely associated with crime and violence. It is a major contributory factor to road traffic and other accidents, resulting in countless deaths and serious injuries. It creates massive costs in terms of both personal and familial unhappiness and distress, it creates economic inefficiency and it imposes a massive burden on healthcare through reducing life expectancy and increasing morbidity (Heather et al, 2001). For some discussants, its costs far outweigh those associated with the use of illegal drugs, yet still it is essentially conceived of and treated in the same old individualised terms that would have been familiar in societies much more than a century ago. In the United Kingdom (UK), radical social policies in response to tobacco smoking have resulted in unprecedented reductions in the proportion of people smoking and the damage done. Yet over the same period, we have seen public policies that have increased access to alcohol and rising concerns about serious increases in alcohol-related problems.

At the same time, the dominant model of treatment for alcohol problems continues to be the '12-step' model with its talk of reliance on a 'higher power'. There can be few social or medical issues in the West in the 21st century that are still framed in such individualised, quasi theological or metaphysical terms. This is a wake-up call for a radical rethink of alcohol and alcohol dependence, building on more recent understandings. That is why this book is so important, because it offers a space to develop such a discussion, which determinedly seeks to move from medicalised, individual, to more social understandings, particularly in relation to a group who have historically received different and inferior treatment in relation to alcohol use – women.

In addition, if we are seeking new and different understandings that may be helpful in reconceiving alcohol problems and the responses made to them, then a particularly fertile field is likely to be the lived experience and experiential knowledge of service users themselves. For this reason, this chapter is concerned with ideas that have been developed by service user movements, particularly the movements of disabled people and mental health service users/survivors. What has conspicuously characterised these has been their *social* orientation.

A social approach

From 11 March until 6 July 2014, the Musée d'Orsay, a museum in Paris, held an exhibition entitled *Van Gogh/Artaud: Suicide by Society*. In 1947, the French actor and writer Antonin Artaud (1896–1948), himself a psychiatric system survivor, who had experienced electric shock treatment among other 'treatments', put forward a thesis that Van Gogh's work so disturbed society that it shunned his art and led to his despair and suicide. He concluded that van Gogh was a man 'suicided by society'.[1] Artaud dismissed simplistic and pathologising psychiatric assessments of van Gogh that even now continue to obscure his life and work. Instead, what he offered was a pre-figurative 'social model of madness and distress'.

A social model approach is generally understood to have been developed first and most comprehensively in relation to disability. While its influence should not be overstated, there is no doubt that the social model of disability has had a major impact on disability policy and practice and also on the lives of countless disabled people. Since the emergence of the 'social model of disability', there have been two additional and related developments. First, there have been far-reaching debates about the social model (Oliver, 2009). Such discussion has often been heated and polarised, with some highlighting what they see as the essential weaknesses of the model, others arguing that it was never intended to be an overarching theory and others still, seeing such discussion as part of its development as a helpful tool for explanation and understanding disability. I include myself in the last group.

The second development has been the efforts made to extend the application of the social model of disability beyond people with physical and sensory impairments – the groups that first developed it – to other groups. This particularly includes people with learning difficulties and mental health service users and raises issues that we will be drawn to later in this discussion (Thomas, 2007).

The distinguishing and innovative feature of the social model of disability is the distinction it draws between 'impairment' and 'disability'. Impairment is taken to mean an actual or perceived impairment to the body, sense or intellect of the individual. Disability is regarded as the hostile social reaction that is accorded to people and groups seen as having such impairments. This negative reaction has been framed in different ways. Thus, it is sometimes presented in terms of the *barriers* or exclusions that operate against people with impairments. These may be attitudinal, communication or physical and environmental barriers, which restrict what disabled people are able to do and stigmatise and negatively stereotype them. It is also conceived in terms of the *oppressions* that disabled people may face in society; oppressions relating to discrimination and stigmatisation, as well as material, social and political oppression. Clearly, these two frameworks are inter-related. Both also highlight the human and civil rights of disabled people and their citizenship and ways in which these are breached and denied.

While as has been said, critically the social model draws a distinction between impairment and disability, to challenge traditional preoccupations with the individual's body and perceived 'pathology', as discussion has developed around the social model, the relationship between the two has also been subjected to further examination. Some disabled feminists have argued that some impairments can exclude disabled people from some activities, even if disabling barriers are removed (Crow, 1992; French, 1993). Other commentators have challenged the idea of impairments as objective, highlighting that these are subject to different understandings, according to time, culture and ideology. Carol Thomas developed the idea of 'impairment effects', where restrictions of activity are related to physical, sensory or intellectual impairments, making clear, however, that impairment and impairment effects should not be seen simply as 'natural' or biological. Instead, she has highlighted that how they are perceived by others and experienced by disabled people, is shaped by the interaction of biological and social factors (Thomas, 1999, 2007). As Cameron (2014, p 77) has suggested: 'At the level of everyday experience, disability and impairment effects interact, which is why it is important to be clear about the distinction between the two.'

These are issues we will return to when we come to explore issues of alcohol, alcohol dependence and 'misuse' in relation to social understandings.

It may be helpful at this stage to draw a distinction between the social model of disability and social approaches to issues such as disability and mental health more generally. There has long been an interest in more social approaches to such issues. In the context of mental health, for example, more recently this has been associated with the production of a growing number of publications (for example, Sayce, 2000; Ramon and Williams, 2005; Tew, 2005, 2011; Tew et al, 2012). However, such sources, while interested in and exploring social factors relating to mental health, tend nonetheless generally to accept essentially medicalised understandings of 'mental health' and the diagnostic system associated with them. These tend to be taken as given, while there has been a concern to extend the search for causation beyond the individual, to their social circumstances. This is in some contrast to the social model of disability, which rejects the traditional dominant Western medicalised individual or 'tragedy' model of disability, which conceives of it in terms of personal abnormality, pathology and 'tragedy'.

So far there seems to have been little consideration of a social model approach in relation to problems of alcohol. A key exception is the contribution by the editor of this book, Patsy Staddon, in her writings (for example, Staddon, 2012). She developed this in 'Theorising a social model of "alcoholism": service users who misbehave', in an earlier edited text on service users in mental health research (Staddon, 2013a). It is not being suggested in the present discussion that alcohol 'misuse' is necessarily the same as disability. Rather, the aim is to see what, if any, helpful insights the social model may have to offer in any consideration of women, alcohol and alcohol misuse.

Women: 'a special case'

Before we turn to this, however, it is important to highlight that there is a critical history to the exploration of women and alcohol, which takes account of social, cultural and gender issues. A key pioneer in this was the research psychologist Shirley Otto. Otto was writing about the particular barriers and oppressions faced by women users of alcohol more than 40 years ago (Otto, 1974). She highlighted the historic 'scandalising of society' of women neglecting their children for the sake of alcohol – 'mothers' ruin' – and their Victorian association with the 'dangerous classes'. She also highlighted that little was done to help the 'woman alcoholic' although she faced particular stigma and opprobrium, 'particularly the woman who is drunk and, worst of all, disorderly' (Otto, 1974, p 28).

> In many parts of our society it is quite acceptable for a man to get 'pissed out of his mind' while even in sophisticated London many women are reluctant to go into a pub alone for a quiet drink, not because they fear assault but for the fear of being misunderstood; women and drink are still associated with sexual promiscuity. (Otto, 1974, p 28)

If the traditional way of understanding disability has been what Oliver (2009) called the 'tragedy' model, then one longstanding approach to representing dependence on alcohol has been the 'farce' model, with the 'drunk' as a figure of fun and ridicule. However, this has tended only to be applied to men. Since Otto was first writing, of course the coupling of women with inappropriate behavior, sexual laxness and disrepute has increased, with modern moral panics about a 'ladette' culture of half-dressed young women partying, getting drunk and vomiting in public (Coslett and Baxter, 2014). Otto's concern was to develop understanding about the issues involved in the 'special case' of women and alcohol in order to increase awareness and improve support. Sadly, all the signs are that progress on both fronts has been hesitant to say the least and been tied to the same old, often stigmatising and punitive thinking. 'Binge drinking' by women is such an issue (Plant and Plant, 2006; van Wersch and Walker, 2009). As Staddon (2013a, p 108) states: 'fury is expressed where women are seen as "binge drinkers" and are seen to be out of control'. She goes on:

> Whatever 'free choices' women may make, they lay themselves open to criticism in a way that men do not 'since most discourses construct femininity in negative terms relative to masculinity'. Concern is frequently expressed about their health, with particular anxiety about their function as future or current mothers. However what seems principally at issue is their *right* to intoxication, indiscretion and inappropriate behavior. (Staddon, 2013a, p 109)

The conventional conceptualisation of 'alcoholism'

Staddon (2013a), in this earlier discussion of a social model in relation to alcohol use/abuse, offers food for thought, which is helpful for the present discussion. She suggests that alcohol service users tend to accept prevailing treatment views of themselves. This is perhaps hardly surprising; these are all they are likely to be familiar with and know. Such medicalised understandings have gained enormous authority and common currency – like traditional medicalised understandings of mental illness and disability. The individual who, for example, rejects the 12-step programme approach, runs great risk of losing both self- and external esteem – if they are unable to maintain 'sobriety'. It is a very difficult but ever-present yardstick to be judged by, in challenging orthodox thinking.

This is particularly true given the complex mixture of moralising and medicalisation upon which prevailing conceptualisations of 'alcoholism' are based. Thus, what is regarded as an inappropriate reliance on alcohol tends to be understood in medical terms variously as alcohol psychosis, as a disease and as a diagnostic category of mental illness. At the same time, such categorisation seems to be inseparable from moral and value judgements. Thus, dependence on alcohol is also seen as immoral, a 'character flaw' and a 'disease of the will', where the individual is inadequate. Women dependent on alcohol are to be blamed and shamed (Munt, 2007; Morgan, 2008; Staddon, 2012, 2013a, p 110).

What has it got to do with disability?

At first glance, this seems some distance away from ordinary understandings of disability, perhaps limiting the likelihood of a social model having relevance or being appropriate to apply. Even in its most medicalised incarnations, we might imagine that disability is about defect and pathology rather than inadequacy and immorality. But more careful consideration of disabled people's own discourse about disability offers a rapid reminder that over the ages right up to the present, attitudes and imagery associated with disabled people have frequently been negative and judgemental and that, in some cultures, there is a continuing association of impairment with wrongdoing (in the person or their parents) either in this or a previous life (Campbell and Oliver, 1996; Fazil et al, 2002; Bywaters et al, 2003).

It is also important to remember the complex issues emerging in developing discussions about the social model of disability. Where efforts have been made to transpose the social model of disability to alcohol 'misuse', a wide range of issues have been identified as the equivalent of disability, experienced by women with alcohol-related problems. These include:

- condemnation of women for behaving in ways that are tolerated, accepted or even commended in men;
- the denial of equal citizenship and rights to women, creating oppression, which can lead them to harmful alcohol use;

- other oppressions that lead women to turn to alcohol use, including child sexual abuse, domestic violence, rape and adult sexual abuse;
- the oppression and social injustice created by the dominant explanatory and treatment models in use (Staddon, 2013a, pp 106-108).

Thus, the equivalent of oppressive 'disability' for women in relation to alcohol, can be seen to extend from women challenging restrictions imposed on them (and drinking more); through the oppressions that led them to over-use alcohol; through to oppressive societal responses to women with alcohol problems.

The equivalent of the 'impairment' of women 'alcoholics' is conventionally seen to range from their being ill, to their 'misbehaving'. Staddon (2013a, p 109) has concluded that 'alcoholism' should be seen as a 'social construction', more to do with social control than health. If we try to explore a social model of 'alcoholism' that is the equivalent of the social model of disability, then as she suggests, 'impairment' may mean '[w]hen the person or the person's social milieu decides that their life, or that of others, is being damaged in a way that is seen to be unacceptable' (Staddon, 2013a, p 107).

At the same time, Staddon has suggested that women's more public, more drunken use of alcohol may be seen as a challenge to the restrictions imposed on them and the different attitudes historically to male and female use of alcohol.

Looking to thinking around madness and distress

Helpful insights for social approaches to thinking about women and alcohol are also to be found in mental health service users' own discussions about mental health. The 'Towards a Social Model of Madness and Distress' national project, supported by the Joseph Rowntree Foundation, focused specifically on this issue. It highlighted, for the present discussion, some of the problems and complexities of seeking to transpose social model thinking, while at the same time offering insights into its strengths (Beresford et al, 2009).

Most service users who took part in the project believed that a medical model based on deficit and pathology still dominates public and professional understanding of mental health issues, shaping attitudes and policy. They largely saw such a medical model as damaging and unhelpful. They felt that the labelling and stigma following from such a medical model of mental illness emerged as major barriers for mental health service users. They saw more social approaches to mental health issues as far more helpful. They felt strongly that broader issues needed to be taken more into account to counter the present individualisation of mental health issues. However, this was not the whole story. At the same time, they had mixed and complex views about the social model of disability and how helpful a related social model of madness and distress could be.

There were several key reasons for this. Most participants in the project were familiar with the social model of disability, understanding the distinction it draws between individual impairment and disability and its identification of disabling barriers in society, which exclude and discriminate against people with impairments. But they were divided about whether it related helpfully to mental health issues. Some service users feared that the association of the social model with disability would add to the stigma they faced. Many mental health service users regard disability as a different issue from their own experience, do not identify as disabled and see it as an additional stigmatising identity. There was also a feeling among a number of them that disability and mental health issues were different and that the idea of 'impairment' underpinning the social model misrepresented the experience of mental health service users. Some mental health service users see their experiences and perceptions that they have as positives, rather than negatives. There may be comparable issues in relation to alcohol, where a case may be made for seeing alcohol use, not as a symptom of disease or deficiency, but as a form of 'self-help' or 'self-medication' for issues that 'might become more problematic either with or without its use' (Staddon, 2013a, p 111).

Thus, in the Joseph Rowntree Foundation project, there were comments such as the following:

> "I think instinctively, at a gut level I've felt 'no, my mental health problems are not an impairment', I don't see that they are an impairment for a range of reasons. So I think that's a limitation in the way I understand the social model of disability at the moment, I don't actually feel that the impairment bit accommodates my experience."
>
> "... I'm not sure I want to be called disabled." (Beresford et al, 2009, p 20)

A further area of concern related to language. There were strong disagreements among service users who took part in the project when discussing the idea of a social model of madness and distress. This was because, while they were generally unhappy with a medical model, they were also wary of non-medicalised terms such as 'madness'. As a result, this made discussion difficult and had helped to discourage it. Typical comments included: 'I stick to my guns and I don't like the word madness. I think it ought to be done away with' (Beresford et al, 2009, p 22). There may be comparable problems in relation to alcohol use by women, where similarly there does not seem to be agreed, non-stigmatising terminology.

There was nonetheless a feeling among some of the study participants that there was a real need for such a social model of madness and distress. While the terminology of 'madness and distress' was an obstacle for some, trying to think about a social model, they highlighted in their comments some of the benefits they could see it bringing and issues that it needed to address: 'Yes, definitely, definitely think it could be helpful. I mean we definitely need to take into account the range of issues that form the problems that we have, and I don't think we can do that just on the basis of a simple medical model' (Beresford et al, 2009, p 24).

One of the benefits seen for such a model was that it would help to create solidarity and shared understandings between different service user groups, strengthening them and increasing their effectiveness, as well as increasing opportunities for collaboration and joint action. It would renew understanding about mental health issues and could help to highlight the links between different people's distress and make clearer how individual distress might be associated with broader oppressions and discrimination. There was also some sense that there needed to be recognition that the barriers that mental health service users face may sometimes be different from, as well as similar to, those that people with physical, sensory and intellectual impairments face.

Developing our own anti-oppressive models

While, as has been said, mental health service users increasingly report the negative and stigmatising effects of dominant, individual, medicalised definitions of their experience and situation, and are very cautious about transferring the social model of disability to mental health, they have not developed an equivalent tool for understanding their own situation. Among mental health service users, this is sometimes explained in terms of people's fears of being further marginalised if they reject dominant interpretations of themselves or of being overpowered by another orthodoxy – this time one of their own making. At the same time, they have become susceptible to highly ambiguous models for reconceiving mental health policy and practice, such as 'recovery', which chime closely with neoliberal political agendas as well as embracing a liberatory rhetoric (Morrow, 2013).

The importance of new and user-led thinking

Strong arguments can thus be made for developing alternative user-led understandings of issues such as alcohol dependence among women. As Staddon (2013a, p 111) has already argued, existing treatment responses seem to be of limited effectiveness, as well as having their own negative associations. User-led re-conceptions of alcohol problems are much more likely than current understandings to engage with structural, cultural, material, relational, equality and diversity issues. They are likely to open the door, as the social model has in relation to disability and mental health issues, to different, more helpful social and treatment responses. They are likely to lead to recognition of the need for greater involvement from women in conceptualising and responding to their situation and difficulties – at both individual and collective levels.

However, this may not be an argument for simply trying to transpose the social model of disability to this different domain, or assuming that it will have comparable benefits. This is emphasised by further findings from the research project discussed above, 'Towards a Social Model of Madness and Distress'. At the time of writing, a second phase of this project is being undertaken. Its aims are to feed back the findings of the first phase to a wider range of mental health service users, using individual interviews and group discussions, in order to share the learning and enable survivors to offer their interpretations of the findings and suggestions for next steps. While this work has yet to be written up, some initial findings are cause for concern. The diverse range of mental health service users involved report increasing difficulties accessing support, with serious cuts in mental health services, as well as increased anxiety and other problems as a result of cuts in benefits relating to so-called 'welfare reform'. These rising difficulties seemed to be having the effect of diverting participants from giving priority to rethinking the conceptual frameworks on which policy and services are based. At a time of crisis and serious loss of supports, such an attitude is not difficult to understand. There still seems to be a significant wariness of being associated with the social model of disability and an identity as disabled.

At the same time, participating service users/survivors have highlighted the importance of encouraging mental health practitioners to work in different, more socially based ways, the importance of user involvement and of peer support approaches. They want psychiatrists, doctors and other health and social care professionals who have a better understanding of their situation and are better able to respond holistically to their various unique needs and circumstances. They also value the support that they can offer each other. A related picture has also emerged from a local user-led research study carried out by Staddon, which explored the support preferences of women with alcohol problems (Taylor, 2010; Staddon, 2013b). The findings from this project indicate that same-sex, service user support for women with alcohol issues, whatever form it took would lead to considerable improvements in women's recovery from alcohol misuse.

Perhaps what is most helpful is not to try to import the social model of disability simplistically across to alcohol misuse issues, but to be sensitive to and be guided by its key aspects and concerns. These include the model's recognition of the oppressive social responses that tend to be applied to people included in groups subject to oppression and/or which are seen as problematic and the need to challenge that categorisation. It means questioning why these groups are both conceived of and responded to negatively. It seems less helpful to seek in women's alcohol misuse exact parallels with disability or to treat it as if it were a parallel expression of 'disability'. Most important, perhaps, it should lead us to placing an emphasis not on imposing external ideas or models on problems and people, but supporting people themselves to develop their own user-led understandings. The developing discussion about the social model of disability has encouraged us to pay attention to the uniqueness of people's personal issues, the crude and damaging uniformity of oppressive responses to them and the importance of matching policy and practice responses both to each person's particular needs as well as their common rights. This seems an appropriate starting point for rethinking both the conceptualisation of women and alcohol misuse and societal responses to them.

Note

[1] www.musee-orsay.fr/en/events/exhibitions/in-the-musee-dorsay/exhibitions-in-the-musee-dorsay/article/van-gogh-artaud-37162.html?tx_ttnews%5BbackPid%5D=254&cHash=66af044067

References

Beresford, P., Nettle, M. and Perring, R. (2009) *Towards a social model of madness and distress? Exploring what service users say*, York: Joseph Rowntree Foundation.

Bywaters, P., Ali, Z., Fazil, Q., Wallace, L. and Singh, G. (2003) 'Attitudes towards disability amongst Pakistani and Bangladeshi parents of disabled children in the UK: considerations for service providers and the disability movement', *Health and Social Care in the Community*, vol 11, no 6, pp 502-509.

Cameron, C. (ed) (2014) *Disability studies: A student's guide*, London: Sage Publications.

Campbell, J. and Oliver, M. (1996) *Disability politics: Understanding our past, changing our future*, London: Routledge.

Cosslett, R.L. and Baxter, H. (2014) 'The drunk woman's manifesto', *New Statesman*, 11 February, www.newstatesman.com/2014/02/drunk-women-manifesto

Crow, L. (1992) 'Renewing the social model of disability', *Coalition*, July, Manchester: Greater Manchester Coalition of Disabled People, pp 5-9.

Fazil, Q., Bywaters, P., Ali, Z., Wallace, L. and Singh, G. (2002) 'Disadvantage and discrimination compounded: the experience of Pakistani and Bangladeshi parents of disabled children in the UK', *Disability & Society*, vol 17, no 3, pp 237-253.

French, S. (1993) 'Disability, impairment or something in between', in Swain, J., Finkelstein, V., French, S. and Oliver, M. (eds) *Disabling barriers – enabling environments*, London: Sage Publications, pp 17-25.

Heather, N., Peters, T.J. and Stockwell, T. (eds) (2001) *International handbook of alcohol dependence and problems*, Chicago, IL: John Wiley.

Morgan, M.L. (2008) *On shame*, New York, NY: Routledge.

Morrow, M. (2013) 'Recovery: progressive paradigm or neoliberal smokescreen', in LeFrancois, B., Menzies, R. and Reaume, G. (eds) *Mad matters: A critical reader in Canadian mad studies*, Toronto: Canadian Scholars Press, pp 323-333.

Munt, S.R. (2007) *Queer attachments: The cultural politics of shame*, Aldershot: Ashgate.

Oliver, M. (2009) *Understanding disability: From theory to practice* (2nd edn), Basingstoke: Palgrave Macmillan.

Otto, S. (1974) 'A special case for treatment: Camberwell Council on alcoholism', *CCA Journal on Alcoholism*, vol 3, no 3, pp 25-28.

Plant, M.L. and Plant, M. (2006) *Binge Britain: Alcohol and the national response*, Oxford: Oxford University Press.

Ramon, S. and Williams, J.E. (eds) (2005) *Mental health at the crossroads: The promise of the psychosocial approach*, Guildford: Ashgate.

Sayce, L. (2000) *From psychiatric patient to citizen: Overcoming discrimination and social exclusion*, Basingstoke: Macmillan.

Staddon, P. (2012) 'No blame, no shame: towards a social model of alcohol dependency – a story from emancipatory research', in Beresford, P. and Carr, S. (eds) *Social care, service users and user involvement*, London: Jessica Kingsley Publishers, pp 192-204.

Staddon, P. (2013a) 'Theorising a social model of "alcoholism": service users who misbehave', in Staddon, P. (ed) *Mental health service users in research: Critical sociological perspectives*, Bristol: Policy Press, pp 105-119.

Staddon, P. (2013b) *Improving support for women with alcohol issues*, 22 September, Bristol: www.wiaswomen.org.uk/uploads/3/1/2/9/3129441/staddon_report_sept_22_2013.pdf

Taylor, C. (2010) 'Extending GP training', in *InnovAiT: The RCGP Journal for aAssociates in Training*, no 3, pp 438-441, doi:10.1093/innovait/inp214.

Tew, J. (ed) (2005) *Social perspectives in mental health: Developing social models to understand and work with mental distress*, London: Jessica Kingsley Publishers.

Tew, J. (2011) *Social approaches to mental distress*, Basingstoke: Palgrave Macmillan.

Tew, J., Ramon, S., Slade, M., Bird, V., Melton, J. and LeBoutillier, C. (2012) 'Social factors and recovery from mental health difficulties: a review of the evidence', *British Journal of Social Work*, vol 42, no 3, pp 443-460, doi: 10.1093/bjsw/bcr076, first published online 15 June 2011.

Thomas, C. (1999) *Female forms: Experiencing and understanding disability*, Buckingham: Open University Press.

Thomas, C. (2007) *Sociologies of disability and illness: Contested ideas in disability studies and medical sociology*, Basingstoke: Palgrave Macmillan.

van Wersch, A. and Walker, W. (2009) 'Binge-drinking in Britain as a social and cultural phenomenon: the development of a grounded theoretical model,' *Journal of Health Psychology*, vol 14, no 1, pp 124-134.

TWO

Alcohol and moral regulation in historical context

Rachel McErlain

Introduction

Women's drinking has been identified as a perennial issue (Nicholls, 2009, p 2) in social and political narratives in which alcohol is considered as a problem. Indeed, women's drinking is discursively constructed as a greater problem than men's drinking (Ettorre, 1997, p 15; Waterson, 2000, p 12). It is possible to argue that the negative discourses of women's drinking cannot solely be related to knowledge about the prevalence of women's problem drinking from epidemiological studies. The construction of women's drinking as a social problem is a product of sociohistorical constructions of femininity. Therefore, women's drinking is the target of gender-specific moral regulation practices.

The practices of moral regulation are a common feature of contemporary alcohol regulation policies. Moral regulation is described as 'an interesting and significant form of politics in which some people act to problematize the conduct, values or culture of others and seek to impose regulation upon them' (Hunt, 1999, p 1). In current alcohol regulation policies, moral regulation acts to impact the behaviour of the drinker through self-regulation. Successful self-regulation among a drinking population becomes more significant in a time when policies governing the availability of alcohol are liberalised (Critcher, 2011, p 182).

This chapter examines moral regulation practices through the campaign materials from alcohol regulation organisations in two historical periods, paying specific attention to the constructions of the drinking woman in these campaigns.

The alcohol regulation campaign materials examined here are from mid-19th-century British temperance organisations and from alcohol regulation campaign groups in the time period 2004–14. The reasons for selecting these time periods are discussed later in this chapter.

However, for now it is important to note that moral regulation was of particular significance in these time periods due to increasing liberalisation of alcohol sales in England.

By examining how the drinking female is presented as transgressing the social norms of femininity through consuming alcohol problematically, the significance of understanding the social context of gendered alcohol regulatory practices are brought to attention. Additionally, similarities and differences in the themes of transgressive femininity and alcohol consumption are drawn upon. This demonstrates how moral regulation practices have used socially constructed gender norms in the production of female-specific drinking norms. It is these gendered drinking norms that alcohol regulatory campaigns have used as tools of self-regulation.

Through the exploration of the presentation of transgressive femininities in alcohol regulation campaigns, some of the implications of resisting or rejecting gendered drinking norms by women are highlighted. This is particularly relevant to understanding how gendered drinking norms perpetuate discourses that prevent women experiencing problem drinking to seek (gender-sensitive) help (Ettorre, 1997, p 64).

This chapter briefly addresses the choice of historical context, explaining some of the reasons why gendered alcohol regulation was important in both time periods. Second, the theoretical approach to examining gender in alcohol regulation campaigns is discussed. A selection of sources from the mid-19th-century temperance campaigns is presented, and this is followed by a selection of sources produced by contemporary alcohol regulation campaigns. The sources from each time period are compared to draw out similarities and differences in gendered alcohol regulation in alcohol regulation campaigns produced within different social contexts. The chapter concludes with the argument for redressing the sexism in gendered alcohol regulatory campaigns, and calls for alcohol regulation campaign groups to be sensitive to the presentation of drinking women in campaign materials.

'Teetotal' abstinence and the dignified female character

The idea of temperance as an organised philanthropic movement began at the turn of the 19th century in the United States (Harrison, 1994, p 97). However, it was in the 1820s that a sustained, organised and collective response to 'the drink question' emerged in England (Harrison, 1994, pp 87-88).

In the 1820s, the temperance movement presented a widely held cultural view of specific forms of alcohol as the source of alcohol-related social problems. At this time, the view was that distilled spirits were the cause of alcohol-related social harms (Shiman, 1988, pp 9-10; Harrison, 1994, p 89; Nicholls, 2009, p 98). The anti-spirits approach to temperance advocacy was one that challenged drunkenness, but not drinking all forms of alcohol. Therefore, drinking wine and beer was accepted practice during this period for temperance affiliates (Shiman, 1988, p 9).

The legacy of the gin pandemic in the mid-18th century, and political advocacy for reducing the monopolising influence of breweries (Nicholls, 2009, p 91), resulted in a populist reform by the Tory government – the Beer Act 1830. This Act primarily reduced the influence of local magistrates from controlling the provision of outlets selling beer, through allowing the establishment of 'beer shops', which did not require a licence to be issued by a local magistrate. The consequences of the Beer Act were significant, as the number of 'beer shops' grew rapidly, with 24,000 beer shops opening in the first year following the passing of the law (Nicholls, 2009, p 92).

In the industrialising North of England, particularly the mill towns of south Lancashire, social reformers quickly acted to point out that the social harms resulting from beer consumption were not unlike the social harms associated with spirit drinking. This led to the formation of a teetotal temperance organisation in Preston, Lancashire, in 1832. The teetotal temperance organisation had noted that policy to impact upon alcohol-related social problems by bringing about a change in the prevalence of beer drinking had failed, as the following colourful description cited by Winskill (1891, p 89) implies:

> Inviting him in, Mr Livesey inquired how he was getting on in his temperance work? 'Bad enough' replied King. 'My people are getting drunk on beer. Thou knows, Joseph, as well as I do, that Preston folk do not get drunk on spirits, and I tell thee that we shall do no good until we get our members to do without beer and all other intoxicating drink.'

The teetotal temperance movement not only affected the extent of abstinence involved for members, but also gave rise to the practice of pledge-signing, reformed drunkards' speeches, structured organisations with roles for the respectable working-class men, and a reformist view of the social good, which could potentially derive from total abstinence (Shiman, 1988, p 21).

The advocates of teetotal temperance sought to reform drinking behaviour through the process of 'moral suasion' – that is, presenting an argument against drinking alcohol, which asserts the immorality of alcohol and the act of drinking. The greatest distinction between moderationists and teetotallers was the approach taken to problem drinkers: 'For the moderationist, the drunkard had failed to exert his willpower and deserved denunciation; for the teetotaller the drunkard's will had been paralysed by alcohol' (Harrison, 1994, p 110). Teetotallers, influenced by non-conformist principles, believed in self-improvement; thus, particular attention was given to reforming problem drinkers (Harrison, 1994, p 111) as well as persuading people who drank moderately to become totally abstinent from all forms of alcohol.

Moral suasion had a significant impact on women within, and outside, the temperance organisations. The place of women in an 'abstinent' society was one in which they educated children on the moral risks of drinking alcohol. It was also imperative that working-class women should seek to emulate the comforts of the middle-class home in order to prevent men from seeking more desirable surroundings, such as in the pub or beer shop. In this way, the need to socialise women into the views promoted through moral suasion was doubly important than targeting men. Abstinent women would ensure sober male workers, and children who would grow up to be abstinent adults. Therefore, women, while acknowledged as less likely to be problem drinkers, were important targets of the alcohol regulation campaigning of the teetotal organisations.

Abstinence and moderation as normative feminine practices

The concepts of 'abstinence' and 'moderation' as feminine practices of alcohol consumption are argued to have emerged in Britain during the 16th and 17th centuries (Warner, 1997, p 98). According to Warner (1997, p 100), literary representations of women drinking in the Medieval period made no reference to abstinence, and in fact used representations of drunk women as a source of humour. The emergence of discourses of abstinence and moderation as feminine practices came about during a period of economic decline (1997, p 103). It was during this time that men's drinking increasingly took place outside the home, with the effect of 'the home as a sanctuary of sobriety, presided over by the long-suffering housewife who rarely, if ever, drank alcohol. Inside the sanctuary are women and children;

outside the sanctuary are men, whose refuge has now become the alehouse or tavern, depending on their social class' (1997, p 105).

Even in periods when drinking alcohol was not high on the agenda of moral reformists, and in times of national increases in consumption, the cultural expectations of female drinking practice as moderate remained. This led to women who were perceived to drink too much to be subject to moral condemnation (Warner, 2004, p 67).

The role of moderate consumption as an ideological construct, reinforcing gender differences, is a theory explored at length by Bordo (2003a). In her essay 'Hunger as ideology', Bordo (2003b) discusses the marketing of food products that reinforce a gendered ideology of consumption in moderation as a feminised practice. These discourses are related to those contained in Victorian conduct manuals, hence she argues: 'The representation of unrestrained appetite as inappropriate for women, the depiction of female eating as a private, transgressive act, make restriction and denial of hunger central features of the construction of femininity ... such restrictions on appetite, moreover, are not merely about food intake' (Bordo, 2003b, p 130).

Relating this theory, here applied to the consumption of food, to the consumption of alcohol, as gender ideology, draws attention to the extent to which normative feminine practice can shape women's drinking practices. This, in turn, impacts upon the feelings of women who are experiencing negative drinking.

Women who drink alcohol do so in a social context in which their experience is heavily shaped by gendered drinking norms. Of course, these norms are experienced differentially depending on how multiple identities shape the meaning of drinking for the individual woman. When women are experiencing negative drinking, awareness of how their practices transgress normative femininities compound feelings of shame (Ettorre, 1992, p 64). Bartky (1990) discusses gender differences in the experience of shame: that women are more 'shame-prone' (1990, p 93) than men. Shame is the experience of self-awareness of failure to meet expectations of standards of behaviour. The contents of these expectations or beliefs are a consequence of the social context of the individual. This is explained by Bartky (1990, p 93), as 'it is the act of being shamed and in the feeling ashamed that there is disclosed to women who they are and how they are faring within the domains they inhabit'. Awareness of gendered drinking norms, and the effect of transgressing these through drinking practices, are differentially experienced by individuals. However, by 'knowing' the gendered drinking norms of a social context, actively drawing attention to the shaming experience of transgressing these norms enables organisations or individuals to impact upon individual drinking behaviour. In this way, shame can be used as a technique in enabling self-regulation.

The role of shame in the experience of transgressing gendered drinking norms is pertinent to understanding how alcohol regulation campaigns seek to impact upon women's drinking behaviour. If, as Bartky argues, women are more shame-prone than men, the use of shame as a technology in gendered alcohol regulation would be an effective tool. The sources discussed in this chapter pay particular attention to how shame is invoked through alcohol regulation campaign materials that are targeted at female drinkers specifically.

Methodological note

The sources used in this study were materials produced by alcohol regulation campaign groups in two historical periods. The first group of sources discussed was identified through hand searching journals and tracts produced by different temperance organisations in the time period 1832–72. The reason for this period is my interest in moral suasion as a technique for enabling self-regulation of alcohol consumption. For further discussion of moral suasion in temperance campaigns during this time period, please see chapter 8 in Nicholls (2009).

The sources used in the contemporary period were produced throughout the period 2004–14 by a range of alcohol regulation campaign groups based in the United Kingdom (UK). The materials were identified through the websites of the organisations, and through photographing sources in situ in public spaces, such as on telephone boxes, in pubs (often in women's toilets) and nightclubs. These photographs were primarily taken in Cambridgeshire, Hertfordshire and Lancashire.

Sources were selected by their direct and explicit targeting of women and girls. They were identified through the titles or main headline of the document making explicit reference to women or girls, and through any images presented in the document.

She tasted – and was undone

The above quote, taken from 'The victim of excitement' (Ipswich Temperance Tracts, circa 1850, no 78, p 15), typifies the melodramatic style of alcohol regulation campaign materials produced in the mid-19th century. The use of melodramatic forms has clear echoes of the temperance fiction of Clara Lucas Balfour (1808–78). The use of dramatic tensions and consequences of drinking served to gain the attention of the reader or listener, and certainly ensured that the dire consequences of drinking would stick in the mind.

Sources such as these are really entertaining to the contemporary reader, and offer an insight into the norms and values the author expected their audience to be familiar with. In this brief overview of the range of documents available from this period, three devices used in the sources will be explored. These are:

- the use of juxtaposition techniques to emphasise the shock value of transgressive femininities;
- the use of the transgressive feminine pose in images of women who drink;
- the role of the 'inappropriate' emotional behaviour of women who drink.

These devices all served to reinforce the ideals of feminine behaviour and practices in the mid-19th century.

The use of *juxtaposition* in the sources is a frequent occurrence. By directly positioning ideal and transgressive femininities alongside each other, the audience is expected to locate one set of behavioural traits as desirable in the ideal female. In the other set of behaviours, it is intended that the audience notes the contrast and defines the behaviours collectively as transgressive, yet still feminine.

One such example is that of the tract previously mentioned, 'The victim of excitement' (Ipswich Temperance Tracts, circa 1850, no 78), which tells the story of a marriage between Anne Weston and Mr Manly. The impending disaster in which this marriage will end is fixed before the marriage takes place, during a discussion between Anne and her friend Emily Spencer on the evening before the wedding. Anne quells her fears about her ability to perform as an ideal wife and, to manage these negative feelings, pours for herself and drinks 'a glass of rich cordial' (p 6). This causes Emily to (unwillingly) voice her concerns about Anne's choice to drink alcohol, that 'I see a speck on the bright character of my friend. It may spread and dim all its lustre. We all know the fearful strength of habit; we cannot shake off the serpent, when once its coils are round us' (p 7). Following the marriage, Emily resides with Mr and Mrs Manly, during which time Mr Manly discovers his wife's intemperance. To prevent Mr Manly from abandoning his wife, Emily pleads Anne's case and 'pledges herself to labour for him, and with him' (p 11). The climax of the melodrama comes with Anne's relapse into drinking when both Mr Manly and Emily are away, causing an accident in which her young child is mortally injured. Upon Mr Manly's return, the scene is thus described:

> His wife, clothed in her richest raiments, and glittering with jewels, lying in the torpor of inebriation. Emily Spencer seated by the side of the bed, bathed in tears, holding in her lap the dying child, her dress stained with the blood with which its fair locks were matted. (p 18)

Here the direct comparison serves to reinforce what the audience is told about ideal and transgressive femininity throughout the story. Anne is bright, vivacious, independent and unused to obedience or enforced monotony. Emily provides the counterpoint of a character that embodies the Victorian feminine ideal. She is passive, abstinent and subservient to the male head of household. In the death scene of the child, quoted above, her tears and lack of vanity (through the blood-stained dress) are juxtaposed with the evident care for dress and failure to perform as a mother through Anne's intoxication. Becoming intoxicated is Anne's ultimate failure; however, it is bound up with a list of other transgressive femininities, in vanity, independence and vivacity.

A second device frequently deployed in the presentation of transgressive femininities in the sources is the *unfeminine pose*. Perhaps it is more accurately described as the unrespectable feminised pose. An example of this is shown in Figure 2.1.

The unrespectable feminine pose in Figure 2.1 is that of a woman who is being carried on a stretcher by four police officers. She is tied to the stretcher, and appears to be in discomfort. She is carried from outside a gin shop, and is surrounded by child onlookers. The accompanying narration of a witness to this scene describes this woman being carried away from Brick Lane in London in a state of intoxication. The meaning of the image for the audience is that this woman's behaviour is the opposite of feminine restraint and poise. The fact that she is forcibly removed from the scene by police officers emphasises the offensiveness of her intoxicated presence. The visible expressions of shock on the faces of the children represented around her highlight the message that the visibility of her intoxication is corrupting.

The body is positioned to shock the viewer, to reinforce the message that female intoxication is dramatically different from normative feminine bodily practice. This technique is repeated many times over, for example in the details of the illustration entitled 'The British juggernaut' (*The Band of Hope Review*, December 1851, p 48). In this image, two female figures are prominent in the foreground. One is

Figure 2.1: 'A sad sight', September 1851

Source: The Band of Hope Review, September 1851, p 34

sitting cross-legged on the floor, her nose darkened to highlight that she is a heavy drinker, clutching a glass; her facial expression is sad with downcast eyes. The other figure is a more extreme representation of transgressive femininity. The figure is kneeling on the floor, surrounded by other intoxicated male figures. Her hair is loose; she is wearing a dress with uncovered arms. Her arms are positioned above her head, holding aloft a bottle and a glass. In both figures the viewer is presented with women who are unrestrained, failing to present themselves as respectable women. These are women of failed character. They are presented to invoke feelings of shame in the viewer, sympathy but ultimately moral judgement of their transgressive femininity.

The final device is that of *inappropriate emotional behaviour*. In the sources, women who are the victims of male drunkenness are often described as weeping; however, their emotional outbursts are contained, conducted in the privacy of the home, and with minimal noise or signs of distress. Conversely, emotional outbursts that are loud, visible and in public places are associated with intoxicated female characters. An example of this is in the tract 'The craving of a drunkard' (Ipswich Temperance Tracts, circa 1850, no 108). In this, a case is noted of a woman 'rescued from the gutter' who is taken in by a group of abstainers. The woman is presented as having the pretence of being fully reformed; however, in the moment she consumes a small amount of alcohol for medicinal reasons:

> The appetite, that til then had slumbered, was roused; and in spite of all the efforts of the most devoted friends that ever strove to save a poor maniac, she was, in an almost incredibly short space of time, actually stripped of her very clothing, and staggering in wretchedness in the street. (Ipswich Temperance Tracts, circa 1850, no 108, p 2)

Intoxication for women is often related to inappropriate emotional behaviours, such as swearing, as in 'Bridget Larkins' (Ipswich Temperance Tracts, circa 1850, no 89) or in complete breakdown as described in the quotation above. The presentation of impropriety affirms to the reader that for women, drinking alcohol results in behaviour that transgresses female norms and practices. These transgressions should be viewed as shaming; as in the example above, the woman is stripped of clothing, symbolic of sexual transgression.

This brief overview has shown some of the devices using shame to reinforce the norms of ideals of feminine behaviour in mid-19th-century England in temperance campaign materials. In these stories it is clear that the outcomes for women who drink and images are extreme. Drinking alcohol for women ends in ruin, concluding with prostitution, sometimes the death of a child, ending with their death, caused by drinking. In contemporary campaigns, the outcomes are not so extreme. I will discuss the relevance of understanding the social context of these campaigns later in this chapter. However, in the discussion of contemporary sources that follows, I wish to show how similar devices for invoking feelings of shame in the viewer are used in contemporary gendered regulation campaigns.

Shame – the other hangover

'The other hangover' was a student-led campaign at the University of Minnesota in the United States in 2009–11 (www.theotherhangover.com, 31 March 2014). This campaign utilised shame as a device for challenging what was perceived to be a cultural norm of binge drinking among students. By direct reference to shame, regret and embarrassment, viewers were intended to identify the behaviours presented in the campaigns as an undesirable consequence of drunkenness. These were utilised in gender-specific campaigns, in which sexual shaming was a prominent feature of the female-targeted campaigns.

The use of shame as a device for reinforcing normative feminine drinking practices has been used in several alcohol campaigns in the UK, particularly by the campaign groups Drinkaware and Alcohol Concern. In the gender-specific campaign materials, women who drink to intoxication are often presented as behaving shamefully, in order to reinforce the ideal of feminine drinking behaviour as 'moderate'. In this section, the ways in which transgressive female drinkers are presented in a selection of campaign materials are discussed. The discussion draws on the three categories of transgressive drinking female identified in the mid-19th-century sources. Through examining how these techniques – of juxtaposing transgressive with ideal femininity, the use of the unfeminine pose and use of the role of inappropriate emotional behaviour – some of the historical continuities in the discursive construction of normative feminine drinking practices are highlighted. The description of the sources is comparatively sparse; however, these materials are easily accessible via the internet, unlike the mid-19th-century sources.

A clear case of *juxtaposition* as a technique for discursively constructing drunkenness as transgressive femininity was in a campaign by Drinkaware called 'Why let good times go bad?', which ran from 2009 to 2012. One example of the campaign materials produced during this period was 'Dance floor – toilet floor' (2011), in which the left side of the poster contains an image of a young white woman dancing, and to the right the same young woman is sitting on the floor, leaning her elbow on the toilet. A shoulder strap on her dress has slipped down her arm. A gap between the images is in the shape of a wine glass. The ideal female figure is placed as on her feet, smiling and with her clothes and makeup intact, and the transgressive female figure is seated, her clothes and hair in disarray. Neither figure is shown holding a drink, yet the viewer can construct a narrative of transgressive and ideal feminine drinking practices from these two images. As with Anne and Emily in 'The victim of excitement', the viewer can identify how failing to perform normative feminine drinking results in transgression of feminine ideals.

Contemporary alcohol campaigns have included several examples of *transgressive feminine poses*, such as being slumped on a toilet floor (as noted above), and in 'Catching up – left behind' (2011) and in 'Laughing with you – laughing at you' (2011) the presentation of females who are intoxicated are slumped or stumbling, thus failing to perform normative feminine drinking practices.

This is reflected in the campaign 'Play your night right' (2009), in which one of the sources features a young woman labelled 'The crier'. Mimicking the game of 'Top Trumps', various scores for behaviour such as 'tantrums', 'hours in the toilet' and 'drunk dials' are listed. Above this is the image of a woman's face, which is covered in mascara-stained tears. The viewer is presented with a construction of transgressive femininity, in which intoxication has led to *undesirable emotional behaviour*. Thus, the act of showing negative emotions presents female intoxication as transgressive femininity. The audience is expected to view this image and identify that the woman will experience shame as a consequence of becoming intoxicated and crying.

The outcomes of drinking for the women in these sources are clearly less extreme than in the mid-19th-century sources discussed earlier. The ideal drinking behaviour here is characterised as moderation, not abstinence. However, the devices used to construct intoxication as transgressing ideal femininity are remarkably similar to those used in the sources examined earlier. The use of shame as a device in the discursive construction of women failing to perform normative feminine drinking practices is apparent in these contemporary sources. The representations of intoxicated women are to invoke feelings of shame by the viewer. The assumed values of the viewer are that a drinking woman who is slumped or unsteady on her feet will feel ashamed when sober. Other behaviours that are directly related to transgressive feminine drinking practices are crying or vomiting, both of which are constructed as making the woman appear unattractive. Failing to meet the standards of normative feminine drinking practice causes the woman to fail to be attractive. This is constructed as undesirable, considering the association of night-life socialising and sexual liaisons (Chatterton and Hollands, 2003). The expectation is that such behaviours should provoke feelings of shame for the drinking woman.

Conclusion

This chapter has sought to illustrate how gendered alcohol regulation, as a form of moral regulation, has used discursive constructions of ideal and transgressive femininity in the reproduction of normative feminine drinking practices.

In both time periods examined here – the mid-19th century and post-2004 – alcohol regulation campaign materials used shame as a device, to affirm to the viewer of campaign materials what normative feminine drinking practices should be.

Yet it is essential to note the impact of the social context on the way female drinkers are presented in these campaigns. In the mid-19th-century campaigns, the aim was to use moral suasion to achieve total abstinence from alcohol. In the post-2004 campaigns, the purpose is to encourage self-regulation of consumption to government-recommended limits. This key difference affects the stories presented by the campaigns.

The outcomes for women who are presenting transgressive femininity in contemporary campaigns are less extreme than those in the mid-19th century. In the mid-19th-century examples, prostitution, insanity and death were the consequences of failing to meet the ideal of femininity through drinking alcohol. In the contemporary sources, the outcomes are related to loss of feminine poise and reputation, especially sexual reputation. The threat of the visibility of being drunk, of recognition of transgressive femininity among peers, is presented as shaming.

In spite of these differences, the devices used in the gendered regulation campaigns are using moral regulation to impact upon drinking behaviours. Contemporary gender discourses, of ideal and transgressive femininity in relation to normative feminine drinking practices, continue to be shaped by Victorian gender norms and values. Women may have achieved greater participation in drinking alcohol, especially in the night-time economy (Chatterton and Hollands, 2003, p 151), yet discursive constructions of drinking women who are seen to fail to be normatively feminine do not reflect this 'genderquake' (Chatterton and Hollands, 2003, p 148). The memory of Victorian gender values endures in the moral regulation of contemporary women's drinking.

References

Bartky, S.L. (1990) *Femininity and domination: Studies in the phenomenology of oppression*, New York, NY: Routledge.

Bordo, S. (2003a) *Unbearable weight: Feminism, Western culture and the body*, London: University of California Press.

Bordo, S. (2003b) 'Hunger as ideology', in Bordo, S., *Unbearable weight: Feminism, Western culture and the body*, London: University of California Press.

Chatterton, P. and Hollands, R. (2003) *Urban nightscapes: Youth cultures, pleasure spaces and corporate power*. London: Routledge

Critcher, C. (2011) 'Drunken antics - The gin craze, binge drinking and the political economy of moral regulation' in P. Hier (ed) *Moral Panic and the politics of anxiety*, Abingdon: Routledge.

Ettorre, E. (1992) *Women and substance use*, New Brunswick, NJ: Rutgers University Press.
Ettorre, E. (1997) *Women & alcohol: A private pleasure or a public problem?*, London: The Women's Press.
Harrison, B. (1994) *Drink and the Victorians* (2nd edn), Keele: Keele University Press.
Hunt, A. (1999) *Governing morals: A social history of moral regulation*, Cambridge: Cambridge University Press.
Nicholls, J. (2009) *The politics of alcohol: A history of the drink question in England*, Manchester: Manchester University Press.
Shiman, L.L. (1988) *Crusade against drink in Victorian England*, Basingstoke: Macmillan.
Warner, J. (1997) 'The sanctuary of sobriety: the emergence of temperance as a feminine virtue in Tudor and Stuart England', *Addiction*, vol 92, no 1, pp 97-111.
Warner, J. (2004) *Craze: Gin and debauchery in an age of reason*, London: Profile Books.
Waterson, J. (2000) *Women and alcohol in social context: Mother's ruin revisited*, Basingstoke: Palgrave.
Winskill, P.T. (1891) *The temperance movement and its workers: A record of social, moral, religious and political progress*, London: Blackie and Son.

Alcohol regulation campaign sources

'A sad sight' (1851) *The Band of Hope Review*, September, www.victorianweb.org/periodicals/bandofhope.html
'Bridget Larkins' (circa 1850) *Ipswich Temperance Tracts*, no 89.
'Catching up – left behind' (2011) Why let good times go bad, www.drinksinitiatives.eu/details-dynamic.php?id=313
'Dance floor – toilet floor' (2011) Why let good times go bad, www.drinksinitiatives.eu/details-dynamic.php?id=313
'Laughing with you – laughing at you' (2011) Why let good times go bad, www.drinksinitiatives.eu/details-dynamic.php?id=313
'The British juggernaut' (1851) *The Band of Hope Review*, December, www.victorianweb.org/periodicals/bandofhope.html
'The craving of a drunkard' (circa 1850) *Ipswich Temperance Tracts*, no 108, http://apps.nationalarchives.gov.uk/a2a/records.aspx?cat=182-druitt&cid=-1#-1
'The crier' (2009), Play your night right, www.behance.net/gallery/Drinkaware-Play-Your-Night-Right/731926
'The other hangover' (2009-11) www.theotherhangover.com
'The victim of excitement' (circa 1850) *Ipswich Temperance Tracts*, no 78.

THREE

Normalisation of hedonism? Challenging convergence culture through ethnographic studies of alcohol consumption by young adults – a feminist exploration

Shane Blackman, Laura Doherty and Robert McPherson

Introduction

This chapter is a feminist exploration of alcohol consumption by young adults, focusing on new patterns of alcohol consumption shaped by the social relations of gender. We seek to restore a sense of agency to young women's alcohol consumption, and show how feminine drinking practices have begun to impact upon consumption by young men. While recognising similarities between the drinking *patterns* of each gender, we identify key gender distinctions between the drinking *styles* of young men and young women; rejecting the notion of a 'convergence culture'. The initial sections critically address how government, newspapers and social media weave negative scrutiny alongside the promotion of neoliberal pleasures through sexualised images of young British women's increased freedom to drink. The data within this chapter are drawn from two ethnographic studies taking place in Canterbury and South London in the United Kingdom. The aim is to use these forms of participation observation to explore the extent to which forms of agency exist for young women and men within these new drinking cultures.

The field of alcohol: an arena of social contradictions and opportunities

For young British adults drinking alcohol is defined by having a good time. Consumption of alcohol increases forms of social confidence, while establishing bonds of solidarity, memory and friendship. The site of young people's motivation for 'getting drunk' is fed by an independent and global corporate culture industry that is defined by profit, while promoting images of responsible drinking (Plant and Plant, 2006). To understand the complexity of these social actions by individuals and institutions, we consider Bourdieu's (1984) concept of *field* as a useful tool to instigate our analysis of alcohol production and consumption as a social and cultural arena where people and institutions at micro and macro levels manoeuvre and struggle in pursuit of power and pleasure. Butler (1999, p 113) argues that: 'Bourdieu's work offers a reading of social practice that reintroduces the market as the context of social power'; adding that his critique is directed at 'exposing false antinomies' (1999, p 126). Specifically within this chapter, *field* operates in terms of change and constraint governed by the market economy and capital in relation to alcohol. Within the *field* of alcohol, we identify competition between different parties, including government, the media, charity organisations and the brewery industry. Young adult hedonistic lifestyles can be defined within Bourdieu's terms as a new 'ethics of fun' (Gronow, 1997, p 23); enactment of which creates and exposes a gender distinction between social competitors within the *field*.

For young adults in contemporary British society, participation in the new consumerist culture of intoxication is based on access, choice and opportunity: the very principles of neoliberalism. Within this study, we identify young adults as the main carriers of Bourdieu's (1984, pp 365-372) hedonistic ethos of consumption belonging to the night-time economy (Hollands, 1995), but at the same time observe young people's struggle within the social space of regulating alcohol as characterised by opposition, conflict and competition. We argue that there are gender and bodily differences in the way that young adults seek engagement in the 'new cultures of intoxication' (Measham and Brain, 2005). Using Bourdieu's emphasis on reflexivity, we present a series of 'ethnographic moments' to highlight his priority on 'fun ethics' as a way to shape the analysis towards restoring a sense of agency via pleasures to young adults' alcohol consumption.

Regulation and rhetoric: a critique of convergence

This section critically assesses the evidence for convergence theory, which suggests that female alcohol consumption replicates male intoxication: becoming celebrated and castigated as binge drinking. In *The government's alcohol strategy* (Home Office, 2012, p 2), Prime Minister David Cameron stated: 'Binge drinking isn't some fringe issue, it accounts for half of all alcohol consumed in this country. The crime and violence it causes drains resources in our hospitals, generates mayhem on our streets and spreads fear in our communities.' This statement is supported by the Office for National Statistics (2012, p 1): 'Young people (those aged 16–24) were more likely to have drunk very heavily (more than 12 units for men and 9 units for women) at least once during the week (27%).' Furthermore, Alcohol Concern (2013) has identified that 'the problems caused by alcohol misuse continue to rise which is putting an increasing strain on our NHS'. In *The Guardian*, Andrew Langford (2012) warned: 'Alcohol abuse has reached crisis point in Britain.' Reports in the tabloid media follow similar patterns:

- *The Daily Express* (20 February 2013) asserted: 'Teenage girls are selling sex for alcohol' (*Scottish Express Online*, 2013).
- *The Daily Mail* (30 September 2013) stated: '293 youngsters were admitted to hospital – a rise of 35%'.
- *The Daily Mail* (19 November 2013) reported a: '"Meteoric rise" in alcohol-related deaths as a result of young people drinking heavily in their teens' (*Mail Online*, 2013a).

Statistically, men remain ahead of women in terms of drinking. Harker (2013, p 3) states: 'In 2010 the prevalence among young men remained at 24%'; corresponding with Peralta and Jauk (2011) who suggest that men are more likely than women to engage in heavier and more frequent drinking. There is an apparent acceptance of binge drinking related to men, whereby the consequent dangers of this normalisation (Parker et al, 1998) seem to matter little. For example, the focus on men and alcohol seems to be represented as less of a priority problem – perhaps slipping into being an unrecognised problem; in *The government's alcohol strategy* (Home Office, 2012), men are referenced four times, while women are referenced 11 times. Further coverage in the tabloid press confirms the centrality of women, sexuality and alcohol. The *Mail Online* shows videos of the drinking game NekNomination[1] portraying women wearing lingerie drinking beer, while there is less coverage of young adult males who have died as a result of the drinking game (*BBC News Online*, 2014). Conversely, an examination of social media images of young adult males photographed when drunk demonstrates a major focus on men being silly, with representations based on humour or practical jokes, whereas the dominant social media image of intoxicated young women is sexualised. We have found that the media interest in young women's patterns of drinking is not only focused on alcohol, but also concerned with gendered behaviour; challenging social expectations of acceptable feminine behaviour, or the apparent 'distaste at "unfeminine" loss of control' (Staddon, 2011).

Challenging images of 'ladette' femininity emerged once the template of 'lad' culture was set by O'Hagan (1991) in *Arena* magazine. In 2001, BBC News reported that 'ladette' entered the *Oxford English Dictionary* under the definition: 'young women who behave in a boisterously assertive or crude manner and engage in heavy drinking sessions' (*BBC News Online*, 2001). 'Ladette' narratives articulated within the media reinforce a culture of convergence. For example:

- Dutchman-Smith (2004) stated: 'They're [women] matching men drink for drink.'
- *The Guardian* (17 October 2003) reported: 'Ladette culture leads to rise in binge drinking';
- Slack (2008) in *The Daily Mail* reported: 'Menace of the violent girls: binge-drinking culture fuels surge in attacks by women.'

Feminine imagery remains under attack from mainstream media in contemporary society, addressed through criticism of the overtly sexualised and provocative dress-style known as 'stripper-chic'. Accordingly, Carey (2011), in *The Daily Mail*, questions: 'Why do young women go out dressed like this?'; continuing the debate by drawing parallels between this style of dress and alcohol consumption, defining young women who drank and wore skimpy outfits as adopting a 'stripper-chic' style. Currently, social media websites have moved beyond the 'stripper-chic' imagery towards what Hebdige (2014) calls 'porn-etration – the penetration of the public sphere by pornography via the internet'. Alcohol companies use overtly sexualised feminine imagery to promote their brands, for example:

- the banned 'Hot Girl Funny Beer Commercial' by Guinness;
- 'Cool Beer';
- 'Thirsty for Beer';
- 'Miller MGD';
- 'Hot Beer Girls and Sexy Girls Playing Beer Pong'.

Within these images, skimpily attired young women are pictured consuming alcoholic products with highly sexual overtones. We identify humour and irony being used to mask the sexual objectification of women to sell products. Numerous pictures of young women in sexual poses on Facebook page 'NekNomination girls' conform to the heterosexual representation of women combining eroticism and alcohol and serving male sexual desire. The *Daily Mail Online* (2014a) posted a video of Rebecca Dagley: 'Woman, 19, walks into a supermarket and strips to her underwear to down can of lager in latest NekNominate dare.' This was followed by videos of other young women: Simone Reed drinking a can of beer dressed wearing a bra, underwear and suspenders in a Teesside job centre (*Daily Mail Online*, 2014b) and Steph-Lou Jones wearing just a thin swimming costume in McDonald's (*Daily Mail Online*, 2014c).

The British tabloid press have also been concerned with the promotion of alcohol and sexual displays in popular music and music videos. For example:

- The *Daily Express* stated: 'Alcohol promoted in chart hits' (*Express Online*, 2013).
- *The Daily Mail* highlighted: 'Pop songs which refer to alcohol brands could be encouraging young people to binge drink and have sex' (30 August 2013) and 'Nearly one in five songs in modern UK top 10s mentions alcohol' (1 October 2013).

A close examination of recent popular music videos shows a new focus on enjoyment through alcohol consumption with a range of messages. For example, consider:

- Pink's *Raise your glass* (2010);
- Katy Perry's *Last Friday night* (2011);
- Lucy Spraggan's *Last night* (2012).

These are celebratory songs of drinking alcohol for the purpose of becoming intoxicated. Jessie J's *Do it like a dude* (2010) follows a similar style, where young women not only want to adopt the exact same behaviour as the men; they also desire the same – albeit male-defined – rewards resulting from intoxication. The theme of exploitation is extended in LMFAO's *Shots* (2009); focusing on female sexual objectification hidden via humour, where drink is used as a means for men to gain sexual pleasure from women.

These are examples of contemporary popular culture's concentration on the visual performance of young women under conditions of alcoholic intoxication wearing 'stripper-chic' style clothes. Constant repetition of these images and narratives of female sexual availability through drinking constructs an image of young women as 'eye candy' where women are viewed through the 'male gaze' (Mulvey, 1975). The social media preoccupation with tight 'high hems' and 'low tops' has a strong voyeuristic appeal, suggesting that alcohol not only loosens female personal inhibition, but also drives female sexual desire. Griffin et al (2012, p 15) argue that young women's drinking practices form part of a 'technology of sexiness', where 'freedom and sexual empowerment' are not only illusory but also increase women's insecurity. It seems that the government's increased concern about alcohol consumption by young women, and the social media focus on hyper-sexual femininity linked with women's drinking, assert that there is a convergence between the sexes in alcohol consumption (BBC News Online, 2006). Women are presented as seeking to drink like men and pursue sexual pleasures previously identified as masculine. Thus, McRobbie (2004) concludes: 'hard drinking marks the corrosion of feminist values'.

The assertion that women's drinking is motivated by sexual desire is both discriminatory and limited. We wish to challenge the notion of a 'convergence culture', and support Measham and Østergaard (2009) who criticise the argument that young women are drinking like men. They maintain that public debate has fallen 'back on stereotypes of gender, age and occupational class and common-sense notions' (Measham and Østergaard, 2009, p 416). Evidence from government that supports this notion comes from Harker (2013, p 3): 'The prevalence of binge drinking among young men and women has fallen since 1998. In 2010 the prevalence among young men remained at 24% while among young women it fell to its lowest recorded level at 17%.' The Office for National Statistics (2012, p 1) supports this statistical decline: 'Between 2005 and 2012 the proportion of men who drank alcohol in the week before being interviewed fell from 72% to 64%, and the proportion of women fell from 57% to 52%.' On this basis, we critique populist coverage of young women participating in heavy sessional drinking on a par with men within contemporary journalism and academic study, which we identify as a new way to increase surveillance on female leisure (eg, Wechsler and McFadden, 1976; Bloomfield et al, 2001).

Storey (1999, p 7) maintains that a naive notion of emulation reinforces a top-down model of culture and communication, which does not allow for different voices outside those of the dominant expression. We argue that social emulation theory is being used to define female consumption of alcohol; impoverishing the complex social and cultural practices of women's drinking. In contrast, we see the new opportunities for young women to be desirably drunk that are intimately linked to the hyper-sexual femininity within the night-time economy as a market device to support neoliberal ideologies.

There is no new acceptability of female drinking culture, but an intensive commodification of drink brands alongside the promotion of female sexual availability (Szmigin et al, 2011). There remains traditional chastisement of women for losing control and market manipulation of female sexuality to sell alcohol. A key contradiction is that young women feel liberated through alcohol consumption, which enhances their social freedom; confirmed by their increased economic independence. This has been identified as a sign of emancipation. Ideas of convergence get mixed with a criticism that feminism is to blame for women's unfeminine behaviour leading them astray. As Phipps (2004) states: 'We demand explanations for women's drinking that we don't ask of men.'

Ethnography

Here we focus on two ethnographic studies researching patterns of interaction by young adult male and females within the night-time economy. The field diaries prioritise 'ethnographic moments' with young people from Canterbury and South London. The aim of these ethnographic moments is to move beyond normalisation of male drinking as an aggressive night-time event and introduce a series of descriptions focusing on the social and cultural competition and contradiction of young adults' consumption of alcohol. Each of the young adult participants and the ethnographic locations are anonymised throughout the subsequent passages.

Pub Golf – two games in one!

Using ethnographic data from a city-centre pub in Canterbury, we apply the 'ethics of fun', revealing distinctions between young men and women as social competitors within Bourdieu's (1984) notion of the *field* of alcohol. Throughout the fieldwork, a common example relates to the group-based game Pub Golf,[2] whereby young men and women drink together to various levels of intoxication. The field diary records that at a pub, a group of 14 – eight men and six women – arrived dressed in colourful, revealing outfits:

> It's 7.30 p.m. on Saturday evening. A mixed-gender group enters the pub together. Alex (the notional leader) immediately approaches the bar, producing a homemade scorecard: 'alright mate, we're on pub golf "hole" number eight. It's gins and tonics in here for us all.' The young men

> and women purchase a drink, marking their scorecards. The group remain mixed, but the young men and women then splinter into gendered groups to consume their drinks. The men urge each other to consume their drinks quick. Alex to Garry: 'Come on you pussy, you struggled in the last place. Man up, get it down you.' Alex tells Kevin: 'Get it down you; don't be such a girl.' The men look drink-weary. The women go about their business with more reservation. They order their drinks with the men, but then survey the scene as the young men drink and cajole each other.

All participants are fully engaged with the ambition of 'calculated hedonism' (Griffin et al, 2009). Initially, it could be argued that Pub Golf supports the notion of a 'convergence' as all participants are expected to follow similar *patterns* by consuming the same alcoholic product within the same predefined parameters of volume and time. But from the outset, a distinction between young men and women's drinking *styles* emerges. The participants split into gendered groups as the physical consumption commences, and the men display greater urgency than the women towards rapid consumption. The competitive edge to the game is male gendered, reinforcing the perception that men's drinking can be framed within a normalised context of 'silliness'; this is acceptable, unquestioned and normalised within the night-time economy. The males also engage in sexualised 'banter' within traditional masculine parameters, exclusive from women. Conversely, as the female participants become incidental to the competition between the men at the point of consumption, it becomes apparent that aspects of gender difference within the 'ethics of fun' emphasise a rejection of convergence; towards distinctly gendered forms of 'calculation':

> Whilst the men are unaware of the women drinking, the young women look and discuss between themselves the scene. Jade to Kelly: 'Shit, they're well on their way now [regarding the young men]; we'll just stick to the rules, but if I can't do it, I can't do it.' Kelly to Jade: 'Yeah, well someone's going to have to clear up the mess at the end of the evening. We'll just take it a bit easier – they'll never know.' The young women also consume their drinks quickly, but do not abide by the 'par' score. Alex sees that the young women are not abiding by the rules: 'Oi, come on, there's rules to this game, girls. We've [the men] all done it; you're letting the side down. Man up.' Gillian to

> Alex: 'Oh shut up, we've done them, haven't we? It's not so easy for us, we're smaller than you.' Jade: 'Yeah, and who'll be making sure that we all get home in one piece, sorts the taxis and everything else later – yeah, that's right, us. You do your thing, and we'll do ours.' This deters Alex from encouraging the women to drink at the same rate as the men. He recognises that the likely outcome is that the young women will provide greater structure to the potential outcomes of the evening: 'Yeah, well, I suppose you're right. Anyway, off to the next hole. Come on everyone.' He shows the group out of the door, directing them to their next 'hole'. As he leaves himself, he leans back inside the door and says: 'I'm fucked mate, shitfaced. I think I'm gonna be sick', before following the group.

The gender distinctions emerging between social competitors support Measham and Østergaard's (2009) rejection of convergence theory and affirm the notion of 'calculated hedonism', suggesting that all participants are engaged in Bourdieu's 'ethics of fun'. While both genders demonstrate aspects of a convergence in their drinking patterns, the differing attitudes towards the outcomes of intoxication offer a critique of young people's drinking, which remains distinctly gendered.

Glamour over consumption

In the ethnography, the women demonstrated that they wished to achieve pleasure through bounded levels of intoxication, exhibiting a 'controlled loss of control' (Griffin et al, 2009), by getting drunk but not 'too drunk'. Alongside intoxication, the women also wanted to maintain a valued feminine identity in the night-time economy, which was deemed as pleasurable, if not more so, than being drunk. For example, while in the women's bathroom in a nightclub, the space allowed women to maintain feminine and hyper-sexualised styles:

> Along the row of sinks and mirrors there is a woman standing in front of each, applying their make-up. They rummage through their handbags, pulling out various make-up items; applying blushers, concealers and brightly coloured lip-glosses. One woman pulls out a brush, backcombing her hair, giving it height and volume. When finished she turns to the woman beside her: 'How do I look?' The woman responds: 'Fabulous!' to which she asks:

> 'I don't look too drunk do I? I think I've had one too many and I don't want to look a state.' The other woman tells her: 'Honestly, you look fine.' She smiles, puts her hand on the other's shoulder, says 'thanks' and leaves.

This fieldwork experience shows how young women feel that alcohol interferes with their feminine status; this is valued over consumption. This coincides with Griffin et al (2012) that women are pulled between the contradictions and pressures of maintaining their 'respectable femininity' and drunkenness. It was also noted that women consumed feminised and 'glamorous' drinks such as cocktails, wines and sweet, fruit-based drinks to portray femininity, but actively restricted their consumption of these to coincide with maintaining a feminine identity. Therefore, women are engaging in pleasurable levels of drinking, but utilising the space of the bathroom to assess their intoxication and femininity, which consequently alters consumption patterns. This form of 'calculated hedonism' (Griffin et al, 2009) – limiting alcohol intake and being feminine/hyper-sexual – also revealed itself to be instrumental to other pleasurable pursuits, including dancing, bonding with friends, meeting new people and sex.

Feminisation of male drinking culture: private and domestic spaces

The ethnography enabled us to explore different forms of male drinking practices, which challenged conventional understandings of male hedonistic alcohol consumption; this included 'preloading' – the practice of drinking at a private residence before going out, a recognised activity for bonding. One evening, Jamie informed one of the researchers that they were going over to a male friend's flat earlier than previously arranged:

> When we arrived Liam answered the door, embracing Jamie in a manly hug, 'Alright mate? Come in', followed by Paul, who received the same greeting. Liam then saw myself [female researcher] and Samantha [research participant] looking slightly sceptical, 'Hiya ladies ... you've come early', and gave us both a hug and led us into the living room. Whilst Liam and the other men were talking to Jamie and Paul, Leo offered to help sort the drinks that we had brought, and showed us to the kitchen to get glasses for the wine. As he was sorting, Leo said: 'I didn't realise you and Samantha were coming over this early, I thought you were coming later?'

The early female presence among the group of men at the flat was clearly unwelcome. Young men frequently made these arrangements to meet up at one another's homes; either completely excluding women to these pre-drinking events or inviting them later. The men engaged in swapping and discussing clothes, listening to music and 'catching up'; talking about the opposite sex and getting ready:

> As we stood in the corridor, the men started talking about their clothes. Jamie asked Paul: 'Does my shirt over t-shirt look OK?' and looked for confirmation from Samantha and I. Paul laughingly said: 'Yes, Jamie, you look really lovely.' Jamie sheepishly asked: 'And what about my rosemary beads, they don't make me look gay do they?' This prompted laughter and he's told he 'looks fine'; which reassures Jamie. David: 'Actually, I usually borrow Mike's clothes, is he is ready yet?' He doesn't wait for an answer and walks to Mike's bedroom door, knocking loudly: 'Are you decent mate? I don't wanna see you with your knob out.' Mike comes to the door and lets David go in without saying anything. David winks back at us as he walks in. Samantha laughs: 'Is there something we don't know about there?' Paul and Jamie start laughing, but it's clear from their faces that David is just messing around. We hear David and Mike talking; after a few minutes they return and David has borrowed Mike's chequered shirt. He says: 'It's cold out tonight, and I look a bit boring with just a plain t-shirt. Now I get to be like Jamie.' He puts his arm around Jamie and they laugh. David turns to Samantha and me: 'This looks better, doesn't it?' We agree and he replies: 'I always borrow Mike's clothes', then goes off to chat with the other males in the living room.

This meeting of young adult male peers in a domestic setting reserved just for men where they could drink, converse and engage in preparation for their night out is comparable to a female 'bedroom culture' referred to by Lincoln (2012); which could explain why the female presence was unwelcome upon arrival. The ethnography follows on when the males enter a nightclub and we see another example of the feminisation of male drinking culture; demonstrating the importance of the male toilets while clubbing:

> Jamie tells me that he doesn't feel well and approaches David to inform him: 'It's time for the old tactical chunder.' David

> laughs and asks Jamie: 'Are you having that sugar rush thing again?' I ask him what a 'tactical chunder' is, and he tells me that when he's had too much sugar or alcohol, he feels a bit shaky and feels unwell – so he just goes to the toilets, makes himself ill and then carries on drinking afterwards because it makes him feel better. After returning from the toilets Jamie says that he succeeded in making himself ill, and feels 'so much better'. I notice that he smells of a strong but pleasant aftershave, and has a lollypop. Grinning like a child, he holds it up high to show us. I ask him why he has a lolly when he just said about having a sugar rush, but he laughs and says: 'I always get a lolly from "lollypop man" [toilet attendant].' Jamie and David proceed to excitedly tell me about their experiences of toilet attendants and phrases they have learned at various nightclubs, including: 'no spray, no lay', 'no splash, no gash', 'no Calvin Klein, no sexy time', 'no cologne, then go home'. Jamie says that the toilet attendant was singing a rhyme to him: 'lollies, lollies, sucky sucky lollies' which he drunkenly attempts to relay.

This account reveals that in a nightclub setting, young men also value the space of the bathrooms, as young women do, to assist them achieving pleasure during nights out. We see how Jamie utilises the space, although somewhat problematically to make him vomit, allowing him to continue to drink in the pursuit of pleasure. Here we see that young men like Jamie are encouraged to pursue pleasure through infantile/youthful products, including lollies, gum and sweets; but also sexual pleasure, which is insinuated by the crude rhymes conveyed by the toilet attendants, and from the display of condoms available. The space offers men opportunities for feminine practices to maintain their bodies, using hygiene products including aftershave, deodorants and hair gels to sustain their appearance and drinking abilities. Here, the 'ethics of fun' within these spaces appeal to previously excluded groups, including women, people from minority ethnic communities and gay populations (Chatterton and Hollands, 2003), but also assist young men in engaging in intoxication and its associated pleasures.

Stigmatised condemnation of women's drinking practices

In the ethnographic studies, we have seen young women structure their night-time drinking and, through their use of domestic and private space, operate methods of control. Simultaneously, we have observed women's condemnation regarding their level of drunkenness. In a discussion with males on the roles of 'street pastors',[3] they maintain the following:

Simon: 'The street pastors are trying to help and make sure that girls, for instance, who take their shoes off and cut their feet and whatever else; they are trying to make sure that they don't actually hurt themselves walking in bare feet.'

Sam: 'They are mainly there for the women. I mean, let's be honest, how many guys do you see bent over a rail outside, women end up on the floor with their hands in their hair, being sick, hunched over. It's women, who pass out! Girls need more attention than the guys, because that's what the girls are doing; rather than a group of lads singing rugby songs as they are walking down the high street.'

The males condemn women for being drunk and stigmatise their associated behaviours of removing their shoes and being sick almost as though they should not be allowed such freedom. They critique women who drink excessively, and implicitly reject the idea of convergence because of the inference that women 'cannot' and 'should not' attempt to drink like men because they 'can't look after themselves' and will 'pass out'. This condemnation was intensified when young adult males labelled women who wore sexualised styles as 'slappers', 'asking for it' or 'have what's coming to them' for being both drunk and sexualised. This stigmatisation is a feature of social interaction between young women and men, as revealed in the following observation:

> As we walked past Subway, a group of four young people were leaving the fast food chain – two men and two women. From the alcohol consumed they were talking loudly, laughing and joking. As we got closer, one of the men pulled up the woman's dress to her neck to reveal her underwear. The woman started screaming: 'What the fuck are you doing?' whilst trying to pull her dress back down, but she struggled. The man who pulled up the dress shouted and pointed: 'Look at that dirty slag, just look at her' and repeated 'what a slag' several times. The other woman shouted: 'That is so out of order, go and help her' to the other man, pushing him and hitting him. The men laughed hysterically and one ran away, grabbed onto a tree, clutching his stomach laughing to himself: 'Oh my god that

> was just too funny.' The woman at this point had gotten her dress back down and went over to her friend – they reached out to each other, stumbling, wrapped their arms around each other and walked away.

The two ethnographic examples show that alcohol and sexuality intensify social competition between men and women. Here, through the act of drinking, women are cast as pitiful objects of attention or opportunities for men to practise public degradation. It is not that drinking has led to women's loss of sexual restraint; they become male targets upon which to direct disapproval. It is the male who has constructed female sexuality as promiscuous. It is not that alcohol makes a woman desire sex more, but for men alcohol promotes an aggressive act. When the young woman's dress is pulled up above her shoulders, stigma comes into play as the males construct female sexual desire as deviant through her nakedness but also their 'deeply discrediting' language use. As Goffman (1963, p 152) notes, a person here is 'fully and visibly stigmatised ... must suffer special indignity.... [The woman has lost humanity and is] ... disqualified from full social acceptance'.

Conclusion

This chapter has sought to argue through critical analysis of media, government and popular culture depictions, that convergence theory denies agency and pleasure to female drinkers. We have argued for a restoration of feminine agency, and focused primarily on a prioritisation of the pleasurable accounts that young people associate with drinking. At the same time, we are in agreement with Hackley et al (2013) – we do not wish to underplay the personal and social consequences of young people's drinking patterns. This is demonstrated through two ethnographic studies, which highlight that contemporary drinking culture has implications for women, including stigma and moral condemnation, which are reinforced within the night-time economy by men. We argue that gendered drinking is a feminist issue, as we found that women construct their own space and autonomy within the night-time economy, while simultaneously encountering social and personal consequences. However, men's extreme drinking is overlooked as being normalised, less problematic or infantile, unless associated with violence as a moral issue.

From the ethnographic fieldwork, we identified that the way in which men are encouraged to drink is intensified by the neoliberal concept of 'pleasure', which reinforces the idea that women and alcohol equal male sexual pleasure. This is partly fed by the commodification of hyper-sexual femininity, where we found young women engaged in practices of female solidarity while fending off sustained forms of social oppression. Thus, women challenged the expectations of the night-time economy by examining their levels of intoxication; managing and pursuing their own valued ideas of pleasure. The data show that alcohol consumption and female expression of sexuality through 'promiscuity' can provide women with a source of fun, pleasure and strength, not merely stigma and vulnerability (Wolf, 1997). The ethnographic data showed that men in the study saw drinking women as not capable of drinking alcohol like 'them', 'pitiful', or degraded as a 'slag'. These examples reveal that males are seeking somewhat unsuccessfully to control women's sexuality through alcohol. However, at the same time, we identified how female drinkers under forms of oppression, also police their behaviour and bodies in order to conform to heterosexual representations that may serve male desires.

Notes

[1] A social media drinking game: a participant is filmed drinking an alcoholic drink, which is then uploaded to a website and they nominate others to do the same.

[2] 'Pub Golf' is a competitive drinking game which regularly incorporates members of both genders. The game is based around the idea that licensed establishments act as 'holes' on a golf course, where an alcoholic beverage is consumed within a 'par' score within each 'hole'. Larger drinks – i.e. pints of lager or ale are commonly given 'par' scores of four (i.e. four gulps to consume the whole drink), bottles of alcopops (for example) a par score of three, whilst spirits and mixers are 'par' two and flavoured shots are given a 'par' of one. Each participant has a printed scorecard where they have to write in their score from each 'hole'.

[3] Street Pastors are trained volunteers from local Christian churches who patrol the streets at weekends, and engage with members of their community. Street Pastors have established networks across the UK and internationally.

References

Alcohol Concern (2013) 'Alcohol Concern responds to latest statistics on alcohol' (online), www.alcoholconcern.org.uk/media-centre/news/alcohol-concern-responds-to-latest-stats-on-alcohol

BBC News Online (2001) 'Ladettes enter dictionary', 12 July, http://news.bbc.co.uk/1/hi/uk/1434906.stm

BBC News Online (2006) 'UK young women "out-drinking men"', 21 March, http://news.bbc.co.uk/1/hi/uk/4824794.stm
BBC News Online (2014) 'Up to five deaths caused by drinking game Neknominate', 22 February, www.bbc.co.uk/news/health-26302180
Bloomfield, K., Gmel, G., Neve, R. and Mustonen, H. (2001) 'Investigating gender convergence in alcohol consumption in Finland, Germany, The Netherlands, and Switzerland: a repeated survey analysis', *Substance Abuse*, vol 22, no 1, pp 39-53.
Bourdieu, P. (1984) *Distinction: A social critique of the judgement of taste*, London: Routledge & Kegan Paul.
Butler, J. (1999) *Gender trouble: Feminism and the subversion of identity*, New York, NY: Routledge.
Carey, T. (2011) 'Why DO young women go out dressed like this? We meet nightclubbers in four major cities to find the surprising and unsettling answer to the question despairing mothers are asking', *Daily Mail*, 30 November, www.dailymail.co.uk/news/article-2067391/Why-DO-young-women-dressed-like-We-meet-nightclubbers-unsettling-answer.html#ixzz30DVsIjHg
Chatterton, P. and Hollands, R. (2003) 'Producing nightlife in the new urban entertainment economy: corporatization, branding and market segmentation', *International Journal of Urban and Regional Research*, vol 27, no 2, pp 361-385.
Dutchman-Smith, V. (2004) 'Is alcohol really a feminist issue?', www.thefword.org.uk/features/2004/09/is_alcohol_really_a_feminist_issue
Express Online (2013) 'Alcohol promoted in chart hits', 2 October, www.express.co.uk/news/uk/433799/Alcohol-promoted-in-chart-hits
Goffman, E. (1963) *Stigma*, Harmondsworth: Penguin.
Griffin, C., Bengry-Howell, A., Hackley, C., Mistral, W. and Szmigin, I. (2009) '"Every time I do it I absolutely annihilate myself": loss of (self-)consciousness and loss of memory in young people's drinking narratives', *Sociology*, vol 43, no 3, pp 457-476.
Griffin, C., Szmigin, I., Bengry-Howell, A., Hackley, C. and Mistral, W. (2012) 'Inhabiting the contradictions: hypersexual femininity and the culture of intoxication among young women in the UK', *Feminism and Psychology*, vol 23, no 2, pp 184-206.
Gronow, J. (1997) *The sociology of taste*, London: Routledge.
Hackley, C., Bengry-Howell, A., Griffin, C., Mistral, W., Szmigin, I. and Hackley, R. née Tiwsakul (2013) 'Young adults and "binge" drinking: a Bakhtinian analysis', *Journal of Marketing Management*, vol 29, no 7-8, pp 933-949.

Harker, R. (2013) *Statistics on alcohol*, 29 March, London: House of Commons, www.parliament.uk/briefing-papers/SN03311/statistics-on-alcohol

Hebdige, D. (2015) 'After Shock: from punk to pornetration to "let's be Facebook Frendz!!"', in Osgerby, W. (ed) *Subcultures, popular music and social change*, Basingstoke: Palgrave, forthcoming 2015.

Hollands, R. (1995) *Friday night, Saturday night: Youth cultural identification in the post industrial city*, Newcastle: Newcastle University, http://research.ncl.ac.uk/youthnightlife/HOLLANDS.PDF

Home Office (2012) *The government's alcohol strategy*, London: Home Office.

Langford, A. (2012) 'Alcohol abuse has reached crisis point in Britain', *The Guardian Online*, 1 February, www.theguardian.com/healthcare-network/2012/feb/01/alcohol-abuse-crisis-point-britain

Lincoln, S. (2012) *Youth culture and private space,* Basingstoke: Palgrave Macmillan.

Mail Online (2009) 'Scourge of the ladette thugs: rising tide of violent crime committed by young women', 30 January, www.dailymail.co.uk/news/article-1131719/Scourge-ladette-thugs-Rising-tide-violent-crime-committed-young-women.html#ixzz30DUr7r89

Mail Online (2013a) 'Meteoric rise in alcohol-related deaths as a result of young people drinking heavily in their teens', 19 November, www.dailymail.co.uk/news/article-2510137/Meteoric-rise-alcohol-related-deaths.html

Mail Online (2014a) 'Woman, 19, walks into a supermarket and strips to her underwear to down can of lager in latest NekNominate dare', 9 February, www.dailymail.co.uk/news/article-2555072/Woman-19-walks-supermarket-strips-underwear-lager-latest-NekNominate-dare.html#ixzz30DWIGlSw

Mail Online (2014b) 'Woman strips to her underwear in the middle of a jobcentre as part of bizarre protest over benefits (but is it just the latest Neknominate dare to end up online?)', 15 March, www.dailymail.co.uk/news/article-2581551/Woman-strips-underwear-middle-Jobcentre-bizarre-protest-benefits-just-latest-Neknominate-dare-end-online.html

Mail Online (2014c) 'McNominate: young woman caught on camera downing pint of lager in McDonald's while dressed in Baywatch costume in latest twist on internet drinking craze', 12 February, www.dailymail.co.uk/news/article-2557473/McNominate-Young-woman-caught-camera-downing-pint-lager-McDonalds-dressed-Baywatch-costume-latest-twist-internet-drinking-craze.html

McRobbie, A. (2004) 'Free to vomit in the gutter', *The Guardian Online*, 7 June, www.theguardian.com/world/2004/jun/07/gender.comment

Measham, F. and Brain, K. (2005) '"Binge" drinking, British alcohol policy and the new culture of intoxication', *Crime Media Culture*, vol 1, no 3, pp 262-283.

Measham, F. and Østergaard, J. (2009) 'The public face of binge drinking: British and Danish young women, recent trends in alcohol consumption and the European binge drinking debate', *The Journal of Community and Criminal Justice*, vol 56, no 4, pp 415-434.

Mulvey, L. (1975) *Visual and other pleasures*, Basingstoke: Palgrave Macmillan.

Office for National Statistics (2012) *Drinking habits amongst adults, 2012*, London: Office for National Statistics.

O'Hagan, S. (1991) 'Is the new lad a fitting model for the nineties?', *Arena*, 27, spring/summer, May/June, pp 22-23.

Parker, H., Measham, F. and Aldridge, J. (1998) *Illegal leisure: The normalisation of adolescent recreational drug use*, London: Routledge.

Peralta, R. and Jauk, D. (2011) 'A brief feminist review and critique of the sociology of alcohol-use and substance-abuse treatment approaches', *Sociology Compass*, vol 5, no 10, pp 882-897.

Phipps, C. (2004) 'Why pick on us? We don't start fights. But like some leering bloke in a pub, the government won't leave women drinkers alone', *The Guardian Online*, 6 February, www.theguardian.com/politics/2004/feb/06/society.drugsandalcohol

Plant, M. and Plant, M. (2006) *Binge Britain: Alcohol and the national response*, Oxford: Oxford University Press.

Scottish Express Online (2013) 'Teenage girls are "selling sex for alcohol"', 20 February, www.express.co.uk/news/uk/378914/Teenage-girls-are-selling-sex-for-alcohol

Slack, J. (2008) 'Menace of the violent girls: binge-drinking culture fuels surge in attacks by women', *Mail Online*, 14 August, www.dailymail.co.uk/news/article-1039963/Menace-violent-girls-Binge-drinking-culture-fuels-surge-attacks-women.html

Staddon, P. (2011) 'Stigma and delight: making sense of women's alcohol use', in proceedings at the conference 'Qualitative Research in Mental Health', Nottingham University.

Storey, J. (1999) *Cultural consumption and everyday life*, London: Arnold.

Szmigin, I., Bengry-Howell, A., Griffin, C., Hackley, C. and Mistral, W. (2011) 'Social marketing, individual responsibility and the "culture of intoxication"', *European Journal of Marketing*, vol 45, no 5, pp 759-779.

Wechsler, H. and McFadden, M. (1976) 'Sex differences in adolescent alcohol and drug use; a disappearing phenomenon', *Journal of Studies on Alcohol*, vol 37, no 9, pp 1291-1301.

Wolf, N. (1997) *Promiscuities: The secret struggle of womanhood*, New York, NY: Fawcett Columbine.

FOUR

Alcohol, young women's culture and gender hierarchies

Alison Mackiewicz

Introduction

The aim of this chapter is to draw attention to the ways in which social factors influence how young women's alcohol issues in the United Kingdom (UK) are understood. Exploring current debates around neoliberalism, post-feminism and consumerism, together with my research on young women's articulations of femininity within the UK's culture of intoxication (Mackiewicz, 2012), I argue that femininity constitutes a hybrid of complex and contradictory discourses, which, in the context of drinking alcohol, is particularly dilemmatic for young women.

Women's alcohol consumption has been the focus of interest, concern and even hysteria for centuries. Historians tell us that there have been 'waves' of disquiet about women's drinking, and while intoxication is seemingly permissible for a man, it is not for a woman; not only has she transgressed the law and social convention, also 'she [has] specifically violated the norms of being a "good woman" – the norms of appropriate femininity' (Broom and Stevens, 1991, p 26). During recent decades, this focus has cultivated a series of 'moral panics' (Rolfe et al, 2009), often promoted by the mass media, of 'the ignorance and prejudices of a world in which there persists a chronic antipathy towards the use of alcohol by women' (Plant, 1997, p viii).

Young women in the UK today have been hyper-actively positioned within the context of a wide range of social, political and economic changes as the privileged subjects (McRobbie, 2009). By inserting and integrating women in these processes of change, various cultural aspects have, in the UK, been deemed 'feminised' (Adkins, 2001), including alcohol drinking. Alcohol plays a key role in UK culture, and young women's alcohol consumption has significantly increased over the last

20 to 30 years, particularly in drinking over the UK recommended weekly limits (Smith and Foxcroft, 2009).

Young women and alcohol consumption in the UK – facts and figures

In 2005, market analyst Datamonitor predicted that the amount of alcohol consumed by young women in the UK would significantly increase over the following five years, with women accounting for 38% of all drinking by 2010 (Rebelo, 2005). However, according to Measham and Østergaard (2009), the rise in young women's drinking peaked around the millennium. For example, average weekly consumption for women aged 16 to 24 years rose from 17% (7.3 units) in 1992 to 33% (14.1 units) in 2002. Additionally, the proportion of young women in this age group drinking more than six units on at least one day in the previous week[1] rose from 24% in 1998 to 28% in 2002 (Richards et al, 2004). Latest statistics from the Health Survey for England, carried out on behalf of the Information Centre for Health and Social Care (HSCIC), a government department, reveal that the percentage of young women exceeding six units decreased to 24% in 2011 (Ng Fat and Fuller, 2012). However, it should be noted not only that changes in the methodology of data conversion (alcohol volume to units), introduced in 2007, resulted in 'some undercounting of the number of units for certain types of drinks' (Goddard, 2007, p 1), but also that there seems to be a variation in the figures published by different organisations. For example, in the UK the General Household Survey (GHS) and the General Lifestyle Survey (GLF) have, between them, been measuring drinking behaviour for over 30 years, and in the GLF 2011 survey (ONS, 2013), the number of young women aged 16 to 24 who were reportedly drinking more than six units on at least one day in the previous week had fallen to 18%, not 24% as noted by the HSCIC.

Despite this decreasing trend in excessive drinking, British women aged 16 to 24 remain the heaviest female episodic or 'binge' drinkers, favouring Friday and/or Saturday nights in their pursuit of what Measham (2004, p 344) terms 'determined drunkenness'. Furthermore, there is evidence that women are more susceptible to the effects of alcohol than men (Alcohol Concern, 2008). With a rise in the number of women suffering from liver disease and other alcohol-related illnesses (Institute of Alcohol Studies, 2008), a number of researchers have pointed out that young women drinking heavily on a regular basis will be on track to develop these physical health complications in years to come (Plant, 2008; RCP, 2011).

While much of the recent academic work on alcohol consumption sees the current drinking culture as a new phenomenon, the British media suggests that 21st-century 'binge' drinkers are a repackaging of 20th-century 'lager louts' (Measham and Brain, 2005); or 'lager loutettes' as the-then British Home Secretary David Blunkett referred to women binge drinkers in 2004 (*Mail Online*, 2004). 'Binge drinking' is often perceived as involving a 'large number of [British] young women supposedly "believing" it quite acceptable to drink heavily and become conspicuously and often loudly drunk' (Plant and Plant, 2006, p 44); a view that finds particular support in countries where drunkenness, especially among women, is seen as socially unacceptable (for example, Southern Europe). Britain also stands accused of 'exporting' excessive alcohol consumption; like a disease 'spread' by British women to such countries as France, whose young female population see 'the excesses of their counterparts as glamorous and exciting, and something to emulate' (Allen, 2011, p 25).

However, despite the intense scrutiny that women's increasing alcohol consumption has come under in the past decade (in the UK press and governmental policies), until recently there appeared to be little feminist work on women's drinking per se (Day et al, 2004). Feminist researchers have examined media constructions of gender more generally (for examples, see McRobbie, 1991, 2004; Gill, 2007, 2009; Ringrose and Walkerdine, 2008), yet it is only in the last few years that we have seen a growing interest in exploring young women's practices of alcohol consumption with a focus on their negotiation of femininities within neoliberal cultures of intoxication (Niland et al, 2013).

Drinking cultures in the UK

Courtenay (2000) argues that health-related beliefs and behaviours, like other social practices that women and men engage in, are a means for demonstrating femininities and masculinities. Femininities and masculinities are negotiated and constructed within a shifting social landscape, and young people construct gendered subjectivities according to place and context in order to fit in with particular social situations. Portrayals of men's alcohol consumption and alcohol problems have often been contrasted with those of female drinkers in several important ways; men's alcohol consumption has been considered primarily as a normal *male* activity (Mullen et al, 2007) and their alcohol problems have been treated as a 'social fact' of masculine excess (Fillmore, 1984;

Lemle and Mishkind, 1989). However, not drinking, or being a light drinker, has been associated with femininity (Plant et al, 2002; Carlson, 2008). In this regard, research on gender and alcohol has a tendency to focus on men's accounts of drinking, showing how they associate drinking with masculinity and traditional masculine identities (Tomsen, 1997; Gough and Edwards, 1998; de Visser and Smith, 2007; Mullen et al, 2007). The relationship between women and alcohol, on the other hand, has been both fraught and complicated, with femininity and alcohol being considered 'unsuitable bedfellows' (Rúdólfsdóttir and Morgan, 2009, p 493).

Some would argue that a lack of rigorous policy and academic work into drinking in Europe and the UK, together with the labelling of 'binge drinking' as a British disease, have led to 'anecdotal stereotyping' (Jayne, et al, 2008, p 88); particularly since the idea that British young people, especially working-class young women, are drunk and 'out of control' seems to dominate political and popular discourse, and is constructed as particular 'classed' and gendered visions of ways of behaving (Skeggs, 1997). These constructions not only contrast with middle-class, cosmopolitan, civilised European drinking practices (Jayne et al, 2008, p 83), but also reverberate earlier-century representations of working-class women drinkers in the UK as immoral and unrespectable.

Nonetheless, facilitated by the introduction of the Licensing Act 2003 and 24-hour licensing, the night-time economy – a phrase often used to refer to night-time economic activity – is now a vital ingredient in the appeal of British town centres. The night-time economy has played a key role in the entertainment and retail provisions of cities at night, designed primarily to cater for 18- to 35-year-old consumer groups (Measham and Brain, 2005). The rapid redevelopment of inner cities, the creation of night-time entertainment precincts and a substantial increase in the number of pubs, clubs and restaurants in many post-industrial cities, have encouraged individuals to 'play with the parameters of excitement and excess' (Hayward and Hobbs, 2007, p 438). Current concerns about binge drinking must be moderated by a consideration of this rigorous commercial development, and the official sanctioning of young adult drinking by changes in licencing policy.

While people in the UK have, it seems, been binge drinking for centuries, Measham and Brain (2005) point to the significant attitudinal and behavioural changes in relation to alcohol consumption since the early 1990s, which arguably make it a new phenomenon; a new 'culture of intoxication', of which binge drinking is a product and involves the 'person in context'. However, in order to understand the emergence of this new culture of intoxication, Measham and Brain argue that we cannot simply link it to alcohol industry developments; rather, we must also take into account how we now live in consumer societies. Not only do young women (and young men) form their identities through consumption, but also the psychology of consumption is centred on the search for gratification, integration and identity formation. Consequently, increased *sessional* drinking is a reflection of this hedonistic leisure culture, fuelled by the economic deregulation of licensed leisure on which the night-time economy relies. A number of feminists have put forward similar arguments in highlighting links between a kind of 'it's about me' (Lazar, 2009, p 375) hedonistic individualism, based on gratification and pleasure, and the neoliberal economic principle (Gill and Arthurs, 2006; Tasker and Negra, 2007).

As a number of social theorists suggest, contemporary societies are consumer societies (Rose, 1991; Bauman, 1999) and consumption has replaced production as a marker of identity (Nava et al, 1997). Marketing campaigns sell goods and services to produce an identity in a lifestyle (Ringrose and Walkerdine, 2008), which is of central importance in a life, characterised by neoliberal governance, in which subjects are reconfigured as 'individual entrepreneurial actors across all dimensions of their lives' (Brown, 2005, p 57). Thus, for example, it could be argued that one of the purposes of licensed leisure is the possibility of consumption and achieving an identity produced through consumption.

Post-feminism and consumer culture

According to McRobbie (2009), freedom is an obligation, rather than liberation, and it is less about what young women ought not to do, and more about what they can do. Surrounded by messages which suggest that feminist struggles have ended, with full equality for all women having been achieved, young women must now enthusiastically embrace 'the constant stream of incitements and enticements' promoting 'success, attainment, enjoyment, entitlement, social mobility and participation' (McRobbie, 2009, p 57). These post-feminist incitements include a particular style of 'girlieness', which McRobbie (2009, p 158) argues is the 'pro-capitalist femininity-focused repertoire'; a style that third-wave feminists such as Baumgardner and Richards (2000) might promote as a form of women's or girl power. This is a style McRobbie (2009, p 158) sees as playing 'directly into the hands of corporate consumer culture eager to tap into this market on the basis of young women's rising incomes'.

Now free to compete in education and in work, girls and young women apparently excel in both, and their involvement, as both workers and consumers, creates new demand for unprecedented forms of technologies and cultural products, which, in turn, create new social spaces and public visibility. Drawing on a neoliberal vocabulary of 'empowerment' and 'choice', post-feminism is a double entanglement. The idea that women can benefit from the equal opportunities now available to them, and secure a 'post-feminist gender settlement, a new sexual contract' (McRobbie, 2009, p 57), is substituted for the disruptive threat posed by feminism. By analysing post-feminist femininity within the cultural context of alcohol drinking, this context has become a key site through which contemporary forms of femininity (and masculinity) are constituted, reproduced, negotiated and transformed, and an expanding body of feminist work has looked at the complex relationship between consumption, gender and identity (Harris, 2004; McRobbie, 2004). Fluid and ever-inventive alcohol marketing practices incorporate feminist and feminine themes into this contemporary consumer culture while aggressively seeking out women as consumers. And while some feminists have celebrated young women's engagement with consumer culture as agentic and pleasure-seeking, others point out that this 'freedom', accompanied by an increased hyper-sexualisation of girls, also works to re-inscribe young women within the disciplinary power of gender subordination (McRobbie, 2009).

Contemporary issues around gender, class and sexualisation might be linked to alcohol initially through the subject position of 'ladette'. In analysing the portrayal of the 'ladette', which first appeared in the UK media in the mid-1990s, Jackson and Tinkler (2007) highlighted how alcohol was central to her identity – she was a 'binge drinker'. 'Ladettes' were troublesome; not only because they occupied space outside the traditional feminine (indoor) domestic sphere, but also, more importantly, because they were presented as vying for space once reserved for men only – public drinking. Ladettes were also portrayed as being either middle class and, for example, part of the 'Bridget Jones' syndrome (Harris, 2001), or as women who could not eradicate their working-class associations. As Jackson and Tinkler (2007, p 255) describe, 'ladette' behaviours, such as those that are excessive (drinking, smoking, sex), disruptive (social order), crude (swearing), aggressive (verbal and physical) and 'open' (sexual), still remain associated with the least desirable, 'unrespectable' elements of working-class lifestyles (Skeggs, 1997, 2004).

Extreme alcohol consumption by young women, such as those occupying the position of ladette, is unsettling for the neoliberal project because of their apparent 'refusal to inhabit the position of responsible, moderate and rational subjectivity' (Griffin et al, 2009, p 470). With the emphasis on obligatory freedom, Griffin (2005) has argued that young women must drink alcohol if they wish to socialise, and alcohol is linked to social identity in the suggestion: 'if you don't have a social life ... then who are you?' (Mackiewicz, 2012, p 146). Yet, it is another practice that must also be, it seems, exceptionally feminine. Traditional and current discourses overlap and co-exist in talk about young women's drinking, with young women's behaviour being simultaneously pathologised as a health issue if they drink too much, and their femininity pathologised, through the figure of the ladette, as transgressive, feckless and not feminine enough (Jackson and Tinkler, 2007). Young women's gendered and sexualised consumption is an outcome of living in a neoliberal, post-feminist society, and although it involves a certain amount of freedom and agency, in dressing up and 'going out' in the public sphere, at the same time, for some women, it is accompanied by exclusion and denigration.

Young women drinkers

Exploring the influence of social factors in producing an identity in the alcohol arena, there has been a noticeable increase in portrayals of sexuality in alcohol advertising; advertisers' use of partially dressed or even nude women has been a technique that objectifies women, but as Gill (2009, p 100) argues, women are now presented as active, desiring sexual subjects who 'choose to present themselves in a seemingly objectified manner because it suits their liberated interests to do so'. As Amy-Chinn (2006) points out, this post-feminist emphasis, on women pleasing themselves, is double-edged, since advertising has become a key site for a hyper-sexual culture. We are witnessing 'a hyper-culture of commercial sexuality' (McRobbie, 2004, p 259) in which women are portrayed as proactively seeking sexual objectification and at the same time 'endorsing the ironic normalisation of pornography' (Amy-Chinn, 2006, p 173).

Alternatively, market researchers suggest that alcohol has been feminised, and this 'feminisation' has had the single biggest impact on the 'on-trade', with the introduction of drinks and venues specifically designed and promoted to appeal to women (Rebelo, 2005). 'Feminisation' as a process, has been applied by a number of theorists in relation to alcohol, starting with Wilkinson's (1994) suggestion that young women had been quietly leading a 'genderquake' revolution, resulting in a feminisation of nightlife culture (Lindsay, 2005; Measham and Moore, 2009). Day et al (2004) also used the term 'feminisation of drinking' to address the popular media's portrayal of alcohol as a pleasurable leisure activity for women. Together, these incentives driven by the alcohol industry have succeeded in increasing women's visibility and spending power in public spaces demarcated for drinking that were previously dominated by men (Measham and Brain, 2005; Plant and Plant, 2006). These changes, towards a supposedly feminised 'culture of intoxication', have also facilitated and contributed to the growing complexity and diversity in representations of femininity and practices seen as appropriate for women (Rúdólfsdóttir and Morgan, 2009).

Feminist theorists have long argued that respectability and (sexual) reputation form key dimensions of contemporary femininity (Skeggs, 1997). However, respectable 'nice' femininity is particularly classed and racialised in ways that limit which spaces young women might occupy. Marked as white and middle class, to secure the sign of 'respectable' femininity requires more than the appearance of femininity alone. It is also a way of behaving and a manner of conduct; it is about how women 'should' behave:

> Femininity requires the display of classed dispositions, of forms of conduct and behaviour, different forms of cultural capital, which are not a part of [working-class women's] cultural baggage: they are unlikely to display 'divine composure', which includes the components of femininity as silent, static, invisible and composed. (Skeggs, 1997, p 100)

Additionally, the contradictions of contemporary femininity are also established through the operation of a sexual/gendered double standard, whereby the agentic, unashamed expression of sexuality generally endorsed as a key marker of masculinity in men is more likely to be derided as a signifier of undesirable sluttishness in women (Cowie and Lees, 1981). Plant and Plant (2006) suggest that, as a result of various cultural shifts, this double standard has been eroded, and in the UK this is reflected in post-feminist discourses, and in terms of young women's drinking – 'ladette culture' (Jackson and Tinker, 2007). Young women, it seems, 'have license now to be badly behaved (drunk, disorderly and undressed …)' (McRobbie, 2004, p 9) and reject traditional forms of respectable femininity. Yet, as research has shown, if young women occupy the position of ladette, matching their male peers in drinking behaviours, they contradictorily risk being seen as unfeminine and failing as women. Furthermore, the policing of young women's drinking behaviour is often carried out by women themselves, and research has shown that for many young women in the UK, the 'new' culture of intoxication cannot be separated from traditional discourses of femininity (Mackiewicz, 2012).

It is important to examine the interaction between young women (and young men) and the social context of alcohol consumption, since perceptions of masculinity and femininity are embedded in drinking practices, and identity is very much about being seen, being somebody, being noticed and belonging. As a number of researchers have found, young women who participate in the UK's culture of intoxication face a particularly difficult set of dilemmas (Griffin et al, 2012; Mackiewicz, 2012). For young women especially, wearing the right 'labels' in terms of clothes, shoes and accessories, and how to drink, where to drink and what to drink in terms of alcohol and drinking establishments, have all become markers of belonging and acceptance (Ringrose and Walkerdine, 2008; Rolfe et al, 2009; Rúdólfsdóttir and Morgan, 2009). Furthermore, it is within the contradictions of neoliberal and post-feminist discourse, such as girl power, that certain aspects of the self are overlooked or hidden; aspects that cannot be displayed such as 'the failure to choose, to be choosable and chosen, [and] to display belonging' (Walkerdine, 2004, p 6). Wearing the 'right' labels is not a guarantee that you have succeeded in portraying a femininity that is respected, respectable and acceptable, as Tyler (2008) explains through representations of the 'chav'.

According to a number of feminists, under neoliberalism, normative femininity is highly exclusionary, premised on middle-class ideals and experiences (eg, Gill, 2007 [1982]; Kehily, 2008; Ringrose and Renold, 2012); and its boundaries are constitutive of 'others': deviant and failed femininity, which is in danger of slipping into unmanageable excess (eg, hyper-sexuality, pregnancy, dropping out of school, or delinquency and violence; Ringrose and Walkerdine, 2008, p 12). Subsequently, many working-class women become discursively constituted through negative discourses because of social and economic restraints. One such example can be found in Tyler's (2006, 2008) analysis of the figure of the 'chav', which, she argues, is part of a resurgence of the *explicit* naming of social class within contemporary Britain media. The word chav has become a term of 'intense class-based abhorrence' (Hayward and Yar, 2006, p 16), and in the case of the 'chav mum' is a typical sexually excessive, single mother: 'an immoral, filthy, ignorant, white, excessive, fat, vulgar and disgusting working-class whore' (Tyler, 2008, pp 26-28).

Skeggs (2005) extends this analogy to include the role that hen-parties have in the shaping of national moral public culture in Britain. As she states, all the moral obsessions once associated with the working class are now contained in one body: the hen-partying woman, whose body is beyond governance. Through her research, Skeggs (2005, p 966) found that 'hens' were variously framed by associations of 'contagion, pollution, danger, distaste and excess'; their loud and tasteless display of excessive femininities, combined with their binge drinking, makes them a target of tabloid newspapers and television media who present them as immoral and unruly, and thus a significant threat to the state of the nation as well as themselves.

This clear demarcation of class difference, through practices of consumption, is not a new phenomenon, since depictions of the white working class in Britain have always pivoted on appearance, and notably on a perceived excess of (bodily) materiality (Tyler, 2008). However, the vilification of young, white, working-class women that we see now can be understood in relation to the emergence of a new set of norms about femininity that reproduce clean, white, middle-class, feminine respectability. And the emphasis on excessive consumption generates the way in which sexuality is read on different bodies. The young woman (including her body) is now effectively under the spotlight, yet achieving neoliberal 'success' is not a reality for many young women and the 'failure' of many women becomes a form of '*othering*' (by women): a categorisation of women 'at risk'. These women are often seen as either most 'at risk' or those most likely to be risk-takers, and this not only ties into ideas of post-feminist neoliberal autonomy and empowerment, but is clearly visible in British drinking cultures where traditional discourses of femininity (eg, respectability and responsibility) come up against new 'sexualised' forms of feminine appearance. As a number of academics have found, there is now a hyper-sexuality within the night-time economy, with alcohol consumption playing a significant role in constructing the identity of the post-feminist woman (Measham and Østergaard, 2009; Mackiewicz, 2012). And the contradiction and complexity that young women face in constructing a feminine drinking identity is all too clear in the following narrative:

> I mean I've got friends that ... I would still consider very feminine ... that go out and get very drunk↑, but I think it depends on the way you act when you're very drunk ... I mean I know you're not in control then, but ... I don't think girls should probably get as drunk as ... guys.... [later in interview]

> I try and look feminine … I wouldn't go out like some girls … you know↑ … like big leather boots and basically … underwear for their clothing. If a girl wants to look feminine, she'd be kind've nicely dressed, she wouldn't look like a hooker … she'd be respectable. (Mackiewicz, 2012, p 151)

Young female drinkers may be more hedonistic and reflecting undesirable forms of femininity, but often these post-feminist discourses are overlaid onto persistent existing gendered dichotomies such as 'good girls' and 'bad girls', or virgins and whores (Jackson, 2006), which represent a form of social control over their behaviour (Fox, 1977). Young women's behaviour is always at risk of being reframed within more negative discourses about female sexuality (Gill and Arthurs, 2006), and one reason for this is that 'good' or 'nice' is a key form of femininity, fundamentally constituted through respectability (Skeggs, 1997). Women's alcohol drinking practices also inform, restrict and contradict these value constructs with dichotomies such as 'nice' and 'slag' still being used in today's neoliberal society. For example, the sassy girl discourse of a 'new fun-loving, independent and assertive young woman' may be, as Griffin (2005, p 11) puts it, a 'new' and up-to-date model that is more progressive than pre-feminist images of *nice* respectable girlhood. However, this apparent post-feminist autonomy and freedom is undermined by the combination of her 'big leather boots and basically underwear' (Mackiewicz, 2012, p 151) and her drunkenness; an outwardly 'appearance' that not only reflects young women's increasing representation as an 'object' of consumption, but is also a 'surface' for condemnation.

This is also apparent in the parlance that today's tabloid newspapers use for presenting women drinkers as 'titivaters' (objects) for their [male] readership (consumption), yet at the same time denigrating them as the deviant figure of drunkenness (Measham and Østergaard, 2009). Thus, this effectively undermines young women's independence and freedom and seemingly relocates women back inside the terms of traditional gendered (and classed) hierarchies.

Cowie and Lees (1981, p 20, emphasis in original) suggest that 'any girl (except perhaps middle-class girls who may have some protection by their class position) is *always available* to the designation slag in any number of ways', and with appearance crucial, this requires not wearing too much make-up or 'sexual clothes'. Furthermore, as Attwood (2007) notes, the term 'slut', or its equivalents (eg, 'slag'), is often used by women *against* women. For example in the following extract, a young woman explains how appearance matters:

> like I say, every girl, whether they are the majority ... will be in competition with each other. Not even for male attention, but for female acceptance … like if you're sort've staggering around drunk, looking, you know, like dress hanging down and looking terrible, they would hate you and say you were a slag. (Mackiewicz, 2012, p 184)

Despite its ambiguous use, sliding between friendly joking and label, the term 'slag' illustrates a very narrow tightrope that young women walk to achieve the impossible state of being sexually attractive 'without the taint of sexuality' (Cowie and Lees, 1981, p 20). This is further illustrated by several young (working-class) women in the author's study (Mackiewicz, 2012):

> [W]e're girls, and we like doing our make-up and we like looking nice, you know, nice dress … but we're not like ... sluts, why should we be called that just because we go out and get pissed. (Mackiewicz, 2012, p 208)

> I go out with ... a lot of make-up on↑ ... wearing not a lot, well, no, that's not, that's not fair ... I'll, I'll wear tight clothes and ... I show off my figure, that's the right way to put it ... and a lot of blokes take that as 'Yep come on', but I couldn't be further from that ... it's for me ... and a lot of people will say 'Oh she's up for it, she's asking for it' … and that's not the case <u>at all</u>.... (Mackiewicz, 2012, p 189)

> [T]here's the 'don't cares' and the 'do cares' but there doesn't seem to be anything in the middle … you know … you're either one thing or another … you can't drink loads, behave how you like and still retain … a certain reputation … good reputation and femininity. (Mackiewicz, 2012, p 170)

Conclusion

Each of the young women's narratives highlights how for many young women, particularly working-class women, in going out in the night-time economy they feel they have to prove themselves through every object, every aesthetic display and every appearance. And 'they care about how they are seen in the eyes of the other' (Skeggs, 1997, p 90) because their bodies, as embodied and experienced 'sites', are sites of doubt; sites where they are never sure if they are getting it right. The pleasure these young working-class women get from dressing up and participating in the 'culture of intoxication' is 'always disrupted by their knowledge of a judgemental external other who positions them as surveillants of themselves' (Skeggs, 1997, p 89). The young women evaluate themselves on the perceived judgements of others, and in so doing continuously create self-doubt. Skeggs refers to this uncertainty as the emotional politics of class, and for these working-class women, in the context of drinking in the night-time economy they can never make use of this social space in the same way as *others* (middle-class women, and men). For young women, in today's neoliberal, post-feminist culture, consuming oneself into being is the basis of 'being seen, being somebody, being noticed and belonging' (Ringrose and Walkerdine, 2008, p 230); yet, without a clear definition/knowledge of what is or isn't *the* 'right way', the process of *othering* is one way of claiming respectability.

Nonetheless, fraught with self-doubt and uncertainty in their attempts to claim respectability, the same young women are surrounded by processes of political and economic change, which depict them as better able to secure their social rights. Immersed in the seemingly neutral neoliberal language of personal responsibility, empowerment and, above all else, choice, young women are now the supposed privileged subjects (McRobbie, 2009), the new consumers par excellence (Harris, 2004). This highlights how femininity poses a dilemmatic problem for young women. Articulations of femininity within the UK's culture of intoxication constitute a fusion of complex and contradictory discourses, which often reinstate gender hierarchies (McRobbie, 2009) and undermine female solidarity. Nights out, being scantily dressed and drinking excessively are not necessarily something these young women perceive as liberating or even something they want to do; rather, it is an obligation. As Griffin (2005) states, young women must drink if they wish to socialise, since, as observed above, 'without a 'social life <u>then</u> who <u>are you</u>?' (Mackiewicz, 2012, p 146). Griffin, in 1982, argued that the dichotomy between 'good' and 'bad' women was not a straightforward ideological division that can be negotiated, and little, it seems, has changed – it is still 'a profound *contradiction* in which young women always lose, whatever they do' (Griffin, 1982, p 556).

The arguments presented in this chapter extend McRobbie's (2009) theorisation of post-feminist sites, which operate in reinforcing gender differences and gender inequalities, to include the 'culture of intoxication' as a 'space of attention'. The night-time economy, of which the 'culture of intoxication' is a part, is an example of this space within which some young women, in striving to negotiate contradictory and complex discourses of femininity, compete and critique each other on the basis of consumption. Furthermore, while some young women do talk of the necessity to drink if they wish to socialise, for others, intoxication may be pursued but not necessarily because it represents a 'pleasure' (Measham, 2004) or enables them to articulate the agentic (drinking) identities characterised by post-feminist discourse. Rather, I suggest that often excessive alcohol drinking is prescriptive; an essential part of being someone, but one with significant risks to be managed and identity dilemmas to be negotiated.

Note

[1] The measure intended to indicate heavy drinking that would be likely to lead to intoxication and set at more than six units for women.

References

Adkins, L., (2001) 'Cultural feminization: "money, sex and power" for women', *Signs*, vol 26, no 3, pp 669-695.

Alcohol Concern (2008) 'Women and alcohol – a cause for concern?', in Factsheet: *Alcohol Concern's information and statistical digest*, London: Alcohol Concern.

Allen, P. (2011) 'France's young binge drinkers upset cafe society with their "British boozing"', *The Observer*, 24 July.

Amy-Chinn, D. (2006) 'This is just for me(n): how the regulation of post-feminist lingerie advertising perpetuates woman as object', *Journal of Consumer Culture*, vol 6, no 2, pp 155-175.

Attwood, F. (2007) 'Sluts and riot grrrls: female identity and sexual agency', *Journal of Gender Studies*, vol 16, no 3, pp 233-247.

Bauman, Z. (1999) 'The self in a consumer society', *The Hedgehog Review: Critical Reflections on Contemporary Culture*, vol 1, no 1, pp 35-40.

Baumgardner, J. and Richards, A. (2000) *Manifesta: Young women, feminism, and the future*, New York, NY: Farrar, Straus and Giroux.

Broom, D. and Stevens, A. (1991) 'Doubly deviant: women using alcohol and other drugs', *International Journal on Drug Policy*, vol 2, no 4, pp 25-27.Brown, W. (2005) *Edgework: Critical essays on knowledge and politics*, Woodstock, NJ: Princeton University Press.

Carlson, M. (2008) 'I'd rather go along and be considered a man: masculinity and bystander intervention', *The Journal of Men's Studies*, vol 16, no 1, pp 3-17.

Courtenay, W.H. (2000) 'Constructions of masculinity and their influence on men's well-being: a theory of gender and health', *Social Science & Medicine*, vol 50, no 10, pp 1385-1401.

Cowie, C. and Lees, S. (1981) 'Slags or drags', *Feminist Review*, vol 9, no 1, pp 17-31.

Day, K., Gough, B. and McFadden, M. (2004) 'Warning! Alcohol can seriously damage your feminine health', *Feminist Media Studies*, vol 4, no 2, pp 165-183.

de Visser, R.O. and Smith, J.A. (2007) 'Alcohol consumption and masculine identity among young men', *Psychology & Health*, vol 22, no 5, pp 595-614.

Fillmore, K.M. (1984) '"When angels fall": women's drinking as cultural preoccupation and as reality', in Wilsnack, S.C. and Beckman, L.J. (eds) *Alcohol problems in women: Antecedents, consequences, and intervention*, New York, NY: The Guilford Press.

Fox, G.L. (1977) '"Nice girl": social control of women through a value construct', *Signs: Journal of Women in Culture and Society*, vol 2, no 4, pp 805-817.

Gill, R. (2007) *Gender and the media*, Cambridge: Polity Press.

Gill, R. (2009) 'Supersexualize me! Advertising and "the midriffs"', in (ed) *Mainstreaming sex: The sexualization of Western culture*, London: I.B. Tauris.

Gill, R. and Arthurs, J. (2006) 'Editors' introduction -- new femininities?', *Feminist Media Studies*, vol 6, no 4, pp 443-451.

Goddard, E. (2007) *Estimating alcohol consumption from survey data: Updated method of converting volumes to units*, Newport: Office for National Statistics.

Gough, B. and Edwards, G. (1998) 'The beer talking: four lads, a carry out and the reproduction of masculinities', *The Sociological Review*, vol 46, no 3, pp 409-435.

Griffin, C. (1982) 'The good, the bad and the ugly: images of young women in the labour market', in Gray, A., Campbell, C., Erickson, M., Hanson, S. and Wood, H. (eds) *CCCS selected working papers*, vol 2, Abingdon: Routledge, 2007.

Griffin, C. (2005) 'Impossible spaces? Femininity as an empty category', *ESRC research seminar series: New femininities: Post-feminism and sexual citizenship*, London: University of East London.

Griffin, C., Bengry-Howell, A., Hackley, C., Mistral, W. and Szmigin, I. (2009) '"Every time I do it I absolutely annihilate myself": loss of (self-)consciousness and loss of memory in young people's drinking narratives', *Sociology: The Journal of the British Sociological Association*, vol 43, no 3, pp 457-476.

Griffin, C., Bengry-Howell, A., Hackley, C., Mistral, W. and Szmigin, I. (2012) 'Inhabiting the contradictions: hypersexual femininity and the culture of intoxication among young women in the UK', *Feminism & Psychology*, vol 23, no 2, pp 184-206.

Harris, A. (2004) *Future girl: Young women in the twenty-first century*, London: Routledge.

Harris, S. (2001) 'Women in their 30s are new "ladettes"', *Mail Online*.

Hayward, K. and Hobbs, D. (2007) 'Beyond the binge in "booze Britain": market-led liminalization and the spectacle of binge drinking', *The British Journal of Sociology*, vol 58, no 3, pp 437-456.

Hayward, K. and Majid, Y. (2006) 'The "chav" phenomenon: consumption, media and the construction of a new underclass, *Crime, Media, Culture*, vol 2, no 1, pp 9-28.

Jackson, C. and Tinkler, P. (2007) 'Ladettes and modern girls: troublesome young femininities', *The Sociological Review*, vol 55, no 2, pp 251-272.

Jackson, S. (2006) '"Street girl": "new" sexual subjectivity in a NZ soap drama?', *Feminist Media Studies*, vol 6, no 4, pp 469-486.

Jayne, M., Valentine, G. and Holloway, S.L. (2008) 'Fluid boundaries—British binge drinking and European civility: alcohol and the production and consumption of public space', *Space and Polity*, vol 12, no 1, pp 81-100.

Kehily, M.J. (2008) 'Taking centre stage? Girlhood and the contradictions of femininity across three generations', *Girlhood Studies*, vol 1, no 2, pp 51-71.

Lazar, M.M. (2009) 'Entitled to consume: postfeminist femininity and a culture of post-critique', *Discourse and Communication*, vol 3, no 4, pp 371-400.

Lemle, R. and Mishkind, M.E. (1989) 'Alcohol and masculinity', *Journal of Substance Abuse Treatment*, vol 6, no 4, pp 213-222.

Lindsay, J. (2005) *Drinking in Melbourne pubs and clubs: A study of alcohol consumption contexts*, Melbourne, Australia: School of Political and Social Inquiry, Monash University.

Mackiewicz, A. (2012) 'New' femininities in the culture of intoxication: exploring young women's participation in the night-time economy, in the context of sexualised culture, neo-liberalism and postfeminism', doctoral thesis, British Library, uk.bl.ethos.582796#sthash.2sSPOxWS.dpuf

Mail Online (2004) 'Lager loutettes "fuel pub violence"', 19 July, www.dailymail.co.uk/health/article-310702/Lager-loutettes-fuel-pub-violence.html

McRobbie, A. (1991) *Feminism and youth culture: From 'Jackie' to 'Just Seventeen'*, Basingstoke: Macmillan.

McRobbie, A. (2004) 'Post-feminism and popular culture', *Feminist Media Studies*, vol 4, no 3, pp 255-264.

McRobbie, A. (2009) *The aftermath of feminism: Gender, culture and social change*, London: Sage Publications.

Measham, F. (2004) 'The decline of ecstasy, the rise of "binge" drinking and the persistence of pleasure', *Probation Journal*, vol 51, no 4, pp 309-326.

Measham, F. and Brain, K. (2005) '"Binge' drinking", British alcohol policy and the new culture of intoxication', *Crime, Media, Culture*, vol 1, no 3, pp 262-283.

Measham, F. and Moore, K. (2009) 'Repertoires of distinction: exploring patterns of weekend polydrug use within local leisure scenes across the English night time economy', *Journal of Criminology and Criminal Justice*, vol 9, no 4, pp 437-464.

Measham, F. and Østergaard, J. (2009) 'The public face of binge drinking: British and Danish young women, recent trends in alcohol consumption and the European binge drinking debate', *Probation Journal*, vol 56, no 4, pp 415-434.

Mullen, K., Watson, J., Swift, J. and Black, D. (2007) 'Young men, masculinity and alcohol', *Drugs: Education, Prevention and Policy*, vol 14, no 2, pp 151-165.

Nava, M., Blake, A., MacRury, I. and Richards, B. (eds) (1997) *Buy this book: Studies in advertising and consumption*, London: Routledge.

Ng Fat, L. and Elizabeth, F. (2012) 'Drinking patterns', in Craig, R. and Mindell, J. (eds) *Health Survey for England 2011, volume 1: Health, social care and lifestyles*, London: The Health and Social Care Information Centre, www.hscic.gov.uk/catalogue/PUB09300/HSE2011-Ch6-Drinking-Patterns.pdf

Niland, P., Lyons, A.C., Goodwin, I. and Hutton, F. (2013) '"Everyone can loosen up and get a bit of a buzz on": young adults, alcohol and friendship practices', *International Journal of Drug Policy*, vol 24, no 6, pp 530-537.

ONS (Office for National Statistics) (2013) 'An introduction', in *General Lifestyle Survey overview – a report on the 2011 General Lifestyle Survey*, London: Office for National Statistics, www.ons.gov.uk/ons/dcp171776_302472.pdf

Plant, M.L. (1997) *Women and alcohol: Contemporary and historical perspectives*, London: Free Association Books.

Plant, M.L. (2008) 'Women: the hidden risks of drinking', *The Observer*, 24 February.

Plant, M. and Plant, M.L. (2006) *Binge Britain: Alcohol and the national response*, Oxford: Oxford University Press.

Plant, M.L., Plant, M.A. and Mason, W. (2002) 'Drinking, smoking and illicit drug use among British adults: gender differences explored', *Journal of Substance use*, vol 7, no 1, pp 24-33.

RCP (Royal College of Physicians) (2011) *Royal College of Physicians' written evidence for the Science and Technology Select Committee's inquiry on alcohol guidelines*, London: RCP.

Rebelo, D. (2005) *New trends in young adults' alcoholic drinks occasions*, London: Datamonitor.

Richards, L., Fox, K., Roberts, C., Fletcher, L. and Goddard, E. (2004) *Living in Britain: Results from the 2002 General Household Survey*, Norwich: HMSO.

Ringrose, J. and Renold, E. (2012) 'Teen girls, working-class femininity and resistance: re-theorising fantasy and desire in educational contexts of heterosexualised violence', *International Journal of Inclusive Education*, vol 16, no 4, pp 461-477.

Ringrose, J. and Walkerdine, V. (2008) 'What does it mean to be a girl in the twenty-first century? Exploring some contemporary dilemmas of femininity and girlhood in the West', in Mitchell, C. and Reid-Walsh, J. (eds) *Girl culture*, Westport, CT: Greenwood Press.

Rolfe, A., Orford, J. and Dalton, S. (2009) 'Women, alcohol and femininity: a discourse analysis of women heavy drinkers' accounts', *Journal of Health Psychology*, vol 14, no 2, pp 326-335.

Rose, N. (1991) *Governing the soul: The shaping of the private self*, London: Routledge.

Rúdólfsdóttir, A.G. and Morgan, P. (2009) '"Alcohol is my friend": young middle class women discuss their relationship with alcohol', *Journal of Community and Applied Social Psychology*, vol 19, no 6, pp 492-505.

Skeggs, B. (1997) *Formations of class and gender: Becoming respectable*, London: Sage Publications.

Skeggs, B. (2004) *Class, self, culture*, London: Routledge.

Skeggs, B. (2005) 'The making of class and gender through visualizing moral subject formation', *Sociology: The Journal of the British Sociological Association*, vol 39, no 5, pp 965-982.

Smith, L. and Foxcroft, D. (2009) *Drinking in the UK: An exploration of trends*, York: Joseph Rowntree Foundation.

Tasker, Y. and Negra, D. (2007) *Interrogating post-femi-nism: Gender and the politics of popular culture*, Durham, NC: Duke University Press.

Tomsen, S. (1997) 'A TOP NIGHT: social protest, masculinity and the culture of drinking violence', *British Journal of Criminology*, vol 37, no 1, pp 90-102.

Tyler, I. (2006) 'Chav scum: the filthy politics of social class in contemporary Britain', *Journal of Media and Culture*, vol 9, no 5, http://journal.media-culture.org.au/0610/09-tyler.php

Tyler, I. (2008) '"Chav mum chav scum": class disgust in contemporary Britain', *Feminist Media Studies*, vol 8, no 1, pp 17-34.

Walkerdine, V. (2004) 'Neoliberalism, femininity and choice', *ESRC research seminar series: New femininities: Post-feminism and sexual citizenship*, London: London School of Economics and Political Science.

Wilkinson, H. (1994) *No turning back: Generations and the genderquake*, London: Demos.

[illegible] (2011) [illegible]
[illegible] (2006) [illegible]
[illegible] (2011) [illegible]
[illegible] (2006) [illegible] London: [illegible]

FIVE

Domestic abuse and women's use of alcohol

Sarah Galvani, with Christine Toft

Introduction

For centuries, society has legitimised men's violence to women at the hands of their fathers or husbands. In their review of the history of men's violence to women, Dobash and Dobash (1979, p 50) highlighted evidence from the 16th to 19th centuries, which saw the 'legitimate use of physical chastisement' meted out to wives, children and servants from the husband or father of the house. In some cultures and families, this belief in a man's right physically to 'chastise' remains, in spite of attempts to legislate against it since the end of the 19th century. Independence and equality are not an automatic right for many women; daring to challenge their father's or husband's ownership and power still results in domestic and sexual abuse and murder. A brief glimpse at current local and national daily news will find yet another woman abused, scarred or killed by the men in her life who are supposed to love her. We still live in a society where almost two women each week are killed by a partner, ex-partner or someone known to them (Coleman et al, 2011). We still live in a society where rates of known domestic abuse are depressingly high (ONS, 2014) and where the legal system struggles to respond (Topping, 2014). Domestic abuse is firmly rooted in our histories and cultures. It is not ideology; it is fact.

We also live in a society where alcohol use and drunkenness have been an integral part of maleness and masculinity but where women's use of alcohol has been frowned upon at best.

This chapter provides an overview of the role of alcohol in the lives of women who experience violence and abuse. It draws on research evidence about women's use of alcohol in the context of violence and abuse, outlines theories of alcohol's role in violence and draws on frontline practice experience to highlight good practice for working with women who experience alcohol problems and domestic abuse.

It begins with a brief overview of the definition of domestic violence and abuse (hereafter termed 'domestic abuse' for brevity) and its impact on women and children.

Domestic abuse

The definition of domestic abuse has developed over the years alongside our understanding of its gendered nature and, most recently, our greater awareness of abuse within young people's intimate relationships.

The Home Office definition of domestic abuse is:

> any incident or pattern of incidents of controlling, coercive, threatening behaviour, violence or abuse between those aged 16 or over who are, or have been, intimate partners or family members regardless of gender or sexuality. The abuse can encompass, but is not limited to:
>
> - psychological
> - physical
> - sexual
> - financial
> - emotional.
>
> (Home Office, 2013)

For the first time in the history of the United Kingdom (UK), the current definition includes 16- to 17-year-olds following evidence that young people aged 16–19 years experience more dating violence than any other age group (Home Office and AVA, 2013). Teen or adolescent violence and abuse to partners, peers and parents is receiving greater attention although child-to-parent violence is still in its relative infancy in terms of recognition and service responses (Holt, 2012).

Who does what to whom

Domestic abuse is gendered. Far more women and girls experience domestic and sexual abuse than men and boys. This is not to devalue the experience of men who suffer domestic abuse; it is simply a matter of fact. In a study entitled 'Who does what to whom', Hester (2009) explored gender and domestic abuse perpetrators in one UK police force. She found the prevalence, intensity and severity of men's abuse and violence to be greater compared with women's abuse and that women were far more likely to be victims of repeated abuse. National evidence supports this. Findings from the Crime Survey for England and Wales show that more than 30% of women aged 16–59 reported suffering domestic abuse in their lifetimes, (4.9 million) with 7.1% of women in the same age group (1.2 million) experiencing domestic abuse in the previous 12 months (ONS, 2014). This compares with 16.3% of men in the same age group in their lifetime (2.9 million) and 4.4% (700,000) in the previous 12 months. However, while these data present the best indication of the prevalence of domestic abuse, they are limited due to the restricted age range (16–59 years only) and also the sensitivity of disclosing such experiences in a public survey. Given the shroud of shame and secrecy that surrounds both victims and perpetrators of domestic abuse, reliable statistics are difficult to attain and the real scale of abuse is thought to be far higher.

The impact of domestic abuse

The impact of domestic abuse can be both intense and short lived and long-term and disabling. While women's responses will vary, what they say clearly is that the bruises and scars of physical abuse heal but the emotional and psychological damage lasts far longer. Among the negative effects are:

- feeling afraid;
- lacking self-esteem and self-worth;
- doubting one's own attractiveness and judgement;
- questioning one's abilities to perform as a colleague, partner, mother or daughter;
- depression, trauma and other symptoms of mental distress.

For women who experience abuse, seeking solace and comfort in family and friends is often not possible where the abuse has involved, or resulted in, social isolation, as well as unemployment and financial dependence on an abusive partner.

Children often witness, or become involved in, the violence and abuse as either victims or perpetrators (Hester, 2009), with many – but not all – young people experiencing negative consequences of the abuse within their own adolescent and adult relationships (Barter, 2009). Young women in particular have been found to suffer more physical harm and injuries, be more fearful and suffer more negative emotional consequences than their male counterparts (Barter, 2009). While the impact on children will vary with age, they learn early on in life to keep secrets because of the stigma and fear around domestic abuse. As with adult abuse, this can lead to social isolation and an avoidance of social occasions because they could not, or would not want to, reciprocate. Children can experience emotional neglect and abuse, psychological or psychiatric problems, behavioural changes and developmental delay. Their care from their parents or guardians can be inconsistent, poor quality, neglectful and overly punitive. Their routines and play time can be disrupted, and they may feel highly conflicted about feelings towards their parents. Importantly, they can feel guilty and responsible for somehow starting the domestic abuse or failing to stop it (for a review, see Humphreys and Mullender, 1999).

In sum, women and girls experience the greater proportion of domestic abuse within their intimate relationships from both partners and family members. This reality is not gender neutral; nor can it be divorced from historical (and current) debates about women's position in society. History clearly shows both the support of abuse to women in national policy and, later on, the lack of application of law prohibiting men's violence to women. It is unsurprising, therefore, that women still experience the majority of recorded abuse and that services that sit outside specialist domestic abuse services are ill-equipped to deal with it. The impact of such abuse is neither short lived nor easily forgotten. For women of all ages who have suffered domestic abuse, they will often seek ways to help them to relax, sleep or escape their physical or psychological pain, including the use of alcohol and other drugs. It is to this latter issue that the chapter now turns.

The relationship between drinking and domestic abuse

There are two main relationships between domestic abuse and alcohol: the relationship between alcohol consumption and *perpetrating* domestic abuse and the relationship between alcohol consumption and *experiencing* domestic abuse. A number of theories have been proposed over decades to try to explain these relationships. Many relate to the perpetration of domestic abuse and are criticised for being overly simplistic and individualistic. Such theories rely heavily on the belief that excessive alcohol consumption alone can cause domestic abuse through its impact on cognition or mood. The evidence simply does not support this view although popular belief and media reports still suggest that the excuse of 'I didn't know what I was doing' is widely tolerated (for a review, see Galvani, 2004).

This is not to suggest that alcohol and other drugs do not have an impact on our bodies – clearly they do. All substances have a direct impact on our central nervous system. However, the resulting behaviour varies hugely from person to person. Even people who have a history of violence and abusive behaviour under the influence of alcohol do not behave that way every time they drink to excess. This suggests that something else is occurring. The question is, what influences some people to behave violently and abusively when drinking and others not?

The evidence suggests that there is a range of additional factors that affect the way someone behaves under the influence of alcohol, including the person's environment, individual characteristics, the relationship with the victim, as well as the potential costs and benefits of their behaviour. This multifaceted approach is reflected in models that explain men's violence to women. In its report on violence and health (Krug et al, 2002), the World Health Organization drew on ecological theory in offering a set of nested factors that contribute to violent behaviour (see Figure 5.1). What is important within this model is its attention to the community and societal influences on individual violent behaviour, in particular attitudes towards women and women's roles.

Figure 5.1: An ecological model for understanding violence

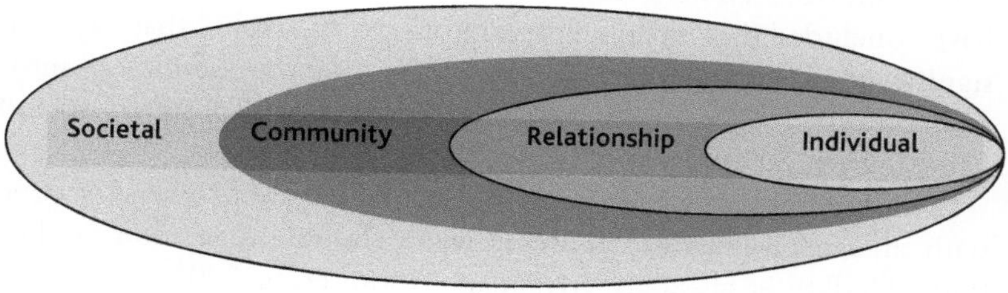

Source: Krug et al (2002)

These community- and societal-level influences have also been posited as important factors in how people behave under the influence of alcohol. In a classic text written in 1969, MacAndrew and Edgerton concluded that 'persons learn about drunkenness what their societies impart to them, and comporting themselves in consonance with these understandings they become living confirmations of their societies' teachings' (MacAndrew and Edgerton, 1969, p 172).

MacAndrew and Edgerton referred to what we currently know as social learning theory and socialisation processes. These are key in considering community and societal influences, in terms of both whether and how we drink and how we behave towards others under the influence of alcohol. They are also key in what we learn about gender and how masculinities and femininities are conveyed through the way we behave. As the historical context suggests, any theory that does not address the issue of gender and the sociocultural context of men's violence to women will ultimately fail to identify and address the key elements of it.

In relation to the victim's use of alcohol, three main relationships have been suggested:

- The victim's drinking is seen as the reason for her partner's violence to her.
- Alcohol is used to help women cope with the abuse they have experienced.
- Alcohol is used as a form of abuse, for example, the victim is coerced into drinking, physically or psychologically. She is then more likely to accede to the perpetrator's wishes.

Research has found little evidence of the victim's drinking as a sole motivator for the perpetrator's violence. The argument would be that the man is provoked to violence and abuse by the woman's drinking and alcohol-related behaviour. Indeed, studies that have explored this have concluded that it is the perpetrator's use of alcohol that has been significant in their perpetration of abuse, not the victim's (Kantor and Asdigan, 1997) or that its role remains unclear (Klostermann and Fals-Stewart, 2006).

Evidence does, however, suggest that women are drinking to cope with their experiences of abuse either in childhood or adulthood or both (Hedkte et al, 2008; Messman-Moore et al, 2009; Devries et al, 2013). The experience of some form of child and adult abuse is common among women who attend specialist substance use services (Bear et al, 2000; Breckenridge et al, 2010). Alcohol is quickly accessible compared with a doctor's prescription, a counselling referral, a divorce process or other potential ways to respond. It may not be a long-term solution but it offers a momentary and fast-acting 'liquid crutch'.

Increasing evidence is also emerging of substances being used as a form of abuse or coercion or to incapacitate victims. This is particularly the case for illicit substances and their relationship with sexual abuse through prostitution (Galvani and Humphreys, 2005; Goldenberg et al, 2012; Drugscope and AVA, 2013). Women have been forcibly injected with drugs or had drugs withheld from them, forcing them into painful withdrawal symptoms unless they did as they were told. Similarly, alcohol and other drugs can be used by victims of abuse simply because not doing so may create additional reasons for violence and abuse. Further, evidence from around Europe has shown the abuse and sexual assault of women who are intoxicated. In a study of 'drug-facilitated sexual assault' (DFSA) in Europe, alcohol was identified as the main substance in almost half the cases of DFSA in the UK (Olszewski, 2008).

Locating women's vulnerability to domestic abuse

Women with alcohol problems and who experience domestic abuse from a partner face a double stigma. Previous chapters have outlined the double standard relating to societal perceptions of women's drinking in comparison with men's drinking. While masculinity allows for and arguably supports men's drinking as an inherent part of many cultures, the same is not true for women (Hey, 1986; Peralta et al, 2010; Wells et al, 2014).

Traditional concepts of appropriate women's behaviour frown on inebriation; in spite of increasing rates of women's drinking in many cultures, society remains less tolerant and more stigmatising of misbehaviour by women under the influence of alcohol (Allamani et al, 2000; Waterson, 2000; Rolfe et al, 2009). Undoubtedly, this double standard relating to women's drinking is at the heart of women being blamed for their experiences of sexual or domestic victimisation. Too often, women continue to be blamed for being raped due to their intoxication and inability to avoid it (Sims et al, 2007).

In sum, there is no evidence of a simple causal relationship between alcohol use and the perpetration of domestic abuse without other factors being present. However, there is evidence that women who have been abused will use alcohol to cope with what are often long-term negative effects of domestic abuse. In doing so, they face further judgement relating to appropriate behaviour as a woman and mother and in failing to avoid their own victimisation.

The extent of problem drinking among women who have been abused

The extent of problem drinking among women who have experienced domestic abuse is not known. Alcohol treatment services are one source of information but most people with alcohol or other drug problems do not attend formal service provision, therefore service data can provide only a partial picture. Alcohol treatment services do not routinely question service users about domestic abuse, therefore prevalence data are limited to figures drawn from individual research studies using treatment populations over a short period of research time. Such research, however, has provided evidence of high levels of domestic violence victimisation among women receiving support for problematic alcohol and other drug use. North American data consistently show 60-70% of women in alcohol or other drug services experiencing physical abuse in the previous six to 12 months (Downs et al, 1998; Chase et al, 2003). UK evidence remains extremely limited but what there is also shows high rates of domestic violence or abuse (Humphreys et al, 2005; McKeganey et al, 2005). One of the weaknesses of such data is that they focus primarily on physical and sexual abuse and frequently fail to record other forms of abuse, for example, financial and psychological abuse. Again, this results in underestimates of prevalence and incidence of domestic abuse among these populations.

Another source of data is the annual Crime Survey for England and Wales. This records various types of domestic abuse, including partner and family violence, sexual assault and stalking. While the survey is limited to people aged 16–59 years, it currently offers some data on recorded domestic abuse and its relationship with the perceived alcohol and drug use of both offender and victim (ONS, 2014). In almost a quarter (24%) of domestic violence cases, the victim said that the perpetrator was under the influence of alcohol and 10% said that they (as victims) had also been drinking. The data also show that those who reported getting drunk more often also experienced partner abuse more often (ONS, 2014). What the analysis does not comment on is the direction of the relationship between the two as this was not part of the original data collection. In other words, it does not comment on whether people are getting drunk more often to cope with partner abuse or whether their more frequent alcohol consumption is creating tension and providing an excuse for their partner's abusive behaviour.

One final source of information is the domestic abuse refuge or shelter populations. In a review of studies based on shelter populations in North America, Schumacher and Holt (2012) found a wide range of prevalence of current or past substance problems, ranging from 22% to 72%. Even at its lowest figure, this represents more than a fifth of women in the shelter system. At its highest it is almost three quarters of shelter residents. Given that many refuges and shelters resist taking women with alcohol or other drug problems, or limit the number they accept, these figures are also likely to be underestimates.

Supporting women who live with alcohol problems and domestic abuse

Women who have problems with alcohol and who experience domestic abuse, be it past or present, can face incredible challenges accessing services. For women with problematic alcohol use, their access to domestic violence services can be restricted at best. Refuges can be unwilling to take women with alcohol or other drug problems due to concerns over managing their behaviour and risk to others, and assumptions about jeopardising the safety of the refuge location. Alcohol services are less likely to discriminate on service entry but often do not engage with the issues around abuse, thereby ignoring an important relationship between the woman's experiences of abuse and her drinking behaviour. It also overlooks an opportunity to assess for issues of safeguarding and to discuss safety planning. Evidence suggests that pockets of good practice exist but it is far from sector wide.

Traditionally, alcohol 'treatment' or interventions have been a white male domain although they are often described as 'gender neutral' (Salter and Breckenridge, 2014). Generally, alcohol services do not meet the additional needs of women drinkers who may have caring responsibilities and are more likely than not to have histories involving violence and abuse (Salter and Breckenridge, 2014). Embedding effective responses to women who are drinking and experiencing domestic violence takes ongoing and concerted commitment and effort. In 2008, the national UK charity Alcohol Concern set up the *Embrace* project to work with alcohol agencies around the UK on their responses to domestic abuse. It offered nine agencies a consultancy and training programme designed to improve awareness of domestic abuse and for this to inform their policies and practice response. The project evaluation found that effective leadership was most likely to result in service-wide changes in policy and practice providing all staff could be engaged, but that agencies should not underestimate the time needed to effect change (Templeton and Galvani, 2011). During the three-year project period, partnerships with domestic violence service providers had been developed informally and all agencies had developed or revised their policy relating to domestic abuse. However, barriers including staff changes and sickness, new commissioning or agency structures served to distract service development in this area.

In the UK, the *Embrace* project[1] and the ongoing work of the Stella Project[2] (www.avaproject.org.uk/our-projects/stella-project/stella-project-resources.aspxhas) led to the production of a number of good practice documents based on their experience of working with agencies and listening to women who use services (Stella Project, 2007; Delargy, 2009; Osman and Delargy, 2009; Bailey and Delargy, 2011). The following summary offers some wider information and guidance drawn from these sources and the professional experience of the authors.

1. Ensure that staff are adequately trained in understanding the links between alcohol and domestic abuse. It is important to understand the interplay between the two issues rather than focusing solely on the potential harm of alcohol consumption or on the domestic abuse.
2. Prioritise safety and safeguarding over and above other agency-based targets. Consider how domestic abuse impacts on someone's vulnerability and drinking behaviour. Even if the focus of the agency's work is the alcohol use, feeling safe and supported is likely to play a huge role in supporting a woman to change her drinking behaviour for the benefit of all. Reflect on the implications for policy and practice within your own service provision.
3. Questions about domestic abuse need to be asked routinely and discussed sensitively in alcohol treatment settings and followed up with joint work with substance use specialists where appropriate. The negative impact of domestic abuse does not stop when the woman is physically away from the perpetrator, particularly where there is shared contact over children.
4. Be aware of the potential for child-to-parent violence and abuse among women with alcohol problems. Do not assume that the woman is safe with the separation from, or the absence of, the adult perpetrator. It will be far harder to support her to control her drinking if she still lives with a loved one perpetrating abuse.
5. Given the close association between domestic violence and child abuse, be aware that other abuse may have been experienced and may be contributing to the woman's drinking. Ask the questions sensitively and be prepared to respond empathically.
6. Become familiar with safety planning – this is the domestic abuse equivalent of harm minimisation. When victims want to remain with the perpetrator, professionals are still able to offer support with safety planning if it is needed. For example, a professional can ask: 'Can you keep a bag of clothes/important personal documents at a friend's house?'
7. Be aware of how some alcohol self-help groups can give messages about alcohol behaviour change that are unhelpful at best and dangerous at worst. Some treatment approaches based on 12 steps or the Minnesota model, for example Alcoholics Anonymous,

emphasise 'powerlessness' over alcohol as part of making changes to people's drinking behaviour. They also suggest making amends to those who have been affected by the person's drinking. These types of concepts and suggested behaviour can be unhelpful to women who have suffered violence and abuse and who already feel powerless and have been blamed repeatedly for their partner's abuse of them. An exploration of these issues and guidance for AA sponsors, professionals and individuals attending AA are available (Grace and Galvani, 2009, 2010).

8. Couples and family work within alcohol services should not take place where there is domestic abuse or any recent conflict that you think could be domestic abuse. This could place the woman and any dependants at risk of reprisals and abuse following the intervention (Galvani, 2007).

Conclusion

Women experiencing domestic abuse live daily with the fear of what will happen next, who will find out and what people will think, and they worry about what the future holds. Many will fear for their own safety and that of their children long after the perpetrator is no longer a part of their daily lives. Seeking a means to escape this psychological and emotional trauma through alcohol consumption may not be a long-term solution nor the best choice for their health and wellbeing, but it is an immediate and short-term coping mechanism. When this coping mechanism becomes problematic and services are involved, women can face further negative judgement, professional control and, if children are affected, coercion from those who seek to support or intervene. While there are no easy solutions to these overlapping and complex issues, the starting point has to be one where an understanding of the impact of domestic violence is matched by an understanding of the crutch that alcohol may offer. The job of the professionals is to work to ensure an approach that avoids further victimising and blaming while at the same time provides an empowering, empathic and informed response with safety at its core.

Notes

[1] The Embrace project was a three-year project run by the national alcohol charity Alcohol Concern. Its focus was on working with alcohol agencies to ensure safe responses to domestic violence for both adults and children, were embedded in agency policy and practice.

[2] The Stella Project is part of AVA, a national charity working towards ending violence to women and girls. The Stella Project focuses on improving service delivery and policy relating to the overlapping issues of substance use, domestic and sexual violence.

References

Allamani, A., Voller, F., Kubicka, L. and Bloomfield, K. (2000) 'Drinking cultures and the position of women in nine European countries', *Substance Abuse*, vol 21, no 4, pp 231-247.

Bailey, K. and Delargy, A. (2011) *Knowledge set three: Families and carers*, London: Alcohol Concern.

Barter, C. (2009) 'In the name of love: partner abuse and violence in teenage relationships', *British Journal of Social Work*, vol 39, pp 211-233.

Bear, Z., Griffiths, R. and Pearson, B. (2000) *Childhood sexual abuse and substance use*, London: The Centre for Research on Drugs and Health Behaviour.

Breckenridge, J., Salter, M. and Shaw, E. (2010) *Use and abuse: Understanding the intersections of childhood abuse, alcohol and drug use and mental health*, file:///C:/Users/sgalvani/Downloads/use_and_abuse-libre.pdf

Chase, K.A., O'Farrell, T.J., Murphy, C.M., Fals-Stewart, W. and Murphy, M. (2003) 'Factors associated with partner violence among female alcoholic patients and their male partners', *Journal of Studies on Alcohol*, vol 64, no 1, pp 137-149.

Coleman, K., Eder, S. and Smith, K. (2011) 'Chapter 1: Homicide', in Smith, K. (ed) *Homicides, firearm offences and intimate violence 2009/10*, London: Home Office.

Delargy, A. (2009) *Knowledge set two: Parenting*, London: Alcohol Concern.

Devries, K.M., Child, J.C., Bacchus, L.J., Mark, J., Falder, G., Graham, K., Watts, C. and Heise, L. (2013) 'Intimate partner violence victimization and alcohol consumption in women: a systematic review and meta-analysis', *Addiction*, vol 109, 379-391.

Dobash, R.E. and Dobash, R.P. (1979) *Violence against wives: A case against the patriarchy*, New York, NY: The Free Press.

Downs, W.R., Patterson, A., Barten, S., McCrory, M. and Rindels, B. (1998) 'Partner violence, mental health, and substance abuse among two samples of women', Paper presented at the Annual Meeting of the American Society of Criminology, Washington, DC.

Drugscope and AVA (2013) *The challenge of change: Improving services for women involved in prostitution and substance use*, http://drugscope.org.uk

Galvani, S. (2004) 'Responsible disinhibition: alcohol, men and violence to women', *Addiction Research and Theory*, vol 12, no 4, pp 357-371.

Galvani, S. (2007) 'Safety in numbers? Tackling domestic abuse in couples and network therapies', *Drug and Alcohol Review*, vol 26, 175-181.

Galvani, S. and Humphreys, C. (2005) *The impact of violence and abuse on engagement and retention rates for women in substance use treatment*, London: National Treatment Agency.

Grace and Galvani, S. (2009) 'Care or control? AA and domestic violence', *Drink and Drug News*, 16 November.

Goldenberg, S.M., Rangel, G., Vera, A., Patterson, T.L., Abramovitz, D., Silverman, J.G., Raj, A. and Strathdee, S.A. (2012) 'Exploring the impact of underage sex work among female sex workers in two Mexico-US border cities', *Aids Behavior*, vol 16, pp 969-981.

Grace and Galvani, S. (2010) 'Care or control? Part II', *Drink and Drug News*, 15 March.

Hedtke, K.A., Ruggiero, K.J., Fitzgerald, M.M., Zinzow, H.M., Saunders, B.E., Resnick, H.S. and Kilpatrick, D.G. (2008) 'A longitudinal investigation of interpersonal violence in relation to mental health and substance use', *Journal of Consulting and Clinical Psychology*, vol 76, no 4, pp 633-647.

Hester, M. (2009) *Who does what to whom? Gender and domestic violence perpetrators*, Bristol: University of Bristol in association with the Northern Rock Foundation.

Hey, V. (1986) *Patriarchy and pub culture*, London: Tavistock.

Holt, A. (2012) *Adolescent-to-parent abuse: Current understandings in research, policy and practice*, Bristol: Policy Press,

Home Office (2013) 'Guidance: domestic violence and abuse', https://www.gov.uk/domestic-violence-and-abuse#domestic-violence-and-abuse-new-definition

Home Office and AVA (2013) *Information for local areas on the change to the definition of domestic violence and abuse*, London: Home Office.

Humphreys, C. and Mullender, A. (1999) *Children and domestic violence*, Totnes: Research in Practice, www.rip.org.uk

Humphreys, C., Thiara, R.K. and Regan, L. (2005) *Domestic violence and substance use: Overlapping issues in separate services?*, London: Home Office and the Greater London Authority.

Kantor, G.K. and Asdigan, N. (1997) 'When women are under the influence: does drinking or drug use by women provoke beatings by men?', in Galanter, M. (ed) *Recent developments in alcoholism – Volume 13: Alcohol and violence*, New York, NY: Plenum Press.

Klostermann, K.C. and Fals-Stewart, W. (2006) 'Intimate partner violence and alcohol use: exploring the role of drinking in partner violence and its implications for intervention', *Aggression and Violent Behavior*, vol 11, pp 587-597.

Krug, E.G., Dahlberg, L.L., Mercy, J.A., Zwi, A.B. and Lozano, R. (eds) (2002) *World report on violence and health*, Geneva: World Health Organization.

MacAndrew, C. and Edgerton, R.B. (1969) *Drunken comportment: A social explanation*, New York, NY: Aldine.

McKeganey, N., Neale, J. and Robertson, M. (2005) 'Physical and sexual abuse among drug users contacting drug treatment services in Scotland', *Drugs: Education, Prevention and Policy*, vol 12, no 3, pp 223-232.

Messman-Moore, T.L., Ward, R.M. and Brown, A.L. (2009) 'Substance use and PTSD symptoms impact the likelihood of rape and revictimisation in college women', *Journal of Interpersonal Violence*, vol 24, no 3, pp 499-521.

Olszewski, D. (2008) *Sexual assaults facilitated by drugs or alcohol*, Lisbon: European Monitoring Centre for Drugs and Drug Addiction, www.emcdda.europa.eu/publications/technical-datasheets/dfsa

ONS (Office for National Statistics) (2014) 'Chapter 4: Intimate personal violence and partner abuse', www.ons.gov.uk/ons/dcp171776_352362.pdf

Osman, Y. and Delargy, A. (2009) *Knowledge set one: Domestic abuse*, London: Alcohol Concern.

Peralta, R.L., Tuttle, L.A. and Steele, J.L. (2010) 'At the intersection of interpersonal violence, masculinity, and alcohol use: the experiences of heterosexual male perpetrators of intimate partner violence', *Violence Against Women*, vol 16, no 4, pp 387-409.

Rolfe, A., Orford, J. and Dalton, S. (2009) 'Women, alcohol and femininity: a discourse analysis of women heavy drinkers' accounts', *Journal of Health Psychology*, vol 14, no 2, pp 326-335.

Salter, M. and Breckenridge, J. (2014) 'Women, trauma and substance abuse: understanding the experiences of female survivors of childhood abuse in alcohol and drug treatment', *International Journal of Social Welfare*, vol 23, pp 165-173.

Schumacher, J.A. and Holt, D.J. (2012) 'Domestic violence shelter residents' substance abuse treatment needs and options', *Aggression and Violent Behavior*, vol 17, pp 188-197.

Sims, C.M., Noel, N.E. and Maisto, S.A. (2007) 'Rape blame as a function of alcohol presence and resistance type', *Addictive Behaviors*, vol 32, pp 2766-2775.

Stella Project (2007) *Domestic violence, drugs and alcohol: Good practice guidelines* (2nd edition), London: The Stella Project.

Templeton, L. and Galvani, S. (2011) *Think family safely: Enhancing the response of alcohol services to domestic abuse and families: External evaluation of the embrace project*, London: Alcohol Concern.

Topping, A. (2014) 'Police referrals of domestic violence cases fall', *The Guardian*, 10 March, www.theguardian.com/society/2014/mar/10/domestic-violence-police-referrals-numbers

Waterson, J. (2000) *Women and alcohol in social context: Mother's ruin revisited*, Basingstoke: Palgrave.

Wells, S., Flynn, A., Tremblay, P., Dumas, T., Miller, P. and Graham, K. (2014) 'Linking masculinity to negative drinking consequences: the mediating roles of heavy episodic drinking and alcohol expectancies', *Journal of Studies on Alcohol and Drugs*, vol 75, no 3, pp 510-519.

Part Two
Different women, different perspectives

SIX

Older women and alcohol

Marian Barnes and Lizzie Ward

Introduction

Alcohol use among older people is a neglected area in research, policy and practice. A large amount of government and media attention on alcohol has been focused on younger people's drinking and in particular on binge drinking and antisocial behaviour in public spaces. When we think about the problematic use of alcohol, we do not tend to think about older people, even though there are indications that drinking is increasing in the older population and that it may be the source of problems for some (NHS Information Centre, 2008; Smith and Foxcroft, 2009; Triggle, 2009). The very restricted research about older people's experience of alcohol means that their reasons for drinking and the kinds of services for and responses they would like to see to alcohol-related health and social problems are not well documented.

This chapter draws on a study that sought to understand the role of alcohol in the lives of older people without starting from the assumption that it is necessarily a problem. The aim was to provide a perspective that previous research has tended to neglect, namely, understanding people's life journeys as they get older, the kinds of issues they face, their problems and concerns and how alcohol may relate to these factors. It was a small qualitative study that involved both men and women in their 50s to 80s, but here we consider the perspectives of the women who took part. We explore how older women talk about the place of alcohol in their lives to consider the ways in which there are both problematic and positive aspects to this.

Within gerontological research, consideration of alcohol use is almost entirely focused on clinical and biomedical questions about the impact of alcohol on the ageing body and the extent to which it contributes to degenerative processes and cognitive function (Johnson, 2000; Peters et al, 2008; Plant and Plant, 2008). There is also a limited but growing body of work from health and social care practice, which deals with issues of working with older people who may have problematic alcohol use (Simpson et al, 1994; Herring and Thom, 1997a, 1997b; Klein and Jess, 2002). However, very few studies have looked at the cultural, social and economic contexts in which older people drink or how these might be connected to transitions and changes related to ageing, and likewise few have sought to understand these issues from older people's own perspectives. Thus, we were attempting to fill a gap in knowledge about older people's drinking behaviour, how this may relate to experiences of ageing and the ways in which this may vary across gender, class, ethnicity, sexuality and place (for full details, see Ward et al, 2008).

Methods

To meet this aim, we developed a participative approach, involving older people in designing and carrying out the research as co-researchers and as members of an older people's reference group. This was a collaborative project involving a steering group from a number of local agencies working in health, social care and housing and a local Age Concern as a community partner. We recruited four co-researchers from Age Concern's volunteer base, whose main role was to conduct the individual interviews, but they also took part in developing the research and in the analysis. The fact that alcohol can be a sensitive topic linked to stigma and shame, and thus a challenging one to research, shaped our approach to designing the research. The older people's reference group was set up to guide and stimulate the research process and offer other older people's perspectives on the topic. By working with the co-researchers and reference group, we were able to draw on our different knowledge, experience and expertise to develop a research approach that we hoped would enable older people to talk openly about their experiences of drinking. Our approach recognised the importance of older people as narrators of their own stories and experts in their own lives. We wanted to enable older people to speak about their experiences of drinking in ways that made sense to them and to construct their own ideas about the place of alcohol in their lives, rather than responding to predefined assumptions about, for example, recommended weekly limits in terms of units of consumption.

We developed a topic guide, which the co-researchers used to conduct 21 individual interviews and three focus groups. The topic guide helped the co-researchers to structure the interview by asking about the 'when', the 'where' and 'who with' of drinking. Participants were recruited from different backgrounds and circumstances in response to a flyer that was circulated through older people's networks, groups, agencies and sheltered housing. Our selection criteria were that participants needed to be over the age of 50 and drink alcohol regularly – we did not refer to either alcohol misuse or abuse. We assumed that describing alcohol as problematic might make it harder to find participants, but moreover we recognised that alcohol can play an important role in sustaining social contact and may be pleasurable in its own right. Of the 21 people who took part in individual interviews, eight were women – three were in their 50s, three were in their 60s and two were in their 80s. Five lived with their spouse, three lived on their own, of whom two were widowed and one was divorced. A further 15 women took part in the three focus groups. Two of these groups were mixed and one was a women-only group. All names given in this chapter are pseudonyms in order to protect the anonymity of participants in the study.

Overall findings

Even within our relatively small sample, it became clear in relation to questions around 'why', 'where', 'when' and 'who with', that people engaged in different drinking practices that were connected to their individual circumstances and biographies and to their social and economic circumstances.

Drinking styles

We identified four different 'drinking styles' in the accounts of the interviewees, as follows.

Social – regular

Typically within the 'social – regular' style, alcohol was seen as something enjoyable and pleasurable. It was connected to positive social interaction and drinking was characterised by an experience shared with spouses or friends. It was, in the main, something that took place at home as part of the evening meal and a daily activity. Three of the women who took part in the interviews typified this style. Jane described sharing a glass of wine with her husband in the evening:

> 'It's probably beneficial ... it's part of my relaxation after work and generally enjoyment. I tend to drink red wine ... and I think it's quite good for me all-round ... definitely part of my relaxing and being at home process ... quality of life.'

All three women, who were married and lived with their husbands, said that they probably would not continue to do this if they were on their own or if their husband was away. Angela explained drinking as very much a shared experience:

> 'I wouldn't open a bottle for myself because it's a social thing. You have a glass of wine and you're talking ... with my husband or when you're cooking.'

Social – occasional

The 'social – occasional' style was similar to the first in that drinking was linked to social occasions and in particular to food or meals out, but less frequently than every day. Four of the women who took part in interviews described this style of drinking. For some, alcohol had never been a significant feature in their life and for others, drinking had been reduced as a result of living on their own as a result of divorce or widowhood.

Heavy lone drinking

The defining features of the third style, 'heavy lone drinking', as the name suggests, were regular drinking in larger amounts, alone and outside of social interaction with others, usually at home. Only one woman described this style of drinking. In contrast to the six male interviewees we identified with this style of drinking who were single, divorced or widowed, Katie was married and lived with her husband.

Heavy drinking in a drinking network

In contrast to being a solitary activity, 'heavy drinking in a drinking network' includes elements of social interaction and takes place in the company of other drinkers. The networks included those whose social contacts were defined by their drinking, as well as friends who drank together. None of the women interviewed described this style of drinking.

Older women and alcohol

In this section we explore the way in which the women in our study made sense of the place of alcohol in their lives and in the lives of others – both those close to them and others they observed in their everyday lives. We relate their personal accounts to the way in which they understood acceptable behaviour for women, and how that had changed during their lifetime.

Women's histories

Any research with older people needs to encompass an understanding of the past as well as the present. We asked women to reflect not only on the current place of alcohol in their lives, but also how this had changed. This revealed some very different relationships with alcohol as a part of social and family life, as linked to work and to financial issues, as well as to both pleasures and problems within relationships.

For two women, alcohol had played a specific role in family employment. Thus, Christine told us that she came from a wine-making family that had owned a vineyard. In spite of this, her early experience was that wine was a luxury, not drunk everyday as it is now. Lily's grandfather had been a publican and Lily (now in her 80s and widowed) described how her mother, as a child, had had everything she could wish for because they were well off. However, she had seen other children with no socks or shoes because their parents had drunk away their money in their pub. Lily's mother had instilled in her the need to be wary about drinks being spiked and not to get drunk "because we don't want you home with an addition thank you".

Most women reflected on their own consumption of alcohol in the context of family and social life. Joanna described a typical experience in her youth of alcohol as only being drunk at Christmas or other special occasions and that, as a young woman, she had drunk very little and could only remember having been drunk once at a wedding. Sue, in her eighties, said that she came from a teetotal family – "my grandparents signed the pledge" – but that when she was a young student and social worker it was an inability to afford alcohol that meant she drank very little. In contrast, Jane said that she had been a regular drinker at weekends when she was a teenager and that alcohol had been a consistent part of her life, but what had changed for her as she grew older was drinking at home rather than in pubs.

Patterns of alcohol use over the women's lifetimes reflected life changes. During her married life, Lily and her husband spent every Saturday with friends drinking in hotel bars, although she said that she only drank Dubonnet and lemonade with the lemonade topped up when she was offered a second drink. Sue related her own and others' drinking to the different places and milieu in which she had lived with her husband. In Japan there was a weekend drinking culture among the professional Westerners living there, but she and her husband did not enjoy this; in the two years they lived in the United States, "I shouldn't think I ever had a drink there because I hadn't really a lot of social life … and I certainly didn't have a lot of money…." But after her husband was diagnosed with Parkinson's disease and they were back in England, drinking wine regularly became part of their lives: "There was very little else that gave him any enjoyment at all and he used to have a glass of wine at lunchtime and in the evening and I would have one in the evening."

Katie, who was in her 50s and younger than the other women in the study, was a current heavy drinker. She originally came from Norway and described her father as an alcoholic and her mother as "liking a drink". She described visits to her parents:

> 'Whenever we were over there, because it is very stressful with my mum as well, we used to have a drink. I always had to make the dinner, so we'd stand in the tiny kitchen and we always had to chat. I didn't have my time there alone. So we used to have a bit of gin … and then for dinner we used to have a glass of wine.'

Her mother had had a stroke, which led to the visits back to Norway to help her get a flat and to decorate this. During this time, "the drink really helped me".

Linda, a divorced woman in her 60s, spoke of an uncle who had a drink problem, although she had never met him and her motivation for taking part in the research was primarily a current concern about her daughter's drinking. It is notable that all the women we spoke to discussed their feelings about drinking in relation to others, in particular family members.

Current lives

Understanding women's drinking in context is not about offering causal explanations for the way women drink, but emphasises the diverse meanings and significance of this behaviour and how it interacts with other aspects of their lives. This becomes more evident when we consider the way women spoke about their current circumstances.

Jane's continuing use of alcohol as an enjoyable and relaxing activity had, as she had got older, shifted from going to pubs to a regular glass of wine with evening meals, and a developing shared interest with her husband for finding out about and exploring different kinds of wine. Angela offered a similar perspective on regular wine drinking as pleasurable and social, as well as more affordable than it used to be. Affordability is linked both to changed personal circumstances and to the reduced cost and more easy availability of alcohol that most commented on.

This current sense of drinking as part of shared lives and adding an element of enjoyment to these was also reflected in accounts of women now living alone following the death of a husband. Thus, Lily, who had associated drinking with sociability, suggested that "a lot of people drink when they get lonely" and she would sometimes have a drink with her meal when she was on her own. She said that if "something had triggered me off" and made her sad about the loss of her husband, she would have a glass of what her son called her "pink lemonade" (Lambrusco Rosé). Sue was more explicit about the way having a drink with a meal with a friend, or sometimes on her own, could feel:

> '… like a return to a happier time of my life, do you know what I mean? When my husband was alive and it was something we could enjoy together, just sitting, having a meal and a glass of wine … just having one always takes me back and I would think that's probably quite important to a lot of people.'

Those women who enjoyed small or moderate amounts of alcohol as a regular part of their lives thus described this as something that added to the quality of their lives without having any detrimental health or financial impacts.

For Katie, the role of alcohol in her life was rather different. She drank every day and in more substantial quantities than the others. She described arriving home from work: "No phone calls, don't want to talk to nobody, and I want my drink. And it is a must." In response to a question from the interviewer, she said that there were times when she also drank during the day "and once I start to get a taste I would like to continue". Katie linked her drinking to the stresses in her life: her mother's condition had deteriorated in the eight years since her stroke; Katie's son had a deteriorating physical health condition, he experienced depression and self-harmed; she described her marriage as difficult; and Katie herself now suffered from depression. She also had a rather negative view of the world in general:

> 'I just find a lot of shit. I don't understand it, I've no clue why we are here, so much sadness around. I see the old people coming in and their eyes die in front of you.'

In this context she described drinking as "an escape … very much a reward, and it's a feeling that you are chilling out, my time". She acknowledged that she probably drank too much (at least a bottle of wine a night), and she recognised that it had adverse effects on her health and her weight, but she sought to control her intake and did not try to hide her drinking. She said:

> 'I don't want to stop. I would like to moderate it, I would like to be able to say I drink weekends and not in the week, or something like that. Three out of four days or something I would be quite happy with. I would like to feel I didn't have to finish a bottle.'

Linda's account of her current life emphasised her involvement with local community activities and, while she did drink as part of this, she said: "It's very little significance, I could live without it." Some of the activities she took part in were held in places with a bar and her strategy then was to buy a drink that was not expensive and would last her the whole evening. She indicated that price was an important factor affecting her drinking, recounting a period when a double whiskey cost "two pounds something" and that this had encouraged her to try this, but she had experienced palpitations from drinking it so "that taught me a lesson" and she gave up drinking whiskey. Being in control of her drinking was important to her financially and in terms of the impact that alcohol had on her. One result of this was that a woman with whom she had made friends at a folk club became angry with Linda for not wanting to buy rounds and their friendship ended. Linda explained:

> 'I'm not going to spend £5 when I've just put £2.50 by and I keep more in control that way and I feel happier for it. And also the dangers of someone buying you a drink at a bar, they could easily slip something into your drink and it means to say that you're not in complete control if you've accepted that drink you know….'

These very different accounts of the place of alcohol in older women's lives suggest that we need to understand drinking as a factor within relationships; as something that can sustain existing relationships and memories of those that are past; but also as something that enables women to give something to themselves when other relationships are difficult and which can delimit those with whom women can and wish to maintain relationships. External factors impacting alcohol use relate to the cost and accessibility of alcohol in relation to the financial circumstances of the women themselves. And all the women in the study, in different ways, wanted to be in control of how and when they drank.

Women who took part in the women-only focus group discussed life transitions for women as they get older and how this might affect drinking patterns. Some of the women felt that as they got older and their responsibilities to family and children had lessened, they had more opportunity and time to enjoy themselves:

> 'I just feel at last, having got rid of the family, I'm … actually allowed, yeah exactly, I can actually afford to treat myself and have a couple of glasses of wine.'(Sonia)

Although this might indicate an increase in women's drinking as they enter later life, it was also pointed out that much of the keeping fit and healthy 'anti-ageing' industry was aimed at women and many may respond to this by drinking less. As Louise explained in relation to her friends:

> 'I mean there's a lot of, we're all living longer and we're all getting fitter as we get older, and there's so many women now taking health things … all these health magazines and going to gyms and looking after their health.'

Highlighting the fact that at different stages of the lifecourse, women are likely to have different priorities and this may relate to their drinking patterns, Winnie commented:

> 'You sort of hit fifty and you have more because you can because your kids have left. Then by sixty you start the tablets ... so you have to cut down.'

In relation to getting older and particular aspects of ageing, many recognised that alcohol may be used as a way of coping. Although some firmly believed that 'drowning your sorrows' was not a solution, there was sympathy and understanding towards older people who may use alcohol in this way if they are lonely or isolated. Maggie felt that it could be a problem for older women who were widows:

> 'A few women who I know, who are widows, slightly older than me, and don't go out much, and to keep on a brave front they pretend they don't drink, and I've happened to call on them and found them under the worse, so I think that is very sad because they're at home, lonely, drinking to forget their loneliness.'

Responses to others' drinking

As the above comment indicates, women spoke about others' drinking as well as their own. Such comments reflected views about what might encourage women in general to drink, and how they felt about why people drink and the impact that this has. There were critical comments about the ways people in general may be encouraged to drink more than they might want. Linda linked this to the social nature of drinking in pubs:

> 'It's a comradeship you know or camaraderie or whatever and the drinking is the same thing [as smoking] so it's almost like you've got to move out of that social group because you can't keep up with them.'

She also suggested that special offers encourage people to drink more because it is cheaper. Linda's interview demonstrated a wish to distance herself from the 'problem' of alcohol and this appeared to derive from both personal experience and her current concern about her daughter. She had been brought up in a convent and described one occasion on which she had made a fool of herself when she had been drinking, but that "I learnt my lesson that time". However, she described one of her daughters as "boozing it" and this obviously concerned her and appeared to inform her view that:

> 'I just feel everyone should try and help to solve the problem you know, and although I sympathise very much with people with a drink problem, I think they have a problem but it impinges on society....'

For Katie it was the increase in the alcohol content of wine that drew criticism: she saw no reason for this to be increased. She was also very critical of alcopops. A number of women acknowledged that the price of alcohol affected how much they drank, without this causing problems.

Lily was critical of women who drink too much: "I don't like to see a woman drink. And as for these ladettes, well they leave me speechless, which is unusual." Joanna was concerned about homeless drinkers who try to get in to her building. Sue recognised the cultural difference in the regularity with which her daughters drank in comparison with her own younger experience, but commented on this without criticism. As we have seen, the women we spoke to demonstrated an awareness of cultural as well as economic changes, which they suggested might account for an increase in alcohol use.

Some recognised that loneliness in old age can prompt alcohol use. As already noted, some spoke about this in relation to themselves, recognising the beneficial impacts of alcohol that do not necessarily lead to harm – "boosting you at the low points" as Sue commented. But they also reflected the potential for this to go further, without necessarily offering judgements on this:

> 'It's a very difficult situation to be left on your own after x number of years. And I think people find their own way of dealing with it … if you've been a coper all your life you continue and if you've needed to fall back on something which will help change your mood then I can understand why people do that….' (Sue)

Katie's experience of needing alcohol to help her cope with the stresses of her life led her to reflect on what would happen to others like her if alcohol is taken away "from the only place I feel happy … in a really rotten world and lonely world". She suggested:

> 'Some people might be able to reach out and get help somewhere else, but older people just really don't care, and they don't want help I suppose, or they want to carry on, but they probably would like to have some contact, somebody to care, even if they cannot be helped.'

Seeking help?

Those commissioning this research wanted to understand what sort of help older people who felt they had a problem with alcohol might find acceptable. As we have seen, most of our interviewees did not see themselves as having a problem and would not have been seen this way by others. Only Katie felt that her use of alcohol could be problematic and so in this subsection we start with what she said about attempts to get help with this.

Katie indicated that she did want to control her drinking and spoke of waking up in the morning telling herself she was going to stop, then by the evening drinking alcohol again. She recognised that she drank four or five times more than the recommended limit and that this was having an adverse impact on her weight and her fitness. The only time she had broached her drinking with her doctor was as the amount of alcohol she was drinking was building up – at that point about half a bottle of wine a day. When she suggested she had a problem, the doctor's response was "well, don't go above that, but don't be too hysterical about it either". By the time we spoke to her it was her poor health and lack of fitness that led her to want to control her drinking, but she was very critical of others who are over-positive and think that "there's a solution for everything". Her view was:

> "I don't mind if I drink myself to death once I'm old enough, if you know what I mean. I don't want to curb my drinking then. I don't need to live to about 80 or 90, I'd rather have a good drink and go out that way."

A number of women suggested that older people would be reluctant to seek help, including from Alcoholics Anonymous (AA), and that more 'user-friendly' services would be necessary. Those identifying a source of help suggested that general practitioners would be the first port of call. Sue's response to this question reflected what might be considered a preventative approach that recognises how older people could be made to feel a 'waste of space' and that there is a need to find both activities that people find valuable (in her case reading) and ways of sustaining relationships with others. Linda's suggested approach was to start much younger in life with an educative approach backed up by legal controls over special offers that encourage more drinking. She did not comment on the specific factors that may have an impact on drinking in older age.

Conclusion

This study on which this chapter is based was small scale and we do not claim to be able to offer generalisable explanations for why older women drink alcohol and why in some instances this may be a problem. Nevertheless, we do think that this research offers some insights into the experience of alcohol use in older age that are important to understand in developing policies and practices that might be helpful in preventing alcohol use becoming problematic.

Growing older is an embodied experience and many of the dominant responses to drinking in older age are based in concerns about the physiological impacts of alcohol use. However, what old age means cannot be understood solely by reference to bodily changes. Older women in particular experience many pressures to retain a youthful appearance as well as maintaining health in old age (see, for example, Hurd Clarke and Griffin, 2008). As we have seen, this may act to limit the use of alcohol, which is understood to exacerbate the bodily impacts of ageing. In contrast, women identify some of the liberating experiences of growing older and no longer having the same degree of responsibilities for others. This creates opportunities for older women to enjoy themselves and for some this can involve more frequent use of alcohol.

But for many women, it is not so much the physical as the emotional and cultural dimensions of ageing that are more problematic. Both the loss of specific people who have been close to them, and the loss of recognised roles, can render older women invisible and generate a sense of worthlessness. In this context, the use of alcohol can both serve as an embodied reminder of happier times and act to fill a space in their lives. If older women are to be encouraged not to use alcohol in this situation, then there is an imperative for an alternative. While some are well able to explore alternative activities that can generate a sense of value, this is not possible for everyone and 'activity' per se may not be the solution.

It is important to recognise the significance of alcohol use in the context of relationships in most instances. In most cases, the accounts of the women who participated in the study suggest that it is the relationships that are important rather than the alcohol, but that alcohol can facilitate and enhance relationships. Alcohol use to replace absent or mitigate difficult relationships is recognised as being problematic. Thus, in most cases, the social use of alcohol is experienced as beneficial, but the private use of alcohol may be more problematic. What we might describe as the 'privatisation' of alcohol use can be encouraged by the easy availability of alcohol via supermarkets and corner shops where it may often be cheaper to purchase than in public venues.

What is clear is that policy and practice responses to the perceived problematic use of alcohol among older women, based on advice about the numbers of units that it is safe to drink, are inadequate. We can draw similar conclusions from work on obesity to suggest that it is mistaken to think that information-based practices that address older women disconnected from the relational contexts of their lives can offer helpful solutions (Henwood et al, 2010). Similarly, brief interventions based in models of individual behaviour change are unlikely to be experienced as helpful.

Rather, if older women do recognise their use of alcohol as problematic, they need a response that is based in a willingness to understand the specific relational context in which a problematic use has developed, and a worker with the capacity to develop a supportive relationship through which they can explore alternative responses. But our research also suggests that we cannot find definitive motivations for alcohol use, or definitive solutions to any problem, solely at the level of individual older women.

References

Henwood, F., Carlin, L., Guy, E.S., Marshall, A. and Smith, H. (2010) 'Working (IT) out together: engaging the community in e-health developments for obesity management', in Harris, R., Wathen, C.N. and Wyatt, S. (eds) *Configuring health consumers: Health work and the imperative of personal responsibility* (pp 194-210), Basingstoke: Palgrave Macmillan.

Herring, R. and Thom, B. (1997a) 'The right to take risks: alcohol and older people', *Social Policy & Administration*, vol 31, no 3, pp 233-246.

Herring, R. and Thom, B. (1997b) 'Alcohol misuse in older people: the role of home carers', *Health and Social Care in the Community*, vol 5, no 4, pp 237-245.

Hurd Clarke, L. and Griffin, M. (2008) 'Visible and invisible ageing: beauty work as a response to ageism', *Ageing and Society*, vol 28, no 5, pp 653-674.

Johnson, I. (2000) 'Alcohol problems in old age: a review of recent epidemiological research', *International Journal of Geriatric Psychiatry*, vol 15, no 7, pp 575-581.

Klein, W.C. and Jess, C. (2002) 'One last pleasure? Alcohol use among elderly people in nursing homes', *Health & Social Work*, vol 27, no 3, pp 193-203.

NHS Information Centre (2008) *Statistics on alcohol: England 2008*, www.ic.nhs.uk/pubs/alcohol08

Peters, R., Peters, J., Warner, J., Beckett, N. and Bulpitt, C. (2008) 'Alcohol, dementia and cognitive decline in the elderly: a systematic review', *Age and Ageing*, vol 37, no 5, pp 505-512.

Plant, M. and Plant, M. (2008) *Alcohol and older people: A review of issues and responses*, Bristol: Centre for Public Health Research, University of the West of England.

Simpson, M., Williams, B. and Kendrick, A. (1994) 'Alcohol and elderly people: an overview of the literature for social work', *Ageing and Society*, vol 14, no 4, pp 575-587.

Smith, L. and Foxcroft, D. (2009) *Drinking in the UK: An exploration of trends*, York: Joseph Rowntree Foundation.

Triggle, N. (2009) 'NHS treating more older drinkers', BBC News, 5 March, http://news.bbc.co.uk/1/hi/health/7922002.stm

Ward, L., Barnes, M. and Gahagan, B. (2008) *Cheers!? A project about older people and alcohol*, www.brighton.ac.uk/_pdf/research/ssparc/cheers-report.pdf

SEVEN

The silences in our dance: Black Caribbean women and alcohol (mis)use

Laura Serrant

Introduction

This chapter explores the historical, cultural and gender-related contexts in which Black Caribbean women are associated with alcohol and alcohol use. Alcohol plays a distinctive social role in the family and community life of Black Caribbean women. For Caribbean communities in particular, it is often central in the great sociocultural rites of passage such as births, marriages and deaths. It graces their religious ceremonies, encases 'mother-love' through the eponymous Christmas cake and lubricates their parties. Moreover, alcohol also embodies some of their regional, geographical and economic identities through longstanding associations in the Caribbean with rum trading, plantation and slavery. For Black Caribbean women, however, the associations with strong liquor and the reflective visions of sexuality, risk and strength provide a subversive text to their relationships with 'strong' (a term used in the Caribbean for alcoholic spirits).

After identifying some of the important terms that will be used throughout this chapter, there follows a discussion of some of the background: the social, historical and cultural factors influencing this discussion, in order to understand the relationships and contexts in which Black Caribbean women engage with alcohol. Without clarification of some of the parameters within which Black Caribbean women are identified, it is difficult to gain an understanding of their drinking patterns or behaviours and how the complex interplay of culture, belief and social expectation has influenced Black Caribbean women's identities.

The Caribbean region and importance of migration

The Caribbean consists of the Caribbean Sea, its islands and the surrounding coasts. It lies southeast of the Gulf of Mexico and the North American mainland, east of Central America and north of South America. The region comprises more than 700 islands, islets, reefs and bays.

The word 'Caribbean' has multiple uses. For the purpose of this chapter, it is used to reflect its identity as both a geographical and political reference point. In this context, the Caribbean is recognised as including territories with strong cultural and historical connections to slavery, European colonisation and the plantation system. The majority of these islands has a long history of colonisation by European countries, which has left imprints of varying degrees on the language, culture and gender roles of Caribbean people and their communities (Chamberlain, 2002). Movement of peoples (both voluntarily and involuntarily) between the Caribbean and the rest of the world is therefore an inherent part of the identities of the people who currently inhabit the region. As a consequence, the Caribbean exists as both a united geographical region with a shared global position and a range of individual islands with diverse sociocultural identities.

Migration from the Caribbean has spanned centuries but in relation to Europe began to increase in earnest around 1953 and peaked around 1961 (Smith, 2005). The majority of the mass migration to the United Kingdom (UK) in particular is epitomised by economic factors and 'invitations' from Western countries such as Britain to travel to the 'motherland' to reinforce the depleted workforce following World War Two. Both the history of migration and the 'similar but different' identities of the Caribbean Islands have a key part to play in this exploration of Black Caribbean women and their relationship with alcohol. This chapter seeks to utilise an insider perspective and explore Black Caribbean woman's complex relationship with alcohol from a Black Caribbean feminist perspective. This insider perspective comes from the positioning of myself as a Black Caribbean woman presenting a critical discussion about my own community. It enables the weaving together of formal evidence from research with the personal 'insider' aspects of that community. In order to help to do this in a structured way, the 'Silences Framework' (Serrant-Green, 2011) is used as a reference point. This theoretical framework was designed to help researchers and other critical readers to explore sensitive issues (alcohol use in this case) from the perspective of marginalised social groups (Black Caribbean women). Here it will help to explain, explore and interrogate the complexities of Black Caribbean women's 'dance' with this strange friend and challenges us to hear the Silences (unsaid or unshared aspects of experience) that scream from with it.

The next section outlines the Silences Framework and identifies how it will be used to help guide our discussion of Black Caribbean women and alcohol use.

The Silences Framework

The Silences Framework (Serrant-Green, 2011) is derived from a concept called 'Screaming Silences'. Screaming Silences (or silences) define:

> areas of research and experience which are little researched, understood or silenced. 'Silences' reflect the unsaid or unshared aspects of how beliefs, values and experiences of (or about) some groups affect their health and life chances. They expose issues which shape, influence and inform both individual and group understandings of health and health behavior. (Serrant-Green, 2011, p 1)

The Silences Framework comprises four core stages and was designed to assist in investigating sensitive issues and/or marginalised perspectives, particularly concerning health-related issues. These stages provide a framework to guide the researcher from conceptualisation of a research question through to structuring the research report. The four core stages are:

- Stage 1: Working in silences (contextualisation)
- Stage 2: Hearing silences (location)
- Stage 3: Voicing silences (revealing)
- Stage 4: Working with silences (recontextualisation)

This chapter utilises the concept of 'Screaming Silences' and the approaches outlined in Stage 1 of the framework (working in silences) to explore the issues pertaining to alcohol use (sensitive issue) and Black Caribbean women (marginalised subjects). Here, working in silences reflects the broader context in which this exploration of Black Caribbean women and alcohol takes place. The chapter then moves on to 'hearing silences', considering the current 'state of play' in the relationship between Black Caribbean women and alcohol, identifying the silences that exist in relation to this subject and the consequences for Black Caribbean women and health. This contextualised, situated exploration of the issues begins by identifying the range and scope of existing knowledge relating to the subject and the social, cultural and personal spaces in which they take place.

The Silences Framework and the Screaming Silences underpinning it are rooted in anti-essentialist viewpoints such as feminism, critical theory and ethnicities-based approaches. While these have differing areas of focus, namely, women, anti-establishment and minority ethnic experiences, they all accept that what we view and experience as the social reality is constructed, rather than objective (Kincheloe and McLaren, 2002). As pointed out by many theorists supporting these approaches, this means that our world, society and places within it are determined by human beings in a particular society at a particular point in time (Williams and May, 1996). This is an important driver in exploring socially and culturally determined issues such as how gender, ethnicity and behaviours in relation to alcohol are experienced or identified in the lives of Black Caribbean women. Such a view of the world encourages us to be open to the existence of more than one reality rather than having a blind reliance on the dominant discourses often presented to us as 'truth'.

Utilising Screaming Silences as a basis for exploring social and cultural concerns places the voices and experiences of those who are seldom heard at the centre of dominant discourses; in this case, Black Caribbean women and their experiences with alcohol. They are situated as 'the listeners', that is, those whose experiences, along with the social and personal contexts in which they occur, are of greatest importance. The aim of any exploration from a silences standpoint is not simply to compare and contrast Black Caribbean women's experiences with reference to the dominant group but to try to present a contextualised 'insider' understanding of the impact of a particular subject (alcohol) on their daily reality and experience.

An important point in the Silences Framework and Black feminist standpoints is recognition that multiple realities are as much of an 'in-group' phenomenon as a 'between-group' reality (Serrant-Green, 2011). That is, multiple realities exist between Black Caribbean women as well as between them and Black Caribbean men, White women or other 'Black' groups. Variations in experiences occurring between individuals or groups of Black Caribbean women in differing social contexts elicit variations in the importance placed on the 'silence' and its perceived importance. This is in line with Black feminists' ongoing battle against traditional ways of viewing Black women as a homogenous group where their lives contrast with the majority on both ethnicity and gender lines, yet are presented as not differentiated from each other (Brah and Phoenix, 2013; Mercer, 2013).

The long-held associations between alcohol and the Caribbean are explored in the next section. In particular, here the reader is invited to consider the often opposing views presented in the commonly held understandings of the role of rum trading, alcohol consumption and slavery with the Caribbean – and contrast these with the lack of discussion (silence) around the experiences of African slaves and Black Caribbean people, particularly women who were at the centre of these activities.

Working in silences: alcohol and the Caribbean

Rum is the primary type of alcohol associated with the Caribbean. Much has been written about the rum trading of the 18th and 19th centuries and the close associations between sugar cane plantations, rum production and slavery (Smith, 2005; Jolliffe, 2012; Brown, 2013; Newman, 2013). Rum, however, did not only have an economic value in the Caribbean. It had an important function in the lives of the plantation slaves in that it played a role in uniting the East and West African beliefs of displaced persons (Smith, 2005).

There are many reports recording the misery and distress caused to native African people brought to the Caribbean as slaves to work on the numerous sugar cane plantations that sprung up on the islands throughout the Caribbean (Brown, 2013). Many of these reports are closely linked to what Durkheim in 1933 termed 'Anomie'; that is, an individual's or group's reaction to the loss of their ethnic or cultural identify as a result of either difficulties of adjusting to migration or feelings of 'invasion' of their communities by mass immigration of 'others' (Caetano et al, 1998). However, few stories reflect consideration of how rum was used in religious ceremonies and belief rituals such as 'Obeah'[1] introducing/teaching (someone) an attitude, idea, or habit by repeated cultural learning and experience in participants' passages to healing and spirituality (Smith, 2005; Browne, 2011; Salter, 2013). There is a silence around the use of alcohol in slave communities and tribal rituals, particularly with reference to providing a social basis for binding communities together. An additional consideration lies in the 'escapism' provided by alcohol, which is often nowadays presented as a negative indicator or an inability to cope with stress and illustrative of distress – the silent stories of Caribbean slaves challenge us to question the acceptance of this dominant medical viewpoint. Alcohol as positive escapism not only allows for the possibility of 'self-preservation' effects on the individual but also the opportunity for groups to develop ways of being, which act outside what is usually expected of them – for the slaves this allowed for 'rebellion', challenging the social order, enabling them to say, feel, dance or display behaviours that would not be acceptable to their masters and to defy the efforts to silence them and render their culture invisible (Browne, 2011; Salter, 2013). In today's Caribbean, slavery traditions linking alcohol, rebellion, rituals and dance continue through soca music[2] and carnival[3] where 'Obeah', 'Sensay'[4] and escapism are celebrated by Caribbeans and in many cases their adoptive countries worldwide. Through continuation of these social rituals and annual events, Caribbean people continue to challenge the politics of the social order through words and rebel against constraints of modern life, while demonstrating the strength of their ties to the past.

Evidence exploring the intersections between Black Caribbean women, alcohol use and misuse is scarce. There are many reasons for this, not least that until relatively recently the reporting of ethnic differences in population healthcare or behavioural research was not the norm. This was confined to studies specifically identifying ethnicity or 'race' as a subject of study. Despite a long history of migration, much of the alcohol research in the United States (US) and the UK focused on dominant White populations with little, if any, reference to the diversity of communities that make up their societies. For example, The National Alcohol Survey in the US began in 1964, but reporting of the impact of alcohol use among minority ethnic peoples only began 20 years later in 1984 (Orford et al, 2004). At this stage there was little differentiation between minority ethnic communities, and 'Black' groups were reported as having higher drinking rates than White groups, with very little discussion as to why or identification of who comprised 'Black' groups. This reflects the start of a trend in reporting alcohol use in Black communities with high-level reports focusing on the negative health consequences in Black communities with no contextualisation of experiences within sociological theory. Instead, the research available reports on either the lack of evidence on alcohol behaviours in Black communities (Andreuccetti et al, 2012), higher risk of alcohol misuse among some groups of migrants (Bécares et al, 2009) or the impact on co-morbidities (Taylor et al, 2013) from the relatively safe and sterile gaze of healthcare and professionalism.

There are even fewer studies that explore alcohol use between minority ethnic groups. Understanding the impact or contexts in which reported rates of alcohol use impact on the lives of individuals is further compounded by 'blindness' relating to the heterogeneity of minority ethnic group identities, leading to the gross generalisation of findings and ineffectual recommendations. A study by the Policy Studies Institute (Modood, 1997) was one of the first to compare alcohol consumption within and between minority ethnic groups in the UK. The focus here was on levels of alcohol use in Black and South Asian populations who migrated before the age of 11 and those who migrated later or were born in the UK. The study was important for two reasons: first, because it incorporated an understanding of the differences between Black and South Asian experiences; and second, because it recognised the need to account for the impact of stage of lifecourse (age and level of education) on alcohol use related to differing migratory experiences. Overall, the study reported lower levels of abstinence among people who migrated before the age of 11 or were born in the UK. Since that study, other population-level studies have followed, which identify numerous factors shaping the drinking patterns and relationships with alcohol among minority ethnic communities. These have been found to include individual ethnic identities, religious beliefs, environmental characteristics and historical and cultural factors (Orford et al, 2004).

This section has illuminated the silence around Black women's experiences with alcohol. However, the Silences Framework encourages us not only to highlight what is easy to find about any subject but also to probe the small spaces where there is discussion to help to gain an understanding of what is 'not heard' (to hear silences). To this end, the discussion will now focus on studies where gender and ethnicity are discussed, or at least referenced together, in relation to alcohol.

Hearing silences: Black Caribbean women and alcohol use

Where both gender and ethnicity were used as identifiers within populations we begin to see how alcohol use among minority ethnic women told a different story from that of men. Orford et al (2004), for example, demonstrated how the 1993 National Mental Health Survey from the Office of Population Censuses and Surveys (OPCS, 1993) indicated lower levels of alcohol-related problems in Black and Asian people compared with the wider population. The survey report illustrated that abstinence and occasional drinking were three times more likely in African Caribbean populations than among White populations in the UK, with minority ethnic women having the highest levels of occasional drinking (less than one unit per week). Furthermore, at the other extreme, very heavy drinking (more than

35 units per week for women) and the reporting of any one of 16 alcohol-related problems were less likely in minority ethnic populations as a whole and minority ethnic women in particular. These patterns at a population level were repeated in other, smaller surveys (McKeigue and Karmi, 1993; Crome and Kumar, 2001), which, while showing variance in absolute numbers between all ethnic groups or between genders within an ethnic grouping, reinforced the same message – measures of harmful drinking to health were lower in women from minority ethnic groups.

Reviewing studies and reports concerning minority ethnic communities, gender and alcohol reveals another concern. It appears that in many cases the identity and presence of Caribbean communities, particularly women, are hidden or 'silenced' within the presented data. Many of the studies highlighting abstinence at one extreme or overt drinking at the other in Black and minority ethnic communities comprise very few Caribbean and/or female participants. While the levels of drinking and alcohol misuse are consistently lower in all minority ethnic women, it is extremely low in women of South Asian origin, particularly Bangladeshi women (McKeigue and Karmi, 1993; Modood, 1997). Thus, in reports of large-scale surveys around alcohol use in minority ethnic women, the 'Black' communities are combined to include Caribbean, African and Asian populations. However, disaggregation of the sample compositions almost always reveals few Caribbean participants, with some studies even justifying the reporting of Caribbean and African communities together as 'similar'.

The work of Orford et al (2004) mentioned earlier, for example, also explored some of the contexts in which relationships between gender, behaviour and alcohol existed within minority ethnic groups. They explored people's perception of the benefits and drawbacks of alcohol and its relationship with their self-identity and social networks. They found that for women, drinking behaviours were most closely associated with their religious beliefs, whether they were employed outside the home, the size of family networks (with close ties) and the strength of their identity with their ethnic group. Furthermore, they discovered that this was not a simple case of women following the directives of a particular religion or set of ethnic group values; there was a complex relationship between social, cultural and religious variables, which resulted, for example, in intergenerational and between-group differences. However, in this study too, the predominant group of minority ethnic women included were from Indian, Pakistani and Bangladeshi communities. There was little discussion of the alcohol-related behaviours of Black Caribbean women, save in relation to the question of 'awareness of parents drinking', which reported that in Caribbean/African households (the groups were combined in the reporting) participants reported a higher level of awareness of their parents drinking and less concern about parents knowing that the participant (under the age of 25) themselves drank alcohol. The observations that followed defined that in comparison to South Asian families in the UK, Black Caribbean women were likely to come from families where drinking was an open activity.

The consequences of this are reflected in the findings such as in the above study, where Caribbean experiences are rendered invisible or silenced by authors resisting making any comment or conclusions on Caribbean perspectives due to small sample size (Johnson et al, 2011). The impact and potential consequences of this for Black Caribbean women and their communities are great. They are rendered both silenced and unaccounted for by omission. The lack of representation of Black Caribbean women's perspectives in alcohol-focused studies means that there is no evidence, data or 'proof' to underpin interventions to meet their needs or to recognise the differences and similarities in their experiences with alcohol. These issues highlight that culturally determined explorations of gender roles is vitally important in any detailed review of Black Caribbean women and alcohol.

The importance of culture

Women's drinking behaviours and drivers for abstinence or excess are influenced by the cultural norms and practices of their ethnic groups as well as other biological and environmental factors (Collins and McNair, 2002). The Silences Framework helps to centralise the personal experiences of Black Caribbean women in discussions about alcohol use, something we are unable to do in the current context. Without a criticalist underpinning, the silence around Caribbean female experience could simply be seen as an issue of poor sampling or the challenges of researching 'hard-to-reach populations'. However, the influence of critical perspectives on society, and experience inherent in the Silences Framework, suggests that research that simply describes experiences, provides insufficient information for it to be fully judged (Scott, 1991). Hence, what is even more concerning from this standpoint is that this lack of representation of Black Caribbean women persists, even when the research studies take place in geographical regions where minority ethnic groups form a significant proportion of the population (Johnson et al, 2011). The Black Caribbean female presence therefore continues to sit as a known entity but a rarely accessed viewpoint in alcohol studies. In this sea of silence it is difficult to see how we will move to understanding ethnically diverse female experiences with alcohol, and be able to interrogate whether they relate to the effects of living in an inequitable society rather than presenting them simply as a matter of personal choice. Ensuring that we move beyond disclosure and 'counting' risk is therefore an important aspect of developing the evidence base, utilising the concept of 'Screaming Silences' and its associated framework. Any examination of issues related to Black Caribbean women's experiences needs to be framed within theoretical, political or action-focused frameworks in order to fully appreciate the variety and diversity of human experience.

One of the most dominant discourses around alcohol use is the issue of acceptable levels of drinking and avoidance of alcohol misuse, due to its effects on health. Furthermore, the stigmatisation of women's drinking is culturally determined by expectations around female behaviour in private and public spaces (Caetano et al, 1998; Okin, 2013). Abbott and Chase (2008) refer to culture as providing a guide for action and acting as a cognitive map or 'grammar for behaviour' – this is overtly played out in relation to women and alcohol where longstanding associations between female gender and questions of morality, duty and femininity complicate the issue of the 'acceptability' of female drinking within different ethnic groups. The association of alcohol use with loss of inhibition, lack of control and inappropriate behaviour has resulted in norms and values that seek to place negative connotations on women using alcohol. Indeed, despite the grand strides made in relation to gender equality, 19th-century views of women as either the 'Madonna or Magdalen' continue to impact on expectations of women's behaviour in the 21st century. Hence, we are surrounded by reflections in the written, visual and spoken media of women 'out of control' or acting inappropriately as a result of alcohol use or misuse. These opposing representations of women must be part of our understanding as factors that influence how women's behaviours are measured and judged in society. But what of Caribbean women? How are they presented as users of alcohol, and what role does alcohol play in their lives?

Locating Black Caribbean women and their experiences

As discussed earlier in this chapter, representations of Black Caribbean women are few in alcohol-related studies, although overall, studies appear to indicate that alcohol use and misuse is less prevalent in minority ethnic women, including Black Caribbean women, than majority White populations (Haworth et al, 1999). However, there appears to be a tension between the surveys reporting Caribbean women's drinking behaviours and studies that suggest that alcohol use by women is more likely in permissive social groups and societies and less likely in those where women are more closely managed and confined. Indeed, some of the studies discussed earlier that focus predominantly on South Asian women have highlighted the religious and ethnic restrictions placed on women's movement and individual freedoms as explaining the low levels of alcohol use and high levels of abstinence. Data relating to alcohol use by Caribbean women appear to contradict this socially constructed viewpoint around women, social freedom and alcohol use (Herd, 1987; Caetano et al, 1998). Caribbean women are identified as being 'freer' with values that are more integrated to Western culture and more likely to be heads of household – all apparent conditions for the sanctioning of alcohol use in public and private. Despite this, the national alcohol surveys in the UK show 55% abstention rates among Caribbean women compared with 39% in White British women. Caetano et al (1998) have suggested that the answer to the higher rates of abstinence and lower rates of reported alcohol use in Black Caribbean women may be due to the 'protective' effects of ethnic and cultural norms.

There are many representations of Caribbean women, which are informed by the social history of the Caribbean and women's role within it. Some of these affect or are influenced by the intersection of gender, alcohol and Caribbean identity. They may go some way towards explaining what some have called the 'protective' cultural factors of minority ethnic identities in relation to risky alcohol use (Caetano et al, 1998). Three of the most dominant representations of Black Caribbean women are that of the Christian woman, the dance hall or soca queen and the matriarch. This next section explores these representations of Black Caribbean women and places them within the contexts of Black women's lives in the Caribbean community.

Christian Black Caribbean women

Black Caribbean women, like other minority ethnic groups, report higher levels of religious affiliation and church attendance (Orford et al, 2004; Taylor and Chatters, 2010), which has been shown to be one of the identified factors influencing lower alcohol use in women (Orford et al, 2004). In the Caribbean the most common religion is Christianity, with Roman Catholicism being the most dominant. However, the intersection of imported Western religions with Caribbean culture has produced a vast divergence of Christian values around alcohol, with a deep-rooted association with the Caribbean history of rum and slave trading. In this arena the social divisions hail back to the 19th century where women were the gatekeepers of family morality. This is reflected in the ways in which Black Caribbean women were judged, or chose to represent themselves, long after the abolition of slavery (hooks, 1992; Chamberlain, 2002; Salter, 2013). Hence, the expectations of women's behaviour espoused through Western Christianity were imported to the Caribbean along with the rum and slave trading. Social traits such as piousness, decorum and keeping oneself under control, began to be adopted within the Caribbean as illustrative of good female behaviour. Over time, as Christianity became established and moulded with the cultural practices of the region, the 'good Christian woman' of the Western ideology began to be recognised as one distinctive representation of Black Caribbean women. Despite the predominant Catholic and African slave rituals rooted across the region (and the close association of alcohol with religious practices in both), the 'good Christian woman' developed to symbolise control and temperance. Initially this was an attempt by settlers to the Caribbean to retain their moral difference from slaves or other migrants and control the activities of the women on the plantation (Sleeter, 2011). However, for Black Caribbean women, post slavery, it began to be adopted as a bi-product of slavery to differentiate between those working in the homes and the fields and developed as a way of illustrating breeding and position, post abolition (Davis, 2011). Today, this representation of the teetotal 'Christian woman' continues to exist both in the Caribbean and the diaspora as a recognised social and cultural positioning for Black Caribbean women, sitting in antithesis to what is often seen as the permissiveness and over-indulgence of the Caribbean culture.

The presentation of the Black Caribbean 'Christian woman' is not the only illustration of how Black Caribbean women's identities and associations with alcohol have been influenced by the social history of the Caribbean region. The 'Christian woman', to some extent, juxtaposes over celebrated representations of Black Caribbean women who mirror what often appear to be the very behaviours frowned upon by that society. Nowhere is this seen more readily than in the celebration of carnival or the dance hall.

Dance hall, soca and carnival queen

As previously discussed, dance, music and gathering together go hand in hand with alcohol use and overt displays of shared celebration in the history of Black people in the Caribbean. From the roots in Africa through to the present day, this has served to reunite displaced peoples with each other and cement a shared sense of belonging despite displacement. Unlike many other rituals, however, the dance, music and associated celebrations encourage and enable mixing of men and women in social spaces. Alcohol had a very clear role to play in this in the past, not so much as a route to excess but as a mechanism for re-enacting traditional rites or temporarily escaping realities of slavery. From times of slavery there were gender-defined segregated roles and places. Carnival grew out of these small periods of rebellion, allowing for the drinking of alcohol (rum) and dancing based on traditional tribal rituals, and inevitably led to opportunities for reduction of stress and free speech, albeit under the influence of alcohol. Women dancers were central to these occasions, with opportunities openly to drink alcohol, and demonstrated tribal dances depicting fertility, courtship and celebrating African gendered (female) identities. Thus, alcohol, rebellion and escapism are inextricably bound to carnival and the Caribbean.

Nowadays, carnival is celebrated by the Caribbean diaspora across the globe as well as in the Caribbean islands. It traditionally takes place before Lent, marking a time before abstinence and return to religious observance (Stevens, 2011). While differing islands have their own traditions, to some extent it fulfils the same role in each as the slave gatherings of the past – uniting displaced peoples and providing a social space for declaring a community sense of belonging. Outside 'carnival season' the dance hall has sprung up to provide a similar outlet for Black Caribbean communities. In both spaces, the representation of women as carnival troupe dancers or dance hall queens has become synonymous with the celebrations. Just as before, here the representation of women in carnival and dance hall allows a platform for a woman, if she so chooses, to display overt sexuality, body adornment and provocative dancing (Carpenter, 2011). Alcohol remains a key part of carnival and even in the 21st century it is seen as an opportunity for escapism with behaviours tolerated (particularly under the influence of alcohol) that would be frowned upon on other occasions. However, just as in the case of the Christian woman, the accepted behaviours of Black Caribbean women with alcohol are not epitomised by over-indulgence. While alcohol is present, and consumed in great quantities, for Black Caribbean women dancers, little if any alcohol is actually consumed by them. It is the escapism and release of the dance that is the draw, particularly for carnival troupes, who can be on their feet for in excess of six hours, as they continue the processions throughout the day until daybreak, or 'Jou'vert'.

Motherhood and matriarch

Other aspects of Black Caribbean culture associated with the female role, such as motherhood, strong family network ties and support through women's relationships, may also act to protect (or restrict) the acceptability of alcohol use by Black Caribbean women and may underpin their patterns of behaviour. The strong matriarchal role is one of the most enduring of the representations of Black Caribbean women (Simpson, 2011). It also stems from the slavery histories of plantation life when women and men were segregated and the high levels of lynching, floggings and ready sale of African men meant that women (by default) were heads of the households (Browne, 2011). At first glance it is difficult to equate this with alcohol use and some have said that the responsibilities of Black Caribbean women to care for children and protect the family, then and today, call for levels of control and vigilance that did not allow for the free use of alcohol as a form of escapism (Davis, 2011). However, the links between alcohol, Black Caribbean women and the family are more closely tied in with the role of family provider, not least in Caribbean cooking.

Nowhere is the link between alcohol and representations of Black Caribbean female identity more culturally enshrined than in the Caribbean 'Christmas cake'. The Christmas cake, also known as Black Cake, is more than simply a culinary exercise. The cake is ceremonial in both importance and production. It is made to mark all important family occasions: the celebration of Christmas, weddings, christenings, baptisms and significant anniversaries. The making of the cake is the responsibility of the matriarch in each household, where the 'family' version of recipe is produced. There is a social and cultural rite of passage between mothers and daughters in the passing on of the recipe and the responsibilities of producing the cake. It is important here to understand that 'family' in the Caribbean sense is often extended so recipes are not always passed directly down a generational line; rather, there is usually one female from each 'branch' of the family who is recognised as the 'head' and/or 'cake maker'. Each role is socially significant. The role of the cake maker is highly regarded and producing the cake is seen as an act of love and reflecting the important role of the woman who produces it. This is the woman without whose Black Cake no family tradition is truly celebrated. Alcohol is the central and key ingredient to the cake – without it, there is no Black Cake. Dried fruits must be soaked in rum for weeks (ideally months) to produce the best cake. This calls for vigilance on the part of the baker to soak the fruit and to watch that the cake does not dry out during cooking. Finally the cake is decorated. The unveiling and cutting of the cake is a key moment in all Black Caribbean family occasions, not simply weddings as in Western traditions.

Interestingly, Black Cake is commonly found at all Black Caribbean occasions, including those in families where abstinence may be ascribed to women. It seems that despite its very high alcohol content, it is not perceived to be contrary to the refusal of 'strong'. Instead it is recast as one part of women's role in providing for the family and uniting issues of identity and family values. This begins to paint a picture that for Black Caribbean women, despite the relative permissiveness of Caribbean culture, there may be stronger sociocultural factors affecting the decision to use alcohol, beyond that of access or acceptability of female drinking.

Conclusion

Without a diverse reference point for alcohol use, we remain restricted in our understandings of the role played by alcohol in the lives of minority ethnic women. In Western discussions, alcohol use and health are inextricably tied up with concerns about substance misuse and the dichotomy of the 'abusive' use of alcohol or 'illicit' drugs. However, identification of the 'abusive' or 'illicit' use of alcohol (or any drug) is itself culturally determined (Abbott and Chase, 2008). As illustrated above, our sociocultural beliefs shape attitudes to alcohol or other drugs and, in addition, social groups develop their own codes of behaviours and internal measures of acceptable use/abuse of alcohol or categorisation of 'what counts' as alcohol use. The Christian woman who eats rum-soaked Christmas cake would most likely not see this as a divergence from abstinence, and if questioned would likely still describe herself as a non-drinker. This highlights further the need to understand the social and cultural factors that not only affect alcohol drinking behaviours but also the use of alcohol in other aspects of the lives of women from minority ethnic communities. Research has only just begun to understand these factors and investigate their relative importance for Black Caribbean women and their health.

In the 21st century, it is apparent that many of the challenges to health and healthcare are situated in the personal experiences of people living in inequitable societies. Much of our understanding of life and health today is based on majority perspectives, whereby minority ethnic experiences are judged and discussed relative to a central (Westernised) reference point. However, by doing this, discourse concerning alcohol use and minority ethnic experience is prevented from developing further. It remains confined to what is known to exist in dominant cultures about alcohol and the broad range of related factors impacting on health and life chances. In the diverse world of the 21st century, sociologists and other researchers are called upon to explore sensitive issues concerning particular minority ethnic communities at a point in time. In addition, exposing how women's experiences differ within and between ethnic groups requires researchers to be able to centralise sensitive subjects or marginalised social groups in studies. This enables an appraisal of the consequences for women and their health 'in the light of' these hidden perspectives, rather than despite them.

The concept of 'silences' was used as a reference point in this chapter, to identify some of the unknown and unspoken relationships between Black Caribbean women and alcohol. These were then presented for the reader so that they could assess and reflect on the role of alcohol in representations of Black Caribbean women's lives. In the silence around alcohol and Black Caribbean women's perspectives, clinicians and health professionals are left to make Eurocentric judgements of care and support needs based on their own cultural reference points (Hendry and Lim, 2006). A valuable goal would be to uncover the sociocultural issues that directly or indirectly influence acceptance, behaviours and ultimately treatment outcomes in alcohol-related conditions. Women and members of minority ethnic communities, and Black researchers in particular, have worked to redress the balance; however, ethnically specific, contextualised accounts focusing on these minority group experiences remain scarce.

Notes

[1] Obeah is a term used in the West Indies to refer to folk magic, sorcery and religious practices developed among West African slaves, specifically of Igbo origin.

[2] Soca music, also known as the Soul of Calypso, is a genre of Caribbean music that originated within a marginalised subculture in Trinidad and Tobago in the late 1970s, and developed into a range of styles in the 1980s and later.

[3] Carnival is a festive season which occurs immediately before Lent. It combines costume, music and dance with origins in west Africa and French Creole.

[4] Sensay is a costume from carnival which is a full dress of long strips of material with a headpiece that may include horns and a mask. The mask is of tribal origin and represents the bad and evil to be driven out of communities.

References

Abbot, P. and Chase, D. (2008) 'Culture and substance abuse: impact of culture affects approach to treatment', *Psychiatric Times* www.psychiatrictimes.com

Andreuccetti, G., Carvalho, H.B., Korcha, R., Ye, Y., Bond, J. and Cherpitel, C.J. (2012) 'A review of emergency room studies on alcohol and injuries conducted in Latin America and the Caribbean region', *Drug and Alcohol Review*, vol 31, no 6, pp 737-746, doi: 10.1111/j.1465-3362.2012.00419.x

Bécares, L., Nazroo, J. and Stafford, M. (2009) 'The ethnic density effect on alcohol use among ethnic minority people in the UK', *Journal of Epidemiology and Community Health*, vol 65, no 1, pp 20-25.

Brah, A. and Phoenix, A. (2013) 'Ain't I a woman? Revisiting intersectionality', *Journal of International Women's Studies*, vol 5, no 3, pp 75-86.

Brown, E.M.L. (2013) 'The Blacks who "got their 40 acres": a theory of Black West Indian migrant asset acquisition, http://works.bepress.com/eleanor_brown/9

Browne, R.M. (2011) 'The "bad business" of Obeah: power, authority, and the politics of slave culture in the British Caribbean', *The William and Mary Quarterly*, vol 68, no 3, pp 451-480.

Caetano, R., Clark, C.L. and Tam, T. (1998) 'Alcohol consumption among racial/ethnic minorities', *Alcohol Health and Research World*, vol 22, no 4, pp 233-242.

Carpenter, K. (2011) 'Introduction to the special issue on sexuality in the Caribbean', *Sexuality & Culture*, vol 15, no 4, pp 313-314.

Chamberlain, M. (ed) (2002) *Caribbean migration: Globalized identities*, London: Routledge.

Collins, R.L. and McNair, L.D. (2002) 'Minority women and alcohol use', *Alcohol Research and Health*, vol 26, no 4, pp 251-256.

Crome, I.B. and Kumar, M.T. (2001) 'Epidemiology of drug and alcohol use in young women', *Seminars in Foetal and Neonatal medicine*, vol 12, no 6, pp 98-105.

Davis, A.Y. (2011) *Women, race, & class*, New York, NY: Random House.

Haworth, E.A., Soni Raleigh, V. and Balarjan, R. (1999) 'Cirrhosis and primary liver cancer amongst first generation migrants in England and Wales', *Ethnicity and Health*, vol 4, no 1-2, pp 93-99.

Hendry, T. and Lim, R.F. (2006) 'The assessment of culturally diverse individuals', in Lim, R.F. (ed) *Clinical manual of cultural psychiatry*, Arlington VA: Psychiatric Publishing.

Herd, D. (1987) 'Rethinking Black drinking', *British Journal of Addiction*, vol 82, no 4, pp 219-223.

hooks, B. (1992) *Black looks, race and representations*, London: Turnaround.

Johnson, M., Jackson, R., Guillaume, L., Meier, P. and Goyder, E. (2011) 'Barriers and facilitators to implementing screening and brief intervention for alcohol misuse: a systematic review of qualitative evidence', *Journal of Public Health*, vol 33, no 3, pp 412-421.

Jolliffe, L. (2012) 'Connecting sugar heritage and tourism', in Jolliffe, L. (ed) *Sugar heritage and tourism in transition*, Clevedon: Channel View Publications.

Kincheloe, J.L. and McLaren, P. (2002) 'Rethinking critical theory and qualitative research', in Zou, Y. and Trueba, H.T. (eds) *Ethnography and schools: Qualitative approaches to the study of education* (pp 87-138), New York, NY: Rowman & Littlefield.

McKeigue, P.M. and Karmi, G. (1993) 'Alcohol consumption and alcohol-related problems in Afro-Caribbeans and South Asians in the United Kingdom', *Alcohol and Alcoholism*, vol 28, no 1, pp 1-10.

Mercer, K. (2013) *Welcome to the jungle: New positions in Black cultural studies*, New York, NY: Routledge.

Modood, T., Berthoud, R., Lakey, J., Nazroo, J. Y., Smith, P., Virdee, S., and Beishon, S. (1997) *Ethnic minorities in Britain: diversity and disadvantage*, London: Policy Studies Institute.

Newman, S.P. (2013) *A new world of labor: The development of plantation slavery in the British Atlantic*, Philadelphia, PA: University of Pennsylvania Press.

Okin, S.M. (2013) *Women in western political thought*, Princeton, NJ: Princeton University Press.

Orford, J., Johnson, M. and Purser, B. (2004) 'Drinking in second generation Black and Asian communities in the English Midlands', *Addiction Research and Theory*, vol 12, no 1, pp 11-30.

Salter, N. (2013) 'Caribbean slave women's resistance as a form of preservation', *Ruptures* (pp 59-66), Toronto: Sense Publishers.

Scott, J.W. (1991) 'The evidence of experience' *Critical Inquiry*, vol 17, no 4, pp 773-779.

Serrant-Green, L. (2011) 'The Sound of "Silence": a framework for researching sensitive issues or marginalised perspectives in health', *Journal of Research in Nursing*, vol 16, no 4, pp 347-360.

Simpson, A. (2011) 'From stigma to strategy: intersectionality and articulated identities', paper presented to the Western Political Science Association Annual Meeting, Seattle.

Sleeter, C.E. (2011) 'Becoming white: reinterpreting a family story by putting race back into the picture', *Race, Ethnicity and Education*, vol 14, no 4, pp 421-433.

Smith, F.H. (2005) *Caribbean rum: A social and economic history*, Gainsville, FL: University Press of Florida.

Stevens, K. (2011) 'Carnival: fighting oppression with celebration', *Totem: The University of Western Ontario Journal of Anthropology*, vol 2, no 1, p 14.

Taylor, R.J. and Chatters, L.M. (2010) 'Importance of religion and spirituality in the lives of African Americans, Caribbean Blacks and non-Hispanic Whites', *The Journal of Negro Education*, vol 79, no 3, pp 280-294.

Taylor, R.J., Nguyen, A., Sinkewicz, M., Jow, S. and Chaters, L.M. (2013) 'Comorbid mood and anxiety disorders, suicidal behavior, and substance abuse among Black Caribbeans in the USA', *Journal of African American Studies*, vol 17, no 4, pp 409-425.

Williams, M. and May, T. (1996) *Introduction to the philosophy of social research*, London: UCL Press.

EIGHT

A drink in my hand: why 'putting down the glass' may be too simple a solution for lesbian women

Lyndsey Moon and Patsy Staddon

Introduction

A complex history lies behind the patterns of alcohol use within the lesbian population. There is no doubt that nowadays alcohol is used among women of all classes and genders, and within most ethnic communities. The use of alcohol in lesbian communities has to be understood historically, relating to societal mores of the past, as well as the broader cultural and national debates influencing societal understanding of sexualities as well as alcohol use. Identifying as a lesbian, as well as differing use of alcohol, are also related to social demographics such as class, religion, race, age, disability, ethnicity and sexuality and cannot be understood outside of these intersectional overlaps. This chapter focuses on the use of alcohol among lesbians in the United Kingdom (UK).

The central theme of this book suggests that issues relating to the way alcohol is used can only be understood properly within their social and environmental context; hence the importance of utilising a 'social model' of alcohol use. A social model suggests that the meaning and use of alcohol is context related (Staddon, 2012, 2013a). It enables us to move away temporarily from distress, from normal social expectations and from 'self-imprisonment' (Gusfield, 1996, p 72). It may be a way of acting out, recreation, even a form of selfhood to which one has a right (Cresswell, 2009; Staddon, 2013a, p 106). To apply this understanding of context to lesbian alcohol use, it is necessary to look at lesbian history.

Lesbian history

Knowledge 'about' the lesbian and her community originally emerged from studies written by those 'outside' of the community. A rhetoric of emotional pathology was constructed via psychiatric and mental health approaches following on from religious and legal sanctimony. The *Diagnostic and statistical manual* (DSM), used globally by psychiatrists, appeared to declare 'open season' on lesbians and gay men throughout the late 1950s to the early 1980s (the DSM only removed homosexuality as a pathology in 1983) by declaring 'homosexuality' as a form of mental illness. It is hard to imagine how lesbians managed to endure life as women throughout these times.

Psychologically, one would want to ask how they managed to 'get out alive' considering the harshness of social life. Imagine the working-class lesbian of the 1950s, living in the North of England. Imagine the way she would need to live her everyday life – refusing to obey the demand to marry and have children alone would be considered outrageous by the standards of heterosexual norms. While this might not have been the only reason to use alcohol, alcohol could in many cases have provided a 'way out' or a 'way of coping' with overwhelming heterocentricity. At this time, finding somewhere to meet with other lesbians had to remain secret, and ensuring that everything remained 'hidden' led to a perilous lifestyle. Lesbians could be openly discriminated against, isolated, hated and feared (King et al, 2003). This was partly as a result of the general desire to control the apparently 'voracious' and 'devouring' (Weeks, 1986, p 47) female sexuality (Vicinus, 1993, p 434). Subsequently, lesbians tended to go 'underground', an apt comment on the kind of spaces and places where lesbian venues could be located – somewhere away from public notability and notoriety.

The outbreak of war, ironically, offered new and exciting ways of meeting other women and the opportunity of lesbian intimacy. The Gateways Club provided the ideal meeting place, on Bramerton Street in Chelsea, London. As far back as the 1940s, the Gateways Club offered women who loved women a space to explore and enjoy bar culture. It must be understood how this would have been considered at that time.

> The years of the Second World War had an enormous impact on London's bar culture, and women's place within that culture. Many women were away from home for the first time, either working in the women's armed services or in other wartime employ. As Rebecca Jennings in *A*

Lesbian History of Britain (2007) has said, 'Distanced from their families and local communities, and with a new disposable income gained from their war work, these women experienced a new freedom and independence.' Jennings goes on to observe the following:

> In London, and other towns and cities around the UK, women took part in a vibrant emerging bar scene alongside male homosexuals and visiting servicemen and women. Pat James remembers the wartime years as a period of great excitement at the Gateways club in Chelsea: 'When I went to the Gateways [in 1944], the atmosphere was fantastic. For a start we had women from overseas coming in, because they were stationed here, so you had all sorts of different people. Very interesting, very crowded, very packed.' (Lost Womyn's Space, lostwomynsspace.blogspot.com/2011/05/gateways-club.html)

The venue became more or less exclusively lesbian during the war when the anonymity and proximity provided by the khaki or blue uniformed women who came to work in London suddenly meant that a far greater number of women, of a certain persuasion, needed somewhere to go that they could call their own. (http://lostwomynsspace.blogspot.co.uk/2011/05/gateways-club.html)

[O]f the years right after the war: 'In a conformist era, the Gateways was a haven for those marginalised by society. Frequented in the afternoons by a mixed, arty Chelsea crowd, its evening clientele was mainly lesbian, at a time when these women felt that the Gateways was the only place they were welcome.' (Lost Womyn's Space, http://lostwomynsspace.blogspot.co.uk/2011/05/gateways-club.html)

'[R]owdies or troublemakers' were often banned immediately. To be excluded, at the time, was more than just embarrassing, it was unbelievably inconvenient -- the nearest alternative lesbian club would have been in Brighton, travelling to which would have made a social life far too expensive to afford.

Dining out with a girlfriend, even in the sixties, would have also cost too much for most women (who would

> have usually been earning far less than men for even comparable jobs in those days). It's difficult to believe now but women wearing trousers were often still banned from most restaurants at the time, while pubs were still risky places for women to visit unaccompanied by men. For a lot of women, the Gateways Club was the only relaxing and affordable place they had to go. (Lost Womyn's Space, lostwomynsspace.blogspot.com/2011/05/gateways-club.html)

Research into lesbian alcohol use

Looking at this historical context is essential if one is to understand the development and meaning of lesbian lifestyles. Research in this area often meant exploring the lesbian 'other' and in order to conduct such research, it often meant investigating the only spaces where lesbians were openly visible in social meeting places. While this was regularly used as the starting point for lifestyle research, it also led to extrapolation about lesbian mental health, as studies were typically based on opportunistic sampling in bars (Ettorre, 2005). Such research claimed that lesbians tended to spend an average of 19 nights a month in a gay bar – and an average of six drinks on these evenings. A few studies show different amounts but concur that drinking was extensive.

Conclusions of this sort are unreliable, given the voluntary nature of self-disclosure both as a member of the lesbian population and as a substance user. Lesbian/bisexual women can choose whether they 'come out' and whether to take part in surveys. Ettorre (2005) confirms that there is disagreement in the field as regards lesbian/bisexual women's greater or lesser use of tobacco and alcohol (Hughes, 2003; Burgard et al, 2005; Fish, 2006; Hunt and Fish, 2008), partly due to the difficulty of sampling. Nevertheless, some remarkable statements are still being cited in current academic publications, such as: 'Sources suggest that one third of the lesbian population is alcoholic [Hughes, 2003]' (Ricks, 2012, p 38).

More recent research by the Lesbian and Gay Foundation has focused on lesbian, gay and bisexual people attending Pride celebrations and their alcohol and drug use. Again, the sampling framework could be critiqued on numerous grounds, since it was based on convenience sampling, but it is perhaps an improvement on studies centred on bars and clubs. This research was part of a five-year study, which to date has concluded that lesbian and gay women are almost twice as likely as others to drink alcohol problematically and are likely to seek help from websites and friends, rather than approaching conventional services (Buffin et al, 2012). However, there has remained little reporting of the drinking patterns of lesbians who do not go to bars or Pride events, and might not declare their sexual orientation, should they seek help with alcohol problems from health services. Certainly, there are many reasons why lesbian women might seek refuge in substances (Roberts et al, 2005) but there are also reasons why they are more likely to need to play the system by disclosing what seems most helpful. Moon, one of this chapter's authors, recently worked with a lesbian client who fully acknowledged her alcohol treatment needs but felt that she would have to 'play the game' in order to receive treatment. She stated that she felt intimidated and could not be herself in the treatment centres. She defined herself as having issues related to gender as well as sexuality and felt that these would quickly be pathologised, as this had been her previous experience.

Younger lesbian drinking

Much has been written about young women's drinking in general (Plant and Plant, 2001; Sheehan and Ridge, 2001; Morrison et al, 2012) and there has been some work on younger lesbian drinking (Bridget and Lucille, 1996; Blackman et al, Chapter Three, this volume; Mackiewicz, Chapter Four, this volume). However, younger lesbians are a particularly difficult group to research, for a variety of reasons. Bridget and Lucille (1996) reported difficulties in obtaining ethical agreement to work with them on an academically funded project and therefore '[t]he research project was completed on a voluntary basis' (Bridget and Lucille, 1996, p 357). They found that there was great fear of identity disclosure and that 'the majority of young women in the sample were facing serious difficulties' (Bridget and Lucille, 1996, p 358). These researchers found that there was a high degree of isolation, lack of self-esteem and a poor personal image. These problems often led to the women becoming overweight and exhibiting other self-damaging behaviours such as alcohol abuse and even suicide.

Young lesbian women are likely to feel outsiders in the heterosexualised leisure scene at school and college; Payne (2007) notes that fitting in is difficult, with heavy peer pressure to conform. The pervasive 'compulsory heterosexuality' 'requires the submission of young women to heterosexuality and normative femininity in order to achieve status in the school culture' (Payne, 2007, p 61). Consequently, adolescent lesbians may well feel disconnected and fearful of being open about themselves. 'In a recent study (Duncan, 2004), 15-year-old girls were asked what characteristic was least likely in a popular girl. The invariable choice was "lesbian"' (Payne, 2007, p 62). Payne (2007, p 76) went on to observe: 'These young [lesbian] women claimed values antithetical to normative femininity; rejected the consumer culture that targets teen girls; and sought recognition for their activities in the arts, sports, and academics rather than through relationships with and to boys.' This interest in health and fitness is a feature of lesbian life at most ages, although it may not necessarily indicate enthusiasm for a moderate drinking style (Ettorre, 2005; Staddon, 2005).

Older lesbians: a snapshot

In February 2014 a snapshot was taken of the role that alcohol plays in the lives of older lesbians today in an English city. How far is alcohol relevant to them? This snapshot was a follow-up to a larger study, funded by Folk.us, which looked into the help women in Devon and Cornwall felt they needed in respect of their alcohol use (Staddon, 2013). The lesbian women in the snapshot were recruited by means of snowball sampling, and were aged between 57 and 68. They were interviewed over the telephone, and described substantial changes which appear to have occurred in the last 20 years in their social lives. More socialising now seems to take place in each others' homes, with wine the preferred drink, and only one or two glasses over the evening being usual. Some women had given up alcohol for health reasons, and one who had not given up observed how important good health was seen to be among older lesbians. All lesbians in this sample were white and they could be seen as middle class in that they usually owned homes and cars, and were not (reportedly) in receipt of state benefits. In these respects they seemed very similar to heterosexual women of similar social status. In general, an alcoholic drink was seen as something pleasurable and relaxing, but not as an essential part of life. However, some interesting cross-cutting themes emerged.

Carol[1] (Snapshot) observed that she only still drank (about once a month) to keep company with a lesbian friend who does like her to drink if she does. This pattern in which drinkers like 'drinking company' was also referred to in the snapshot by Lennie, who is a musician and finds that there are problems for her now that she has stopped using substances for reasons of health and personal safety:

> 'As a lesbian in a band I am more aware of my personal safety than the others are. I know I am more likely to be attacked [on the way home].'

> 'So not drinking does interfere with the social bonding that goes on for the others with alcohol and dope. [But also] I think I am more aware of the importance of making the most of my time. Using substances is good for the unconscious mind but as an artistic day-dreaming person I find I do that anyway and I have to use Diet Coke to get into a 'get up and do it' mode!'

In contrast, snapshot participant Alice, who is very fit and active, and often does stop drinking for a few days for health reasons, usually has a drink on a daily basis. She says she drinks a good deal more than her friends, often finishing up other people's bottles at dinner parties, and admits: "If I couldn't drink any more I'd feel a sense of loss – disappointed. Some of the glitter would go out of life."

Holly, another snapshot participant, had to give up alcohol ten years ago because of serious health issues which necessitated taking (prescribed) morphine. She is able to relax with her cats and her drawing but:

> 'It has affected my social life. It's much harder to go to new things – to meet people – and it's hard to relax without it [in a social context].'

It seems that alcohol still affects these older lesbians' lives, whether directly or indirectly, but not to a great extent. It also seems to be the case that many older lesbian and bisexual women are very aware of their health in general, as was clear from the snapshot study mentioned above, and this might be expected to make them more likely to see themselves as being at risk of alcohol problems and so to be more likely to address any alcohol issues than heterosexual women. Barnes and Ward (Chapter Six, this volume) consider the issue of older women's drinking in general and there are interesting similarities.

Different lesbian drinking patterns

Staddon's personal experience of lesbian drinking is that what distinguishes it from that of the drinking of more mixed groups is a greater tolerance of different drinking patterns among friends and acquaintances, and a less panic-driven approach to over-drinking. There may be a sense that lesbians have all 'been there' in some way, as 'deviants' who have suffered to some extent from society's heterocentrism (Szymanski, 2006). As recently as 2005, lesbian participants in Staddon's research were enjoying an outsider status similar to that of Cohen's (1972) 'delinquent boy' group. They might feel stress and anger at finding themselves in an outsider position in society, and might choose to deal with this by behaving aggressively, dressing distinctively and drinking in an 'unfeminine' way. These tactics might reinforce their sense of self-worth, while irritating and angering others. However, like Mods and Rockers (Cohen, 1972), they could easily discard such outward proofs of cultural identity, and melt away into social invisibility, or 'the day job' (Fifield et al, 1977).

For example, Fran[2] had embraced, and even celebrated, negative aspects of her very heavy alcohol use and low income, embodying them in a way that alleviated her difficult circumstances (Cohen, 1972). How she lived, for her, expressed who she was. She was often depressed, but was proud of being 'a bit different'. Although her life was restricted by poverty and agoraphobia, and centred on being able to acquire enough money for her daily alcohol intake, she did not seem to be particularly unhappy about the fact that many people on her run-down council estate laughed at her, because they sometimes saw her drunk. Although she paid lip service to acceptance that her alcohol use was bad for her health, she showed no other signs of concern and met the many ups and downs of her life philosophically. Her identity as a lesbian and a nonconformist sat well with her acknowledgement of herself as being someone whose behaviour around alcohol was unconventional and a source of anger to some other people. It was as if she had achieved the difference she wanted by being and looking like a drop-out and a drunk; for her it seemed a positive identity, even with its drawbacks.

This was also true for Wendy, who took part in the same research project. She too had dropped out of a series of chances at further education but loved to dance, to drink and to dream. She had a very laid-back approach to life. She did not seem to feel a need to conform in any way, including the pursuit of conventional career paths, or the completion of her various degrees. She had worked out ways to manage her alcohol intake so that it did less damage:

> 'I do try [to look after my health] … I don't allow myself to drink at home … I only drink socially, with other people ... I try to drink no more than twice a week but I do tend to, on the whole, binge drink. And I know I used to drink on an empty stomach.'

Fran and Wendy seemed comfortable, and often happy, with being different, with being outsiders, even when it might mean depression and loneliness. Neither had particularly strong links with the lesbian community but both felt confident about their identity, despite some depression and a degree of isolation (Camp et al, 2002). They had perhaps already experienced rejection in a heteronormative world, and developed a variety of ways to develop a sense of self-worth (Bostwick et al, 2005).

Lesbians and alcohol treatment

This sense of self-worth may be hard to find or to maintain for lesbians seeking treatment for a mental health and/or substance use problem. They are less likely than heterosexual women to have a positive experience.

Substance use counsellors have negative or ambivalent attitudes towards lesbian, gay, bisexual and transgendered (LGBT) clients, in particular towards transgendered people, and lack knowledge of their needs (Eliason, 2000, quoted in Fish, 2006, p 45).

Typically, although not invariably, alcohol treatment has focused not on the reasons for women's over-drinking but on a model of abstinence, and acknowledgement of personal failure. In promoting these goals, rather than those of social learning theory (Heather and Robertson, 1985), treatment has adopted a moral stance (Warner, 2009). It might be seen to be infringing human rights; what Cresswell (2009) terms 'experiential rights', whereby people suffering from a condition may be made to suffer further by their experience of treatment. A woman who has already had to cope with the stress and loneliness of stigma as a lesbian is now expected to acknowledge ownership of a spoiled identity as 'an alcoholic' (Kertzner et al, 2011). She will be seen to be of less value as a human being and to have been shamed (Staddon, 2012). While alcohol may have enabled her to behave inappropriately, or in an 'unfeminine' way, this in turn will have damaged the extent to which she is seen to be an acceptable member of 'normal' society.

Attention to different causes of and treatments for lesbian and bisexual women's alcohol problems has been slower to appear outside the pathologising of sexual identity described by Hall (1993, p 111): 'Medical writings in the first three quarters of this century were frequently disparaging of lesbians [Stevens and Hall, 1991].... Drinking was thought to cause covert homosexual tendencies to appear overtly.' Hall further affirms that cultural interpretations affect the understanding of alcohol issues so that 'medicalization of addictive problems, beliefs about alcohol use are still framed in moralistic terms ... concepts like codependency have special implications for a stigmatized subculture in which family structure and social support differs greatly from that in mainstream society....' (Hall, 1993, pp 109-110).

Cultural assumptions about women's appropriate behaviour, which inform much treatment, are particularly problematic for lesbian women:

> As lesbians, we may be suspicious about the motivation behind current mental health treatments on offer.... When lesbians seek help for alcohol issues and are open about their sexuality, the labels, 'lesbian' and 'alcoholic', indicate to clinical staff that they are socially dysfunctional ... lesbians 'are much less likely to present to these services for a variety of reasons ... (including) ... fear of their sexuality being pathologised if they do present. (Malley, 2001, cited in Staddon, 2005, pp 73-74)

Alcohol treatment services frequently still make use of the phraseology and the philosophy of Alcoholics Anonymous (AA), and encourage attendance at its meetings. As Galvani (2009) explains, such an approach is particularly damaging for women with experience of domestic abuse, and such experience is known to affect the majority of women with alcohol issues. Galvani (2009, pp 6-7) has also observed:

> In order to 'recover' fully, the AA programme emphasises the need for people to admit their powerlessness, acknowledge their defects, turn their will over to God/higher power, and admit their wrongs and shortcomings, among others. This is particularly concerning for women suffering abuse, many of whom have already had their 'will' broken, their life controlled and have been repeatedly told how useless they are.

The 12-step model of treatment, which owes its source to AA, invokes a patriarchal ideology and an individualisation of issues. This presents particular problems for lesbians, for whom cultural understandings are crucial. They may not be acknowledged by their families, and suffer the stress caused by leading a 'deviant' lifestyle (Goffman, 1963). Lesbians can become unhappy and depressed because of their families' incomprehension of their lesbianism, their inability to share in the lives of heterosexual workmates and their being ignored by the health providers and educators. If the lesbian scene is not for them, they may experience loneliness. For them, alcohol can be exciting and pleasurable: 'You get what you need from drugs' (study respondent quoted in Raine, 2001, p 23, cited in Staddon, 2005, p 72).

Among lesbian and bisexual women, depression and anxiety are believed to be common, as is suicidal behaviour, as a result of homophobia (King et al, 2003; Alcohol Concern, 2004). There is evidence that depression often results from feeling different, fearing the consequences of sexual orientation becoming known, either while a child or as an adult in the workplace, and feeling unable to share personal details such as loss of a partner (Bent and McGilvy, 2006).

It would not be surprising if some lesbians misuse alcohol and feel unable to control their alcohol intake. Some research indicates that stigma, alienation, discrimination and the cultural importance of bars place lesbians more at risk of developing problems with alcohol than heterosexual women (Drabble and Trocki, 2005). Other research supports the idea that lesbian drinking is more problematic than that of heterosexual women (Jaffe et al, 2000; Staddon, 2005, pp 72–73).

Treatment providers, from general practitioners to alcohol specialists, frequently present themselves as being unaware of their important positions as agents of social control within a medicalised society (White, 2002). Their answer is too often to 'put down the glass', before help of any sort may be offered. Awareness of the relevance of both LGBT identity and of the complexities surrounding disclosure, is uncommon, particularly regarding lesbian women (Daley, 2010, 2012).

For example, although it may be suggested that a certain number of units of alcohol can be drunk per day without 'harm', this may not be a base around which drinking socially can be easily monitored and patterns of drinking tracked. It may not be realistic to expect people continually to monitor their intake of alcohol, and it is unclear as to the extent to which this would promote change. There are particular difficulties here when we explore the factors affecting lesbian drinking, with its history of clubbing and grouping for friendship and 'family' support, as discussed above.

The difficulties encountered by lesbians in alcohol treatment have been mentioned by Staddon (2005), Cochran and Cauce (2006), Fish (2006) and Ettorre (2007). One such difficulty is invisibility. Neville and Henrickson (2006) note that more women than men report that their doctors presume that they are heterosexual, and that homophobia continues to operate in this area effectively. For example, there is the clinical staff's assumption, referred to above, that someone who is known to be both 'lesbian' and 'alcoholic' must be socially dysfunctional (Staddon, 2005).

Lesbians may well suffer more than heterosexual women in 'treatment', usually concealing their sexual identity for fear of its being pathologised (Staddon, 2009). Some may be able to draw comfort from AA, finding there an opportunity to express regret at their behaviour, while also being offered continuity and even a second chance at acceptability. However, the majority seem to draw away from the organisation quickly, recognising the same kind of restrictive culture and moral opprobrium that had been an ingredient in their need to drink (Moncrieff, 1997; Sweanor et al, 2007; Staddon, 2009).

A different perspective is needed to help lesbian women who have issues with alcohol. Doctors and treatment specialists have been inclined to see 'sexual deviance' as the root of the problem (King et al, 2003). The challenge to this way of looking at mental health issues, based on a heteronormative construction of health, is still inadequately addressed in the literature about substance use (Ettorre, 2005; Staddon, 2005). However, the principle of unconditional positive regard (Rogers, 1975, cited in Nelson-Jones, 1982, p 211) has helped many lesbians to come to terms with who they are, develop positive identities and take up their lives, with alcohol ceasing to be their focus.

> 'I know it sounds odd but I don't even think of alcohol now – I go out with my friends, and they all have a glass of wine or something, but I have Coke or Perrier. It's just lost its appeal – I suppose I drank a lifetime's worth in the years I was at it!' (Jennifer, a participant in the snapshot research: Staddon, 2013b)

For those fortunate enough to find groups of lesbians such as those referred to in this chapter, who are not particularly concerned with how much the person drinks, but who are interested in the person herself, there are benefits and aids to recovery less available to heterosexual women. For example, for many lesbians, the experience of having alcohol problems lacks the shame factor that so damages self-worth in many women. It can even be a style, as in Fran's case – part of who they are, social renegades and deviants:

> Some lesbians may be scornful of traditionally feminine behaviour such as looking smart and tidy, not being noisy in public and not being seen to be affected by alcohol. This attitude is likely to make it easier to admit to yourself and your friends that you have a problem with alcohol, since

> you are not perceived as being socially disgraced in the same way. (Staddon, 2005, p 73)

This might well indicate that no matter how damaging past experiences of heteronormative society may have been, and how unsuitable the alcohol treatment, lesbian women have a better chance of survival from alcohol dependence and alcohol treatment, especially if they have the support of other lesbians. Lesbian culture itself tends to criticise and perceive as worthless the traditional ways in which women have been able to attain self-worth in a patriarchal society, and these include sobriety.

Positive regard of oneself has usually been acquired in a combination of ways and over time, although the giving up of alcohol (or its ceasing to be a problem) often seems like a sudden event. This has been described as the cycle of change, whereby small alterations in the way the person understands their alcohol use may change over time, so that it may be seen by them in different ways, and their use of alcohol may change in consequence (Prochaska and DiClemente, 1983). Counselling may have been of help, or supportive friends, usually but not always of the same sex, but an overall acceptance of the self has been the signal factor (Aaronson, 2006). For lesbian women this is likely to involve more socialising with lesbian friends, more awareness of a lesbian identity, which is rewarding and life-strengthening, and a refusal to allow regret to become shame and self-castigation (Staddon, 2012, 2013a). Unfortunately, as explained above, this may prove difficult within traditional treatment settings. Lesbians without such support might be more at risk of suicide or self-harm than those lucky enough to find it (Rivers and Carragher, 2003; Liu and Mustanski, 2012).

Conclusion

It is by now apparent that when the words 'lesbian' and 'treatment' are used in conjunction, a wide area of debate and contention is opened up. At least two areas of dissent are present: that of belonging to an alternative group with different ways of understanding and responding to life; and being groomed in treatment to belong in a world whose ways of understanding relationships and socialising may not be your own. Cross-cutting themes include lesbian motherhood (Pelka, 2010), lesbian employment (Cocker and Hafford-Letchfield, 2009) and lesbians as carers (Parslow and Hegarty, 2013). Writers stress the risk of losing lesbian identity within roles that largely mirror heteronormative models, and the importance of remaining connected with the lesbian community. Lesbian/bisexual women often do share a supportive alternative culture similar to that of the extended heteronormative family (Staddon, 2005), even though women as a whole are more likely to be poor, due in part to continuing inequality of earnings, and the fact that they are more likely to be single parents (World Bank, 1990). Countercultures, or 'dissenters' forums', often emerge as a result of being seen as deviant, both challenging the social order and sometimes indirectly reinforcing it. Positive alternative identities may be constructed, but the outward structures of the heteronormative world impact on a daily basis: "I get tired of listening to the chat at work. I can't really join in – my life is too different. Sometimes I lie about what my weekend has been like; or I keep them talking about theirs. But it's lonely" (Lennie, a participant in the snapshot research: Staddon, 2013b).

These stresses in lesbians' daily lives are multiplied in many ways in conventional alcohol treatment, as mentioned above, so the development of new ways of understanding their alcohol use is urgent, if indeed lesbians are increasingly using alcohol in a damaging way. Their need to experience authenticity (Holt and Griffin, 2007; Liu and Mustanski, 2012) should be fully met, in the same way as for people from minority ethnic communities and disabled people. Authenticity has been confirmed as a crucial part of modern identity, perhaps experienced with particular acuteness in gay and lesbian bars. Rebellion may be crucial for women growing up in a social straitjacket and may well involve:

> finding lesbian friends who were neither drinkers nor judgemental about my drinking ... [I met] women who were interested in feminist issues, and made me feel welcome.... In lesbian bars, we are not outsiders and can take pleasure in our differences.... For the first time in twenty-eighty years, I could manage without alcohol. (Staddon, 2005, pp 70–71)

A social model of addressing lesbian alcohol use recognises that an oppressed and largely invisible minority may develop a variety of damaging conditions, including self-injury, problematic alcohol use, depression, isolation and an inbuilt fear of physical and mental attack. At the same time, it recognises that great strengths may emerge from oppression, such as the development of political vision and a feeling of solidarity and of looking out for each other. Where lesbian women are finding that they have problems with their alcohol use, they need access to alternative spaces where they can get help from other women in dealing with the difficulties of being from a minority culture. Alcohol services need to be freed from funding contingencies that mean they cannot build a service without thinking of how to activate funding opportunities.[3] If services were guaranteed funding then they could get on with the job of finding out how to access other populations, for example trans women, younger lesbians and lesbian mothers. The current lack of vision dysfunctionalises the lesbian community.

Alcohol use is not predominantly a medical issue but a social one. To develop and make use of this perspective we need to contextualise how we offer assistance, if indeed such assistance is required. One of the many necessary steps must be specialist centres for lesbian health and social care, together with the freedom to learn from childhood that 'lesbian' is not a dirty word but a proud one.

Notes

[1] All names given in this chapter are pseudonyms.

[2] Fran was a participant in a 2005 research study by Staddon for Avon and Wiltshire Mental Health Trust entitled 'Making a Start'.

[3] For example, project Antidote in London had to change founders and is constantly under local authority funding pressures. Money needs to be ringfenced, especially as the LGBT community is a significant contributor in terms of tax.

References

Aaronson, R. (2006) *Addiction: This being human: A new perspective*, Bloomington, IN: Authorhouse.

Alcohol Concern (2004) *Draft Mental Health Bill 2004: Submission of evidence to the Joint Committee by Alcohol Concern*, 28 October, http://wwwwww.publications.parliament.uk/pa/jt200304/jtselect/jtment/1127/1127se03.htm

Bent, K.N. and McGilvy, J. (2006) 'When a partner dies: lesbian widows', *Issues in Mental Health Nursing*, vol 27, no 5, pp 447-459.

Bostwick, W.B., Hughes, T.L. and Johnson, T. (2005) 'The co-occurrence of depression and alcohol dependence symptoms in a community sample of lesbians', in Ettorre, E. (ed) *Making lesbians visible in the substance use field*, New York, NY: The Haworth Press.

Bridget, J. and Lucille, S. (1996) 'Lesbian Youth Support Information Service (LYSIS): developing a distance support agency for young lesbians', *Journal of Community & Applied Social Psychology*, vol 6, no 5, pp 355-364.

Buffin J., Roy, A., Williams, H. and Winter, A. (2012) 'Part of the picture: lesbian, gay and bisexual people's alcohol and drug use in England (2009-2011)', http://wwwwww.lgf.org.uk/documents/sep_12/FENT__1347531966_10584_POTP_Year_3_ReportFINALL.pdf

Burgard, S.A., Cochran, S.D., Mays, V.M. (2005) 'Alcohol and tobacco use patterns among heterosexually and homosexually experienced California women', *Drug and Alcohol Dependence*, vol 77, no 1, pp 61-70.

Camp, DL.; Finlay, W.M.L. and Lyons, E. (2002) 'Is low self-esteem an inevitable consequence of stigma? An example from women with chronic mental health problems', *Social Science and Medicine*, vol 55, no 5, pp 823-834.

Cochran, B.N. and Cauce, A.M. (2006) 'Characteristics of lesbian, gay, bisexual, and transgender individuals entering substance abuse treatment', *Journal of Substance Abuse Treatment*, vol 30, no 20, pp 135-146.

Cocker, C. and Hafford-Letchfield, T. (2009) 'Out and proud? Social work's relationship with lesbian and gay equality', *British Journal of Social Work* (2010) vol 40, no 6, pp 1996-2008, doi: 10.1093/bjsw/bcp158

Cohen, S. (1972) *Folk devils and moral panics*, Abingdon: Routledge, 2002.

Cresswell, M. (2009) 'Psychiatric survivors and experiential rights', *Social Policy and Society*, vol 8, no 2, pp 231-243.

Daley, A. (2010) 'Being recognized, accepted, and affirmed: self-disclosure of lesbian/queer sexuality within psychiatric and mental health service settings', *Social Work in Mental Health*, vol 8, no 4, pp 336-355, doi: 10.1080/15332980903158202

Daley, A.D. (2012) 'Becoming seen, becoming known: lesbian women's self-disclosures of sexual orientation to mental health service providers', *Journal of Gay & Lesbian Mental Health*, vol 16, no 3, pp 215-234, doi: 10.1080/19359705.2012.680547

Drabble, L. and Trocki, K. (2005) 'Alcohol consumption, alcohol-related problems, and other substance use among lesbian and bisexual women', in Ettorre, E.(ed) *Making lesbians visible in the substance use field*, New York: Haworth Press. Also co-published in special issue of *Journal of Lesbian Studies*, 2005, vol 9, no 3, pp 69-78.

Ettorre, E. (ed) (2005) *Making lesbians visible in the substance use field*, New York, NY:The Haworth Press.
Ettorre, E. (2007) *Revisioning women and drug use: Gender, power and the body*, Basingstoke: Palgrave Macmillan.
Fifield, L.H., Lilene, H. and Lathem, J. David D., with Christopher Phillips, C. (1977) *Alcoholism in the gay community*, Los Angeles, LA: (Los Angeles Gay Community Center.)
Fish, J. (2006) *Heterosexism in health and social care*, Basingstoke: Palgrave Macmillan.
Galvani, S. (2009) 'Care? Or control?', *Drinkanddrugsnews*, 16 November, www.drinkanddrugsnews.com
Goffman, E. (1963) *Stigma: Notes on the management of spoiled identity*, Harmondsworth: Penguin Books, 1968.
Hall, J.M. (1993) 'Lesbians and alcohol: patterns and paradoxes in medical notions and lesbians' beliefs', *Journal of Psychoactive Drugs*, vol 25, no 2, pp 109-119.
Heather, N. and Robertson, I. (1985) *Problem drinking*, Oxford: Oxford Medical Publications, , 1997.
Holt, M. and Griffin, C. (2003) 'Being gay, being straight, and being yourself: local and global reflections on identity, authenticity, and the lesbian and gay scene', *European Journal of Cultural Studies*, vol 6, no 3, pp 404-425.
Hughes, T.L. (2003) 'Lesbians' drinking patterns: beyond the data', *Substance Use and Misuse*, vol 38, no 11, pp 1739-58.
Hunt, R. and Fish, J. (2008) *Prescription for change: Lesbian and bisexual women's health check 2008*, London: Stonewall, http://wwwwww.stonewall.org.uk/campaigns/2365.asp
Jaffe, C., Clance, P.R., Nichols, M.F. and Emshoff, J.G. (2000) 'The prevalence of alcoholism and feelings of alienation in lesbian and heterosexual women', *Addictions in the Gay and Lesbian Community/ Journal of Gay & Lesbian Psychotherapy*, vol 3, nos 3-4, pp 25-36.
Kertzner, R.M., Barber, M.E. and Schwartz, A. (2011) 'Mental health issues in LGBT seniors', *Journal of Gay & Lesbian Mental Health*, vol 15, no 4, pp 335-338, doi: 10.1080/19359705.2011.606680
King, M., McKeown, E. and Warner, J. (2003) 'Mental health and quality of life of gay men and lesbians in England and Wales', *British Journal of Psychiatry*, vol 183, no 2, pp 552-58.
King, M., Smith, G. and Bartlett, A. (2004) 'Treatments of homosexuality in Britain since the 1950s—an oral history: the experience of professionals', *British Medical Journal*, vol 328, no 7437, pp 427-429.

Liu, R.T. and Mustanski, B. (2012) 'Suicidal ideation and self-harm in lesbian, gay, bisexual, and transgender youth', *American Journal of Preventative Medicine*, vol 42, no 3, pp 221-228.

Moncrieff, J. (1997) *Psychiatric imperialism: The medicalisation of modern living*, www.academyanalyticarts.org/moncrieff.htm

Morrison, P.M., Noel, N.E. and Ogle, R.L. (2012) 'Do angry women choose alcohol?', *Addictive Behaviors*, vol 37, no 8, pp 908-913.

Nelson-Jones, R. (1982) *The theory and practice of counselling psychology*, London: Holt, Rinehart and Winston.

Neville, S. and Henrickson, M. (2006) 'Perceptions of lesbian, gay and bisexual people of primary healthcare services', *Journal of Advanced Nursing*, vol 55, no 4, pp 407-415.

Parslow, O. and Hegarty, P. (2013) 'Who cares? UK lesbian caregivers in a heterosexual world', *Women's Studies International Forum*, vol 40, September–October, pp 78-86.

Payne, E. (2007) 'Heterosexism, perfection, and popularity: young lesbians' experiences of the high school social scene', *Educational Studies: A Journal of the American Educational Studies Association*, vol 41, no 1, pp 60-79.

Pelka, S. (2010) 'Observing multiple mothering: a case study of childrearing in a U.S. lesbian-led family', *ETHOS, Journal of the Society for Psychological Anthropology*, vol 38, no 4, pp 422-440.

Plant, M. and Plant, M. (2001) 'Heavy drinking by young British women gives cause for concern', *British Medical Journal*, vol 323, no 7322, p 1183.

Prochaska, J. and DiClemente, C. (1983) 'Stages and processes of self-change in smoking: toward an integrative model of change', *Journal of Consulting and Clinical Psychology*, vol 5, no 3, pp 390-395.

Ricks, J.L. (2012) 'Lesbians and alcohol abuse: identifying factors for future research', *Journal of Social Service Research*, vol 38, no 1, pp 37-45, doi: 10.1080/01488376.2011.616764

Rivers, I. and Carragher, D.J. (2003) 'Social-developmental factors affecting lesbian and gay youth: a review of cross-national research findings', *Children and Society*, vol 17, no 5, pp 374-385.

Roberts, S.J., Tarmina, M.S., Gatson, C., Patsdaughter, C.A. and DeMarco, R. (2005) 'Lesbian use and abuse of alcohol', *Substance Abuse*, vol 25, no 4, pp 1-9, doi: 10.1300/J465v25n04_01

Sheehan, M. and Ridge, D. (2001) '"You become really close…you talk about the silly things you did, and we laugh": the role of binge drinking in female secondary students' lives', *Substance Use and Misuse*, vol 36, no 3, pp 347-372.

Staddon, P. (2005) 'Labelling out', in the special issue of *Journal of Lesbian Studies*, vol 9, no 3, pp 69-78, also co-published in Ettorre, E. (ed) *Making lesbians visible in the substance use field*, New York, NY: Haworth Press.

Staddon, P. (2009) 'Making whoopee'? An exploration of understandings and responses around women's alcohol use', PhD thesis, Plymouth University, http://hdl.handle.net/10026.1/415

Staddon, P. (2012) 'No blame, no shame: towards a social model of alcohol dependency – a story from emancipatory research', in Carr, S. and Beresford, P. (eds) *Social care, service users and user involvement: Building on research*, London: Jessica Kingsley Publishers.

Staddon, P. (2013a) 'Theorising a social model of "'alcoholism'": service users who misbehave', in Staddon, P. (ed) *Mental health service users in research: A critical sociological perspective*, Bristol: Policy Press.

Staddon, P. (2013b) *Improving support for women with alcohol issues*, report for Folk.us

Sweanor, D., Alcabes, P. and Drucker, E. (2007) 'Tobacco harm reduction: how rational public policy could transform a pandemic', *International Journal of Drug Policy*, vol 18, no 2, pp 70-74.

Szymanski, D.M. (2006) ''Heterosexism and sexism as correlates of psychological distress in lesbians', *Journal of Counseling & Development*, vol 83, no 3, pp 355-360.

Vicinus, M. (1993) *'They wonder to which sex I belong': The historical roots of the modern lesbian identity*, London: Routledge.

Warner, J. (2009) 'Smoking, stigma and human rights in mental health: going up in smoke?', *Social Policy and Society*, vol 8, no 2, pp 257-274.

Weeks, J. (1986) *Sexuality*, Hemel Hempstead: Ellis Horwood and Tavistock Publications.

White, K. (2002) *An Introduction to the sociology of health and Illness*, Los Angeles, LA: Sage Publications.

World Bank (1990) *World Bank's world development report*, http://econ.worldbank.org/external/default/main?pagePK=64165259&theSitePK=469372&piPK=64165421&menuPK=64166093&entityID=000178830_98101903345649

NINE

Been there, seen that, done it! An auto-ethnographic narrative account of alcohol use

Lyndsey Moon

> We must learn how to connect (auto)biographies and lived experiences, the epiphanies of lives, to the group and social relationships that surround and shape persons. As we write about lives we bring the world of others into our texts. We create difference, oppositions, and presences which allow us to maintain the illusion that we have captured the 'real' experiences of 'real' people. In fact, we create the persons we write about, just as they create themselves when they engage in storytelling practices. (Denzin, 2014, p 6)

Introduction

According to those who believe in an underlying genetic misfortune leading to 'alcoholism', my future is not looking too bright. My brother, paternal aunt and grandmother and maternal grandfather all died alcohol-related deaths. My father has illnesses complicated by years of 'drinking', my parents' relationship has been marred by alcohol, while I binged my way through my mid-twenties to thirties. To be frank, a disease model offers me an easy way out, a set script to frame my 'alcoholism' as a genetic malfunction that denies me agency for the future. It would add that my only hope would be total abstinence and any slippage from this would lead to either a lapse (a partial but recoverable return to alcohol) or relapse (which means less chance of recovery), while both are more than likely to lead to more years of helplessness and hopelessness as I fight my 'demons'.

The alternative – a social learning model that allows for a better understanding of social context in relation to alcohol use, and suggests that alcohol is a way of coping but has the potential to lead to physiological dependency – has all but lost out in the past few years. Constant reductions in funding have led to services being slashed and only those most willing to compromise their work to rationalisation and efficiency can possibly survive.

I am in favour of the social learning model. Twenty years of working with people who had alcohol-related problems has told me that no one woke up one morning and decided to drink until they dropped. Patterns of drinking sit inside social systems that influence attitudes, approaches and understanding about the use and serious abuse of alcohol. Such systems expect the National Health Service (NHS) and voluntary sector organisations' services and treatment services to deal with those who find themselves in a messy place with alcohol. Some argue that very little should be provided, and that people should be charged for wasting the resources of the precious NHS. Perhaps there is an argument to be heard as we head towards even more austerity. Personally, I would advocate more services with a wider range of approaches and funded from the coffers of those who make alcohol so freely available. Far more preventative work needs to be carried out, especially around young children and teenagers, while the vilification of those who use alcohol should be ended. Of course, readers may say 'You would say that' once they have read the story that follows. Well, yes I would!

This chapter explores personal issues by presenting two stories. The first is my understanding of a particular time and event that relates to alcohol. It is a 'real' story that was told to my therapist (just to clarify, it is a fictional therapist in the sense that I have seen many therapists and it is an amalgam of their responses) who then made a series of interventions or interpretations. This is followed by a more reflexive auto-ethnographic account where I offer an alternative and contemporary story (but it is still a story) that helps to make sense of the original account. This latter creation is a reflexive and reflective understanding that I deliberately put together from the social facts as I understand them today, in a way that removes it from a therapeutic narrative to a story that reveals the context of all those involved in relation to gender, sexuality, age, ethnicity, disability and so on. The chapter unpacks 'taken-for-granted' narratives framing alcohol use, how they are subject to ongoing pressures that have opened up fissures in treatment approaches and how creative ways of addressing alcohol-related issues can benefit from a feminist approach to alcohol care.

A critical humanist approach

The chapter relies on a critical humanist approach to understand the underlying historical scripts and issues that influence decisions to use alcohol and inserts an auto-ethnographic account of my life and relationship to using and 'misusing' alcohol. Critical humanism is selected because it 'takes the human being as an embodied, emotional, interactive self, striving for meaning in wider historically specific social worlds and an even wider universe' (Plummer, 2001, p 255). It provides a narrative of the self as embedded in the historical and social context at any given time. There is an emphasis on the self-reflective and self-reflexive self – the human as intersubjective and self-aware. The human is part of a community of ongoing communication, a thoughtful and compassionate person, a human being who has feelings and responds empathically to others, regardless. A critical humanist approach lends itself to an auto-ethnographic methodology that allows consideration of the perspectives about alcohol and how these socially shape everyday meanings. Looking at journal articles about alcohol from an auto-ethnographic perspective (Grant, 2010), they read like confessional stories where alcohol is the 'very bad guy' and somehow the reader is a victim of their demons. They are pretty miserable and do not seem connected to a wider, social context that may challenge a number of taken-for-granted meanings. There seems very little 'cultural consciousness' where there is an awareness of the relevance of culture to autobiographical experiences (Chang, 2007). I try to reclaim a 'cultural consciousness' in this chapter.

An auto-ethnographical account means considering the story within a context shaped by gender, sexuality, race, ethnicity, class, disability, age and so on and these are all considered. It is about transgressing the 'structures of domination' (Denzin, 2014, p 6). Auto-ethnographies always consider 'the other', while auto-ethnographic texts 'are raced, gendered, class productions reflecting the biases and values of racism, patriarchy and the middle class' (Denzin, 2014, p 6). In this sense, auto-ethnography can mean understanding 'what's going on here' (Goffman, 1974) from the standpoint of trying to deconstruct and reconstruct facts and 'truth' as they are shared between and about people, times and events. Access to a 'reality' or 'truth' is shaped by text because there is no experience 'outside of text' and therefore the story told by the auto-ethnographer relies on interrogation of the 'social' experience as embedded in a much wider social story.

The story in this chapter is a duo-ethnography in the sense that there are two stories merged into one (rather than two people merging two stories into one) and the stories occupy completely different meanings in the interpretation of events. The first story is told and interpreted via a therapeutic trope, highlighting the way my story became an inner dialogue immersed in a psychological explanation after being shaped in a therapeutic encounter. Therapy tropes are conceived of predominantly by the middle classes, embedded in overwhelmingly white privilege and often demonstrating an almost wilful ignorance in relation to the story of 'the other' (Moon, 2011). Therefore, in the stories that follow, the first addresses the story as revealed to a therapist inscribing an intimate, individualised therapeutic analysis while the follow-up story is a self-reflexive monologue set within a critical humanist project, demonstrating the way an alternative meaning may be applied to go further by visiting the broader human context and interconnections that are often dismissed in therapy. In effect, I provide the wider context for understanding the narrow therapeutic story.

Let us begin.

Vignette 1

> It is 1968 and the summer holidays have arrived. We are off to Jersey. By 'we' I mean my mum, dad, brother and myself. We arrive at Manchester airport when the tannoy suddenly blasts: 'Will a Mr Moon please come to information.' My dad is told his mum is in hospital and he must go to her because she collapsed into a diabetic coma and is struggling to stay alive. My dad has to leave and we go ahead. My mum is more than annoyed. She reminds my dad that this is because my nan mixes insulin injections with a drop of brandy and port and how she has always done this and why now. There are countless accusations to do with her drinking behaviour and how she has been a 'drunk' for years. It is pretty unpleasant. There is little empathy for 'that woman' in a coma. We have to wave goodbye to him.
>
> My dad arrives on the second week.
>
> His mum had died.
>
> He is quiet and we are unable to understand what is happening. He seems unwell and starts on the whisky and while it is quiet drinking, it seems lonely and out of place.

I only ever mentioned this in therapy once. Immediately the therapist wanted to know what it was like to share this scenario and what the impact of the loss my grandmother had on my family. The therapist was interested in the details of the relationships and how these may be played out in the present. How did the people involved relate? What was it like to be in a different country without my father? What did I imagine the impact of my grandmother's death had on the members of the family at that time, especially my father and how was this felt by each of us? And what did his drinking mean in retrospect? All useful and reflective pieces on which to contemplate and I leaned upon some useful soul-searching. The therapeutic narrative extended into my thinking, providing one tiny fragment of a story where thousands of pieces appear to re-make and re-construct my subjectivity.

Now, many years later, the story is far more complex than I originally imagined. In fact, I have needed to ask my father about details that seem remote yet significant when I begin to interrogate them. I am left wondering if these details are gradually being erased by therapy tropes that seem unlikely to make them count. My grandmother was born into a poor, northern, working-class life in 1901 as the third of five girls and one boy (deceased). She was hardly educated and started work in the mill at 14 years old. My grandfather worked on the railways as he had done from the age of 14, working himself up from fireman to driver. They married when she was 27 years old because she was pregnant with my father – not an ideal start, especially as my grandfather did not want to marry her. She was unwanted and so was my father. She gave birth to my father in 1928; her second (male) at 29 years old, who died and she gave birth to a third (female) child at 31 years old, who survived. Most of her working life was spent in a cotton mill, which was the typical unskilled labour for most women and later she was a 'clippy'[1] on the buses around Preston. At 39 years old, her husband, my grandfather was killed on the railway. It was through sheer negligence but there was no union fighting on his behalf and the company (LSM) took no responsibility. They (my grandmother, father and aunt) were immediately thrown into poverty – there was no such thing as benefits, while the death led to a small pay-out to cover the rent on the house. It was the start of the war years. Everything was rationed and her partner was dead. She could not manage. She relied on my father to do everything. There was no income other than her wage although she received some support from her mother. My father was so poor he had to sit at school in a coat all day because his shorts had holes in them. A year later, he had to start work on the trains as a fire 'man' at age 14. My grandmother had no opportunity to think about death. Perhaps she did not want or know how to reflect on her life. Regardless of the reasons, she would have 'a drink' and later 'didn't know when to stop'. When my father married, she was 50 years old. She seemed unable to behave as a woman should behave – drinking and smoking became part of the story. She was referred to in rather unspeakable terms by my mother who wanted her to remain unseen. Gradually, my grandmother became unwell, developing diabetes (because of the alcohol the pancreas was unable to work as it should) and continued to drink regularly and heavily, often bringing on diabetic comas and needing my father to be with her. It caused problems that were all too clear. In our family, lines had been drawn about acceptable and unacceptable behaviour. There were tensions and hatreds and unkind words about my grandmother – she was written off as a woman with very little virtue; she was 'a tramp', 'trash'. Nothing worth remembering. I remember my grandmother as a little bit wild, I remember her smelling of brandy, cigarettes and perfume, wearing fake fur and always with gloves. She always seemed to be putting on bright red lipstick and she showed me how by sliding it over my five-year-old lips. I remember her in a kind but distant way, as though her life had simply passed me by.

In a sense, this shifted into my life fairly quietly. I think of this working-class, white woman who really had quite a small and ordinary life, in a way that leads me to consider certain injustices. How did thousands of children become engaged in manual labour in such a way that the cotton mills of England made vast profits? And what of the injustices perpetrated when some innocent worker like my grandfather died? How could the private company refuse to share its wealth with those who worked and died in the making of that wealth? And what of education? Health? Social security? How could a woman who had been left to survive possibly cope? Perhaps she chose the wrong method. But alcohol became her friend and her foe. At 68 years old, she died of an alcohol-induced diabetic coma. Nothing grand, nothing startling. I ask myself if I would like that life. If I had that life, would I cope any better considering the conditions?

Vignette 2

> It is 1979. Punk is on its way out. I am 18 years old and doing my 'A' levels and tomorrow is 'A' level English Literature. I am at a fee-paying, all-girls Convent school to help me 'get somewhere'. It's a nice enough place and lovely girls, but I don't really fit in. I am quiet and nervous and not very bright. Certainly not as clever as my brother, who is a handsome 15-year-old and quite talented. I wanted to be an artist or a footballer and neither are options, so I have ended up with a team of 'A' levels that are completely a waste of my time, it seems to me: Geography instead of an easel, Bismark instead of a football. What's the point? It is nearly 9pm and I should be revising. But there is also too much

> tension in the air. My dad is now 50 years old. He hasn't been home for three days and any second he could come through the door and that will be it. Hours and minutes sweat by on the hands. All the doors are locked. There is no way he will be able to get in. This isn't going to work.
>
> It's midnight. Lights are off but I am wide awake. Waiting. There is the faint sound of a car engine. One, two, three....
>
> Suddenly, there is a loud bang on the front door that is wooden and framing a large piece of pretty, patterned glass pressing against horrible, gold, wrought-iron leaves. There are two more loud bangs and my mum shouts to tell my dad to 'Go back to where you came from' before there is the sound of glass cracking, crashing and then silently landing on the carpet in sharp-edged pieces all over the floor so that it is impossible to walk on without heavy shoes. My dad opens the door from the inside and almost falls onto the glass but manages to get his balance and somehow stumbles sideways and falls onto the settee in the room to the right. He lands full length, face down and just falls asleep. He is snoring. The stench of alcohol is overwhelming. My mum has had enough she says and leaves the room. She returns with a hammer. She raises it above my dad's head and as it moves down I gently lift it from her grasp. Would she?
>
> I go upstairs. In just a few hours it is English Literature. I find a valium that belongs to my mum and swallow it down with some left-over cider from a 'jolly' (a good night drinking and laughter).
>
> I can hardly see the paper the next morning.

My therapist seemed quite disturbed by this account. Personally, it wasn't any different from what most of my friends had experienced and we went through it too often to be traumatised. He reckoned on some form of post-traumatic stress disorder. I reminded my therapist that my mother quite enjoyed serial murder stories and cooking. Well, I thought it was funny. My therapist seemed to be focusing on my relationship to both parents and asked how this event reminded me of their relationship. I felt uncomfortable and was upset by the memory and the distress caused. We could have focused on the event forever. It was a lonely experience as I remember. Who would ever know what was happening the night before English Literature? It was a tremendous story in itself. Far more entertaining than the rubbish on the exam paper. No one knew. And no one was likely to ask. There were no school counsellors in those days. It would be possible to see this as the consequence of drinking, neglect, ignorance and stupidity. Hardly likely to be said by my therapist but definitely a possibility in the context of present-day therapy.

Now I can see the event differently and perhaps with a critical humanist focus. I am aware of the ongoing encounters and the meaning of events I was proxy to and yet all accumulate into these 'moments' in history. At the time this event took place, my father was being medicated on gold salt injections. This was yet another 'magic cure' for rheumatoid arthritis and meant literally being injected with a mixture of gold compounds. It caused a list of side effects – it damaged the kidneys, made the skin itch and turn grey and ulcerated the mouth. It didn't kill the pain. Mixed with beer and whisky after a 10-hour day of window cleaning, didn't help. My father would lose days out of his life. And ours.

What I never realised and did not understand was the level of uncontrolled pain he was in on a daily basis. He had been diagnosed with rheumatoid arthritis at the age of 31 in 1960, shortly after he had turned self-employed as a window cleaner. The doctors believed that it was caused because he simply could not manage the series of life events between 1955 and 1960. Within five years my parents had gone from being happily married to experiencing the death of their first child, an accident to my mother's brother, Terence, aged 17, which paralysed him from the neck down, and the death of my mother's father. Distressed by the death of his child and carrying the coffin alone, my father has only spoken of that day once in his life with me – while we stood together in a London pub after closing time. That death was added to by the tragic and unnecessary accident to Terence. While at work on a freezing cold morning, pushing containers of wood on a tiny track, the cart toppled and the wood fell onto his body, forcing down his neck until it broke. Paralysed from the neck down, Terence was later awarded £15,000 because it was due to negligence and a lack of health and safety. It paid for the specially made bed he needed so he could be cared for by his family when he could go home from Southport Hospital. My father saw Terence as if he were his younger brother. He loved him. And so he would cycle three times a week for five years from Preston to Southport – a round-trip of 120 miles a week. It ended with the brave young boy's death at the age of 22. My parents didn't cope. Why should they? Who would? My father was in the wrong job to be ill.

I wonder now if the events were also triggering a much deeper loss for my father – that his own father had been killed when he was just 13 years old. After a row, his father had hit him and sent him to bed. He never saw his father again. The next day, his father was scalded to death in a railway accident. My father had to take over earning an income and was sent to work on the railway himself less than a year later. It was a life of brutality and poverty. And despite trying to move into the 'swinging sixties', life for many young post-war men and women was a reminder of the poverty and horrors they had lived with for most of their life. For my parents, these experiences were simply intolerable and they had no idea how to help themselves or each other. And the rheumatoid arthritis, I realise now, left my father exhausted and in pain every day. The illness was a metaphor, my therapist said, for the pain of his life. Not helpful. It is hard to imagine all this, never mind live with it. And so my father started using alcohol to kill both physical and emotional anguish. It seems quite obvious now. But not that night. There we were, my mother and father in their big house, which showed that they were 'successful' working-class parents, sending their children to a better school, to have a better chance – so we would give them access to the gold salt of professionals. How much they wanted to be able to know doctors and lawyers and people who were 'proper'. How much they wanted to afford nice carpets and curtains, a good car and good schools – to leave behind the sadness and losses and simply have a better life. Perhaps the crashing of glass was inevitable really. It strikes me even now how the death of my uncle and my grandfather were unnecessary consequences of working-class life. They were not heroes, were never written about, never remembered outside close family. And yet, all these years later, they are part of my memory, part of who I have become because I believe in the need for trades unions and political responsibility to workers and their families and I believe that profit ultimately causes pain.

Vignette 3

It is 1992. I am out as a dyke and I live in a housing cooperative in North London. I work in an alcohol and drug agency on a part-time basis. It is the annual Gay Pride weekend. We will head for Kennington Park on Saturday. There is one dilemma and that is my cousin's wedding in Preston. I am expected to attend. Every single one of my extended family will be there. Except me. I stand my ground. I stay for Gay Pride. I drink myself stupid on the day. Fantastic. We laughed, all drank for days, took drugs, played around and eventually slept it off. It is the year my

> brother is awarded his wings as a Flight Lieutenant in the RAF.

My therapist focused on the feeling of exclusion from my family and whether this had a long-term effect on relationships and asked how I felt as I discussed this issue. Personally, I revel in memories from Pride as a moment of community glory and I talk through how much I enjoyed the day with friends. My therapist asked about drinking. I explained that many of us drank – it was part of 'the scene', an opportunity to meet others and to just have fun.

Today, I see that time with a more socially aware understanding – one that remains beyond therapeutic discourse. By 1992, living and working in London meant finding subsidised housing and housing cooperatives provided exactly that opportunity. Embedded in the 1970s' system of cooperative living as a way of community, the system is based on elected democracy and rents are kept low because of a cooperative population of tenants who meet regularly and are led to think about their welfare and that of other tenants. It is a unique and social way to live in a vibrant and expensive city. Back then, the labour market for lesbians and gay men usually meant being involved in types of social care and often in local authority-funded voluntary projects. It was always necessary to be careful in being 'out' because while some projects were supportive of lesbian, gay and bisexual (LGB) people, others were afraid. Rarely could you openly admit to living as anything other than heterosexual until working out who in the organisation was tolerant and what being 'out' would mean for personal safety. Only left-wing local authority-funded projects took the risk to employ 'others' and push for all forms of equality – to the point where it was a regular part of a staff team meeting. It was the Thatcher era of 'pretended family relationships' and local authorities were terrified of being 'outed' by the press as gay-friendly otherwise they could lose their funding.

Most of us worked for local authorities such as Haringey, Camden or Lambeth – branded left-wing and 'dangerous' as they took the lead in defying the homophobic and intolerant Conservative Party. Union activity was high on the agenda pursuing health and safety and working towards human rights for LGB people. The work was often with grassroots groups such as homeless people, people with drug- and alcohol-related issues and sex workers. At that time, there was no kudos in this work. It was simply dedicated, hard-working people who sedimented rights for those of us who were unrecognised at a national level.

The annual Gay Pride event was, at this time, the signifier of a longed-for freedom by and for lesbians and gay men. It involved a march through London followed by a free event at a park, hosted usually by a 'leftie' local authority. Actually, it was always a do-it-yourself event put together by a voluntary team of lesbians and gay men. As time went on, this voluntary-run event became a jewel of gay commodification. But at that time, we desperately needed somewhere to take Gay Pride because we needed to fight intolerance with the right to recognition, regardless of the hostile press, government and lay people, and the event was so much more than a sing-a-long in the park.

The march is now for entertainment, while lesbian, gay, bisexual and transgender (LGBT) communities are allowed to congregate at Trafalgar Square rather than their own space. Drinking and drug taking are still part of the day. I mention this because although a number of LGBT people do have problems with drug and alcohol, the oft-reported statements that LGBT communities are somehow disproportionately more involved in drug taking and drinking than the heterosexual communities are a fallacy. The reports often fail to include the vast population of LGBT people and instead narrow down investigation to those in bars and clubs. It would be like basing statistics for alcohol and drugs only on heterosexuals who go to parties, festivals and bars.

Something of my history around activism and militancy persists. It was the reason why, in 2006, I joined the Greater London Drug and Alcohol Alliance (GLADA) Women's Expert Advisory Group. In 2005, under the leadership of Ken Livingstone, London's City Hall set up a campaign to help the women of London to explore their options around their relationship to drugs and alcohol. With various stakeholders (the NHS, the STELLA project working to prevent domestic abuse, the London Drug and Alcohol Network – LDAN – and the Federation of Black and Asian Drug and Alcohol Workers, to name a few), the aim was to provide ongoing support and advice to women and their alcohol- and/or drug-related concerns. In 2006, this moved centre stage, with City Hall offering access to their building for free, employing a senior policy officer whose remit was drugs and alcohol and who made it her task to find women and organisations who would and could work together. GLADA advertised in the alcohol and drug units across London, asking women who had experiences related to alcohol and/or drugs and were willing to work in partnership with each other, if they would be willing to join forces. Women who attended the very first meeting at City Hall on 17 July 2006 were represented in relation to class, race, ethnicity, sexuality, disability and age. There had been a sea-change in the way the general public thought about LGBT people and perhaps a more compassionate and less hostile political approach to drug and alcohol issues that were surfacing as ongoing problems within London, and in particular for women.

GLADA provided a unique project that reached out to women who wanted to work on policy and events that would show the role of alcohol and drugs in their life. The uniqueness of the project was astounding. For the first time in my professional history (and by then I had worked in the alcohol and drugs field in the voluntary sector and NHS for 18 years), a group of women were brought together who had used alcohol/drugs (A/D), were using A/D, worked in A/D and/or made policy that would affect women in relation to A/D. In a fully cooperative way, all the women brought up vastly interesting issues related in one way or another to alcohol and/or drug use and although these stories were shared, the remit of the group was to connect with women in London. Perhaps this is why GLADA made such an impact on me personally. Years of working in NHS and voluntary sector settings had shown how truly difficult it was to engage with women in such a way that they would be interested in bothering to look at the information about an alcohol or drug project. Government strategists had no idea, while cutbacks in funding public provision was always top of government agendas in the hope that services would be fully privatised and show no recalcitrance to imposed regulations from the business in charge. I had never had much time for the 'private' sector because listening to the voices of those in treatment always seemed a much better way of managing drug- and alcohol-related problems than trying to impose a costly and fairly ineffective top-down management system. I also did not agree with the privatisation of social ills as a way of making profit.

So, GLADA proved to be innovative. All women involved worked together and the system allowed for cooperation as a central principle underpinning the group. Once every six weeks we would meet to plan what we would do next. Within the year, we decided to put on an exhibition at the 2008 'Capital Woman' event. Although we didn't realise it then, that event would be the final event, as it was inexplicably shut down at the time the newly elected Mayoralty in City Hall was established. While ensuring that policy was discussed and feedback given to London's policy makers in the field of drugs and alcohol, it seemed equally important to make sure that we remained visible. The event was followed by several more independent projects in publicly funded settings where we would each contribute poetry, art, music and ideas where women could be brought together to talk about their losses, their hopes, their history and their life. It became immensely rewarding. As a group we travelled around London, put on exhibitions, talked to the press and represented women in isolation, in prison, in detox in need of help. We did this as a voluntary project and we gave it 100% time and effort. It ended in 2008 when the new Mayor was voted into power and there was no longer the same appeal to 'our' project. However, what it showed was how organisations, stakeholders and volunteer participants can make an idea a reality if they have the will.

Vignette 4

> It is 2007. Monday, 16 April, 3.00am. I am in bed but wide awake. The phone rings. It is my brother's wife saying 'I am sorry …'. My brother is dead. I have to think how I will tell my mum and dad their only beautiful son has died. I don't know what to do. Or say. I get dressed and just lie motionless on the bed in solitude. I have no idea what to do. 'I loved you', I say over and over.
>
> It is now 7am. I have to ring home. I have to tell my parents the awful news. I have to think that someone needs to be with them and so I ring my uncle and ask him to go to my mum and dad. It is the first time I have to say: 'Guy has died.'
>
> I ring home and each ring is sickly. My mum answers. She says in a trembling voice: 'Hiya luv.'
>
> I say: 'Hi mum….' and she just says:
>
> 'Our Guy's died hasn't he?'
>
> 'Yes, mum, he has.'
>
> 'I have to tell your dad.'
>
> Guy had been admitted to hospital after vomiting blood at 11pm on Sunday 15 April. His stomach had haemorrhaged. He had been drinking a bottle of vodka a day.

My therapist asked about the death and allowed me to cry from the depths of my saddened body uncontrollably. Of course, weeks of this and my therapist was really wanting to know why, if the death was so long ago, I was still so upset. The therapist was unable to understand why grief was wordless, feelingless, just desolation. He asked me how my family had responded and I was forced to add that certain members who worked in the NHS saw my brother as genetically flawed because of evidence about my father's history with alcohol. Even my dentist said that it was all down to genes. My therapist could not offer his opinion.

Of course, looking at the 'evidence' it could support the statement that a genetic factor must have been behind my brother's 'alcoholism'. In fact, in everyday life, most people would look at the evidence from the narrow perspective of what they have read in the media or what they think must be the cause of drinking to excess. However, the story of a successful pilot officer who witnessed the death of 37 of his 'mates' over a decade goes unheard. The death of 12 of these young men in a helicopter crash, and the fact Guy lived in the room next door to one of them he considered as close as a brother, goes unheard. The fact Guy had to find out about the crash on the news and that he was chosen to tell the parents that their beloved son had been so horribly burned he could not be identified and had to be buried in a lead casket, had to go unheard. This was a turning point for my brother. From a happy 'lad' who so much wanted to join the RAF as a boy, and who was so overjoyed when he made it through by overcoming 300 applicants in 1984, to a young man who in the late 1980s was severely depressed and not coping very well. I remember him visiting me in 1990 and as usual we all went out for a meal and a drink and then to a bar where I remember him drinking a few pints rapidly, then quietly slipping to another part of the room. As I walked over I noticed him sitting with his head in his hands and as he raised his head, I saw tears running down his face. He was destroyed and yet had nowhere to turn. There was no welfare, no counselling in this flight 'family'. His time in the RAF was brought to an end in 1994 when he crashed his car at 130mph after a night of drinking to celebrate a flying trip where it was suggested he should be made Captain. Having recently returned from the Falklands, he was showing signs of stress and trauma but turned to flying and driving to hide his feelings, I now realise. He had returned to his friend's house, had gone to bed but for reasons of his own thinking, he decided to leave and to drive. He left the RAF because he was forced to resign his commission. No one wanted to listen. I found a letter to an Air Vice-Marshall, never posted, telling them he wanted to be a top pilot in the RAF and wanted to continue. Too late. He was collected from Lyneham RAF Station by a family friend accompanied by my father. When they returned home they cracked open a bottle of whisky. Ten years later we discovered some of the atrocities he witnessed while in the RAF. It is estimated that such traumatised men and women in the forces have a survival rate of 13 years after leaving the forces before their delayed trauma disturbs or kills them (http://science.howstuffworks.com/ptsd.htm). The estimate is exactly right.

I find solace with my friends at GLADA. They seem to understand far more than anyone else – certainly therapists. They have all experienced the same feelings. I simply no longer have to explain. In 2007, we (GLADA Women's Voices) held an event to mark the first International Remembrance Day on 21 July in Kennington Park in London. 'We' are the people who have lost someone to alcohol and/or drugs and the event was held in their memory. Over a hundred people attended. I was asked to read the story of my brother, while later a man who had been drinking throughout the ceremony simply picked up his guitar and sang a stunning version of the song *Wish You Were Here* before just walking away. It was the first time people who had died of alcohol or drugs could be commemorated openly, lovingly and with pride.

These accounts are means of understanding the way alcohol can be inscribed into a family legacy and everyday life. As a narrative it seems remote, something in isolation. Yet, as I have shown, the story is a complex web of interactions and meanings. Would it really be possible to talk about this history of alcohol use in a therapeutic setting without some form of interpretation or underlying hidden pathology? I doubt it. Yet, if we change the approach to alcohol and allow ourselves to experience a kindness by creating new spaces where there is cooperation and integration, then it can alter the way we understand those who use alcohol and drugs in a more open and loving way. I am willing to do this. Are you?

Note

[1] A 'clippy' is old British slang for a female bus conductor.

References

Chang, H. (2007) 'Autoethnography: raising cultural consciousness of self and others', in Walford, G. (ed) *Methodological developments in ethnography* (Studies in Educational Ethnography, Volume 12) (pp 207-221), Bradford: Emerald Group Publishing.

Denzin, N.K. (2014) *Interpretative autoethnography* (2nd edn), Chicago, IL: University of Illinois.

Goffman, E. (1974) *Frame analysis: An essay on the organisation of experience*, Cambridge, MA: Harvard University Press.

Grant, A. (2010) 'Writing the reflexive self: an autoethnography of alcoholism and the impact of psychotherapy culture', *Journal of Psychiatric and Mental Health Nursing*, vol 17, no 7, pp 577-582.

Moon, L. (2011) 'The gentle violence of therapists: misrecognition and dis-location of the Other', *Psychotherapy and Politics International*, vol 9, no 3, pp 194–205.

Plummer, K. (2001) *Documents of life 2: An invitation to a critical humanism*, London: Sage Publications.

Part Three
A social approach to women's alcohol treatment

TEN

The right 'space' for women: examining effective treatment in primary care for women's dependent and problematic alcohol consumption

Jeff Fernandez

Introduction

This chapter looks at what can be done to encourage a greater number of women to attend substance misuse services and how the location of the service can be an important part of encouraging women to attend. It examines the community detoxification audit based in primary care. It discusses how women are more likely to attend a service where there is a non-judgemental approach and easy access to services, with minimal waiting times. It also illustrates that services situated in general practice can be seen as a non-stigmatising 'space' and therefore easier to attend for substance misuse services.

A service that is provided in a 'safe space' aligns with the social model of alcohol treatment (Introduction, this volume) in that it perceives women's issues as being different from men's, and responds by offering a social approach. Gender, together with race and ethnicity, are key factors shaping Western industrialist capitalist societies, and lead to persistent structural inequalities, and hence divisions and differences (Haralambos and Holborn, 2000). In healthcare, gender factors can influence presentations (Gabe et al, 2004). Women are much more likely than men to be frequent presenters to primary care, partly because of their responsibilities for young children. They are also more vulnerable to poverty and hence to increased health problems. Some studies have shown that women are more prone to stress and to seek help from primary healthcare services for this (Brady, 2009). Consequently, they are also more likely to use mental healthcare services and to present to their general practitioner (GP) for disorders such as depression. On the other hand, men may be more likely to use and misuse drugs and alcohol.

In the area of substance misuse, the ratio for men and women using treatment services is 4:1 (Jones et al, 2009). This is a very marked difference in favour of men. Jones et al (2009) have suggested that this could be due to men as a group being more vulnerable to alcohol and drug misuse problems and therefore making them as a cohort more likely to present to these services. It is not clear how much of this difference is due to the greater reluctance of women who do have alcohol issues to access services. The gender ratio has long been recognised by services and some approaches have been adopted to try to address this. For example, some women-only clinics and women-only 'spaces' in drug and alcohol services have been set up. This has met with limited success. There is evidence that the low number of women in substance misuse services may reflect fears around child protection.

These factors, coupled with a 'medical approach', in which social factors are often ignored, can limit success in reaching some populations such as women (Rhodes and Johnson, 1997). What is certain is that services need to look at what can be changed or structured successfully in order to address the problem. A way to provide greater access for women is to provide an accessible 'space' for women and in Islington in London this is provided at the local GP surgery. This approach is explored in this chapter.

Gender and alcohol and service provision

Women's alcohol consumption may appear to have increased in the UK over the last two decades. One reason may be that there are increasing numbers of women in paid work in the UK, and some of these have entered professions where drinking is encouraged (such as journalism). Here, drinking 'after work' and also socialising with alcohol are often 'spaces' where women are drinking more often than before. Also, women's drinking in public in the UK is more accepted than two decades ago (Blackman et al, Chapter Three, this volume). Some people have argued that binge drinking is a growing problem. Certainly, young women are more likely to be noticed when behaving in this way than are men (Gilmore et al, 2008). These factors highlight how the phenomenon can be seen as gender specific and a particular problem for women. In turn, women who drink alcohol dependently are thus more noticed and open to stigma and demonisation in society.' [Ed: There is in practice some evidence that most women may not be drinking as much alcohol as they did, although levels for some remain problematic – see 'Changing trends in women's drinking', Institute of Alcohol Studies website, http://www.ias.org.uk/Alcohol-knowledge-centre/Alcohol-and-women/Factsheets/Changing-trends-in-womens-drinking.aspx (accessed 2 April 2015).]

Women often have different reasons for excessive alcohol consumption than men who drink dependently, which makes accessing effective treatment difficult (Staddon, 2012). In primary care, common factors include:

- domestic violence;
- childhood sexual or other abuse;
- undiagnosed depression;
- postnatal depression;
- a poor relationship with significant family members;
- significant family members using drugs/alcohol;
- a partner being alcohol dependent.

It is estimated that 15% of women in England and Wales are drinking in a way that damages their health, and there is a drive, as mentioned, by healthcare services to try to address this (Centers for Disease Control and Prevention, 2012). Research has indicated that young women are increasingly more likely to die from alcohol and drug misuse (Shipton et al, 2013). What are drug and alcohol services doing to address this increasing and worrying picture?

As mentioned above, the national ratio for treatment in terms of gender is 4:1. This ratio in favour of men has been stable for many years, despite efforts being made to attract women who have a problem with either alcohol or drugs to services. However, women who do access services, and are able to use treatment, are more likely to use those services effectively and leave the treatment system 'drug or alcohol free'. Of the women who detox the first time, 70% manage to stay off alcohol for over three months and 45% over six months. Of women who detox the second time, 85% stay dry for over a year. Of the women who detox the third time, 94% stay dry for over one year (www.nta.nhs.uk, 2013).

Location of services seems to be a key factor and can result in larger numbers of women accessing healthcare if it is right for them. It is argued here that primary care is a sector of healthcare services that women are not afraid to access. This should be the place to start examining whether good access for women with alcohol dependency problems can be achieved.

Women seeking treatment in Islington

There are many reasons why women have been reluctant to access treatment for alcohol dependency in primary care. One of the main reasons cited is that some GPs have, in the past, been judgemental, holding a 'moral' perspective (Gabe et al, 2004) on the use of alcohol by women. Women often feel their alcohol use is seen as a moral issue in treatment services, increasing feelings of guilt and inadequacy (Staddon, 2012). Much has been done in the past decade to try to get GPs to understand substance misuse as an 'illness' that needs to be treated like any other. The Royal College of General Practitioners, which is responsible for educating and updating GP practice, has developed a teaching module entitled 'Certificate in the Management of Alcohol Problems in Primary Care Level 1'. Many GPs in London have asked for this training and the Primary Care Alcohol and Drug Service (PCADS) conducts such programmes in Islington for them to practise in the addictions field (www.smmgp.org.uk).

There could be many reasons for women's wish to detoxify from alcohol and be 'alcohol free'. There is the fear of imminent referral to social services due to either the mother's or the grandmother's problematic or dependent drinking, which raises concern for their ability to care for their children or grandchildren (Fernandez, 2006) Often the fear of involvement of social services and the loss of residence of children is the main driver. If the woman achieves abstinence from alcohol, social services may be satisfied with her and her family and they may disengage with them.

The area of alcohol detoxification will now be examined, to illustrate how women are able to use a primary care service effectively to achieve their goal of being alcohol free. It is suggested that a clear clinical approach can be delivered without being judgemental and moralistic. In primary care, services can be more easily accessed, and these elements of a quick service and non-judgemental approach may, it is hoped, be adopted by other boroughs in England so that they too may improve service outcomes. Most importantly, it enables women to be treated in an NHS service and space (primary care) that they already feel comfortable in accessing.

Recovery

'Recovery' has been the new word on the block in the United Kingdom since the coalition government came to power in 2010. It was thought that there was too much emphasis on retaining people in the treatment system and not enough of a focus on enabling people to achieve the goal of being drug or alcohol free (Public Health England, 2013). This thesis has been insufficiently examined. However, the government's approach has been to orientate drug and alcohol services to try to achieve the goal of patients being 'drug and alcohol free' as the main focal point for substance misuse services. This change will be driven through by a system of 'payments by results' being the way that services will be commissioned.

This is a big ideological shift from a 'harm reduction' approach, which focused on reducing harm to the individual and society foremost, with abstinence an end signpost. Harm reductionists have argued that the goal of abstinence was always part of the approach and was incorporated in its ideology. However, it was not central to its structure. Abstinence as a goal in planning an individual's care is now central to treatment and is 'the ideology'.

'Recovery' has been adopted by all drug and alcohol services across England but most services have remodelled themselves to build towards a patient being drug or alcohol free after two years in treatment (Public Health England, 2013). For PCADS and alcohol work conducted in primary care in Islington, the focus of the service is to get the patient alcohol free for the long term. In fact, most patients who access the service state that this is their goal, when they are assessed. Women tend to be more focused on a treatment goal than men. They often state that the idea of being alcohol free is why they came to the primary care service. Many do complete a community detoxification and do become alcohol free after a period in treatment.

PCADS offers a service with 'recovery' as a central part of the patient-centred approach, as well as alcohol reduction. This chapter illustrates what can be done to enable women to access services and what can encourage them to achieve their goal of being alcohol free. The role of detoxification will be outlined, and the chapter will show how this may enable women to achieve alcohol-free outcomes.

Detoxification

The PCADS in Islington assesses patients who present to the service asking for help to control their alcohol and drug consumption. Women are more likely than men to ask to detoxify from alcohol; as mentioned, they have clearer goals for treatment when presenting to the PCADS.

In primary care, a community detoxification is a process by which clients are enabled to withdraw safely from alcohol while remaining in a primary care setting. This is achieved with a combination of support, a reducing regime of medication and ongoing monitoring.

This process takes between five and eight days. The PCADS nurse offers alcohol detoxification as in primary care, which commences with an assessment and moves onwards through community detoxification to relapse prevention and rehabilitation to support the client's goal of being alcohol free.

Box 10.1 sets out the PCADS criteria for community alcohol detoxification. As they indicate, the patient should not have the potential to suffer from fits, and there must be no overt liver damage or physical symptoms such as Ascites (indicating advanced liver damage), which would need a higher degree of monitoring and therefore lead one to look at an in-patient detoxification regime.

Box 10.1: PCADS criteria for community alcohol detoxification

The patient:

- is not severely dependent and their alcohol consumption is less than 200 units per week
- is aged 18–65 (service remit)
- is not confused, nor has hallucinations or delirium tremens (DTs)
- has no history of uncontrolled or unexplained seizures while on medication
- has no acute physical illness including history of reduced respiratory function, cardiac failure or severe liver damage
- is not pregnant or breast feeding
- is not physically compromised or has unsteady gait
- is not dependent on benzodiazepines or chaotically misusing illicit drugs
- has no presenting signs of Wernicke-Korsakoff syndrome
- has not suffered from unstable or severe psychiatric illness including a risk of suicide, frequent self-harm or impaired cognitive function
- has no history of uncompleted medication-assisted withdrawal or is likely to disengage with services for monitoring during withdrawal.
- has a supportive home environment and is not vulnerable, easily influenced or mistreated by others
- is able to give valid consent for treatment (see also Mental Capacity Act 2005).

The patient must be able to comprehend the regime and be able to comply with the way the regime is designed. Also, for a community detoxification the patient must agree to a minimum degree of monitoring as this can reduce the likelihood of undertaking a detoxification in primary care. This usually means visiting the surgery to be assessed by the specialist nurse three times a week.

Librium is used in primary care in Islington as there is less risk of respiratory arrest and it is tolerated better by patients. It is given in a sliding-scale, decreasing dose regime, tailored to the individual. Hemeneverin is discouraged for use in detoxing patients from alcohol in the community and is best used in in-patient settings.

Methodology

For the research on which this chapter is based, the details of the women who detoxified from alcohol were analysed from the data collected from a wider study conducted for PCADS. This wider study was an evaluation from the year January 2010 to January 2011. A database was kept, which logged all patients who completed a community detoxification from the PCADS team; this is now repeated annually. The database recorded:

- units consumed prior to detoxification;
- ethnicity;
- date of birth;
- gender;
- number of detoxification regimes in the period 2010–11 (total)
- aftercare;
- post-detoxification prescribing: Acamprosate/Disulfiram.

The database recorded the number of units that the clients consumed over a period of one week. As the guidelines indicated that the threshold for community detoxifications was 200 units per week, the number of units was recorded to try to see if this criterion was adhered to, and whether it was effective.

The ethnicity of the clients was recorded and this showed that the majority of the patients were White British, with very few coming from other ethnic categories.

Aftercare data were also recorded with information as to whether anything was prescribed post detoxification such as Acamprosate or Disulfiram and whether they were monitored post detoxification as the guidelines indicated.

The database was created in Excel and the categories analysed in sections to show some interesting correlations. As mentioned earlier, the main purpose of this chapter is to show an adherence to the guidelines and also that the assessment criteria screened for a potential population could have good outcomes, as well as be safely managed by the PCADS nursing team.

Results

This study included 53 people. Figure 10.1 shows the proportion of men to women in primary care alcohol treatment services in Islington which is near to 1:1, with only a slight (53:48) percentage ratio in favour of males, compared to the national ratio of 4:1. In Figure 10.2 we see a gender split of the clients who were detoxified in Islington in 2010–11 whereby 56% were men while 44% were women. This shows that there is a greater percentage of women presenting for alcohol primary care in Islington than is evident in the national ratio for substance use, where the ratio for PCADS is shown to be 60:40 in favour of men.

It has been suggested in the literature that women are more able to use talking therapies than men (Rhodes and Johnson, 1997). It has been noted from previous research that, in primary care services in Islington, men are keen to use medication, to help with stopping drinking, while women are more able to use talking therapies and have greater insight and motivation to treatment (Fernandez, 2006). This will hopefully be verified by further research to update these points later in 2015.

In primary care, the figure for women entering treatment such as a detoxification regime is higher than is suggested by the national figures for treatment across all services for drug and alcohol use. This may be

Figure 10.1: Gender of all patients in Islington primary care alcohol treatment services

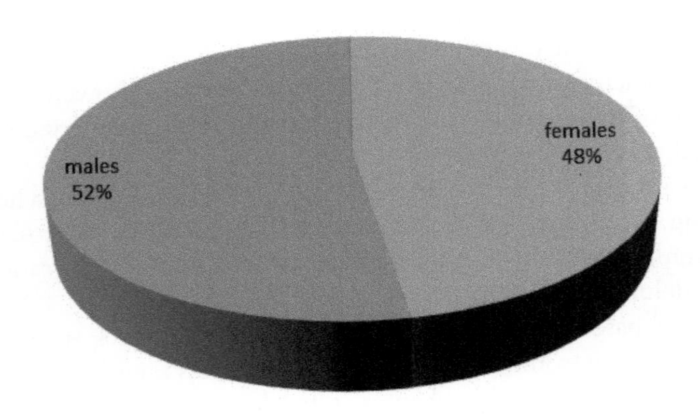

Figure 10.2: Gender split of detoxifications in Islington, 2010–11

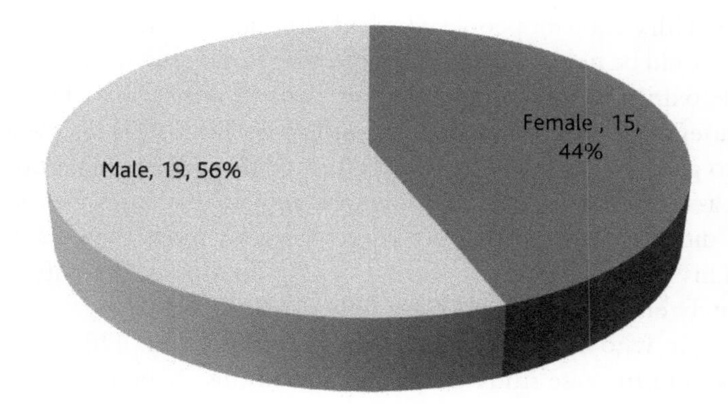

because such a service is structured to be more accessible to women; or, it could be that it is situated in the right 'space' for women to access services, that is, nearer to their home and without the stigma of being a specific 'alcohol or drug service' but simply a service located in primary care.

Anecdotally, it is common knowledge that people who complete a detoxification for the first time have a high relapse rate. The total number of regimes completed in the period 2010–11 as shown in Figure 10.3 was 53. Of those, 43% had more than one detox.

Figure 10.3: Number of detoxification regimes, 2010–11

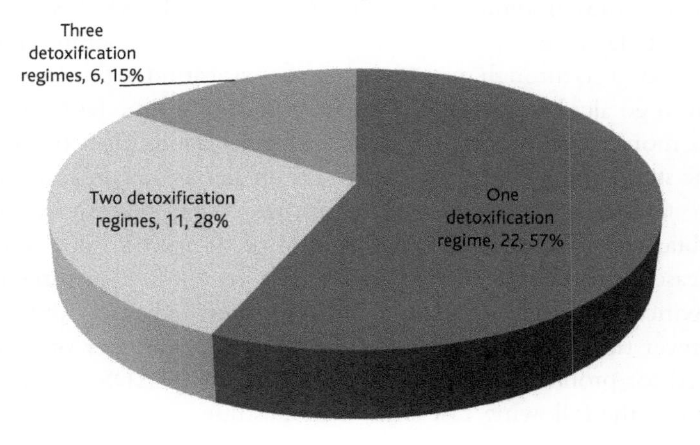

There is always a significant population in any year who complete 'dry-time' for 2–3 months after detoxification. Figure 10.4 shows the length of 'dry' time for people who had just one detoxification in 2010–11. It should be noted that those people who had undertaken more than one detoxification all completed more than 12 weeks 'dry'. However, for patients who only had one detoxification in 2010–11, 28% were able to go dry for between one and four weeks, which was a positive result as there was no one who did not complete this timescale. In fact, some did even better by going eight weeks or more than 12 weeks dry. This was achieved with the use of Disulfiram post detoxification, definitely enhancing people's dry time. This is particularly advocated for people who are new to an alcohol detoxification. This is further explored in the case study described later in this chapter.

Figure 10.4: Dry time for people who just had one detoxification in 2010-11

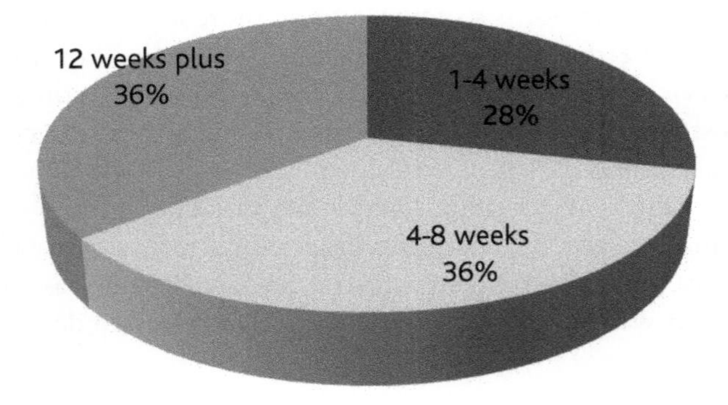

Therefore, the community detoxifications were on the whole successful in all people achieving their aim of being alcohol free, although they may need to go through more than one detoxification regime to enable them to go alcohol free for a significant period of time (at least three to six months). As Figure 10.2 shows, a significant number of women in the study completed detoxification from alcohol. Nationally, it has been stated that women as a group do better than men in treatment in obtaining their goal of being alcohol or drug free. This was not the case in this study as in general all who entered treatment for detoxification from alcohol at PCADS achieved good outcomes whatever their gender. However, the significant number of women treated for problematic/dependent drinking in PCADS needs to be noted, as the following case study will illustrate.

Case study

A case study is now examined to explore some of the findings from the results of the evaluation from 2010 to 2011. It was chosen for its high degree of typicality of the people analysed for the evaluation. The woman's name has been changed to protect her anonymity.

Helen, aged 47, had first attended the service in early 2006. She was referred by her GP, who has a Certificate in the Management of Alcohol Problems in Primary Care Level 1 (a course run by the Royal College of General Practitioners). Helen had a good relationship with her GP and often used primary care, where this relationship became established. She felt very confident that she would be able to talk about her alcohol problems without being too embarrassed. Since she had had detoxification in the past, Helen felt a failure in that she was back with her GP, asking again for help to detoxify from alcohol.

It is known that many GPs have taken a moralistic and judgemental stance, in some women's experience of treatment, but this was not the case for Helen. Although this was her third time of asking for a detoxification, she felt that her GP, being female, would be of help. Her GP seemed to understand and 'get' that she had a real problem with alcohol and this was linked to the stress of being a mother with three young children. Helen had previously suffered from postnatal depression and her previous (male) GP managed this in primary care with the use of psychology services in the GP practice. Despite this intervention, her depression still continued after therapy. She was aware that this depression could be a factor in her alcohol intake. She discussed with her GP the role of alcohol as a self-medication for her depression. Her daily alcohol intake was the consumption of one litre of vodka.

She completed a community detoxification with the specialist alcohol nurse as she was supported by her husband, a non-drinker. She detoxed successfully in 2006 and was then referred for psychotherapy at the local service. This therapy was of 18 months' duration and very beneficial for her. She was alcohol free for three years. She described her mood as much better but she still did not feel completely 'right'.

After the birth of her fourth child in 2010, she again began to suffer from postnatal depression. She started drinking again to help cope with the depression but this made her mood even lower and she struggled to get out of the house. She realised that the same pattern was occurring again and she went to see a nurse at the doctor's surgery. She felt that this really helped her, and she had a good relationship with the nurse and surgery.

Helen attended her appointment with the nurse together with her partner. It was planned for her to undertake an alcohol detox. She had completed one before, a year ago, and understood the regime, and had some experience of being 'dry' from alcohol. A further detoxification from alcohol was arranged quickly for her, as an assessment for depression was needed. Helen was detoxified from alcohol and then referred for a psychiatric appointment to assess her depression by a psychiatrist attached to the PCADS service. She was diagnosed as suffering from depression and she was started on Sertraline (an anti-depressant). She was also started on Disulfiram post detoxification.

Six months later Helen described her mood as good and she was still dry. She was still taking the Disulfiram, but not every day. She described the services as very helpful but she learnt a lot the first time she engaged with the service. However, this time once she was detoxed and taking an anti-depressant, she was confident she would be able to stay dry long term. She had previously felt embarrassed for not being alcohol free and going back to her GP felt a failure. However, the professionals she came into contact with did not make her feel that way. In fact, she stated that they encouraged her and she felt a growing confidence in herself as a result.

The psychiatrist she saw was a female but that did not matter much to Helen by then as her positive experiences of the services she received did not make her think that gender was relevant at that stage. But the psychiatrist was also very non-judgemental, emphasising a problem-solving approach to her problem, which in the end was an anti-depressant.

Helen feels that treatment does work, and that professionals (GPs and nurses) are now more able to see beyond alcohol and look at other factors such as undiagnosed depression, which for Helen was linked to her postnatal depression. She would rather attend her GP rather than a specialist alcohol service as this does not have the stigma attached. Being treated at the GP surgery may normalise alcohol dependency and she feels that this is important.

Conclusion

From these results it can be said that, compared with the NTA figure for women accessing alcohol services overall for drugs and alcohol (Public Health England, 2013), there is more access to detoxification treatment for women in the primary care service in Islington. Importantly, the case study shows that social approaches may be influential for women engaging in alcohol services. Helen felt a degree of kinship with her female GP who was also a mother. This encouraged her to return to treatment. In England, there are now increasing numbers of GPs who are women (Brady, 2009). This could be useful for women attending general practice for a whole range of illnesses, not just alcohol dependence, so if there are more female GPs in GP practices this can only encourage greater numbers of women to engage in primary care. Importantly, Helen's GP was also trained in alcohol, and this played a part in enabling her to be more confident in dealing with problematic alcohol use (www.smmgp.org.uk) and in turn enabled the patient (Helen) to engage better.

The enlightened attitudes of professionals were also important, as Helen did not feel judged or 'guilty' for having an alcohol problem, which some women who have attended treatment services for alcohol have felt (Staddon, 2012). She felt more confident and enabled to deal with her problem, which resulted in a good outcome for her. This is the very essence of what healthcare services should be about, enabling the patient.

A further study on the women who access PCADS would be likely to confirm these data. The case study examined here has a high degree of typicality and therefore the findings have a degree of validity. Overall, the case study also illustrates that women can engage with a primary care alcohol service and that they are able to recover from alcohol dependency through a community detoxification regime.

Local, non-residential treatment is very important as it is often experienced by patients like Helen as non-judgemental yet retaining a clinical approach. It is also easier for women with children to access a non-residential service, as they can continue to care for their children at home. Treatment, if well delivered and well received by patients, can transform lives.

Therefore it is important that primary care provides a 'space' for alcohol treatment, which for Helen 'normalised' her condition for treatment. It also provided a clinical approach that was non-judgemental and supportive to her, enabling her to use the service offered effectively. Therefore providing a non-judgemental and easily accessible 'space' is important for women to engage in services with a degree of confidence. This confidence can then be used to achieve an effective outcome. It will be important to explore this further as it can be potentially influential in attracting women into alcohol and drug services.

Further expanded qualitative research would be useful to examine why women engage well with the alcohol service in primary care in Islington. Indeed, such research is being planned, to offer further insight into these interesting findings.

References

Brady, H. (2009) *Medical sociology: An introduction*, London: Sage Publications.

Centers for Disease Control and Prevention (2012) 'Alcohol use and binge drinking among women of childbearing age', *Morbidity and Mortality Weekly Report (MMWR)*, vol 61, pp 534-538.

Fernandez, J. (2006) 'Attracting the opposite sex? A more psychological approach in primary care', www.smmgp.org.uk (resource library/ other resources).

Gabe, J., Bury, M. and Elston, M.A. (2004) *Key concepts in medical sociology*, London: Sage Publications.Gilmore, I. and Rieuss Brennan, B. (2008) 'Excessive drinking in women', *British Medical Journal*, vol 336, no 7650, pp 952-953.

Haralambos, M. and Holborn, M. (2000) *Sociology: Themes and perspectives* (5th edn), London: HarperCollins.

Jones, A., Weston, S., Moody, A., Millar, T., Dollin, L., Anderson, T. and Donmall, M. (2009) *The drug treatment outcomes research study*, DTORS baseline reportwww.dtors.org.uk/

Public Health England (2013) *Medications in recovery: Best practice in reviewing treatment: Supplementary advice from the Recovery Orientated Drug Treatment Expert Group report*, London: The Stationery Office, https://www.gov.uk/government/news/medications-in-recovery-best-practice-in-reviewing-treatment

Rhodes, R. and Johnson, A. (1997) 'A feminist approach to treating alcohol and drug-addicted African-American women', *Women and Therapy*, vol 20, no 3, pp 23-48.

Shipton, D., Whyte, B. and Walsh, D. (2013) 'Alcohol-related mortality in deprived UK cities: worrying trends in young women challenge recent national downward trends', *Journal of Epidemiology & Community Health*, vol 67, no 10, pp 805-12.

Staddon, P. (2012) 'No blame, no shame: towards a social model of alcohol dependency – a story from emancipatory research', in (eds) *Social care, service users and user involvement: Building on research*, London: Jessica Kingsley Publishers.

ELEVEN

Responding to women's alcohol problems through adult community learning provision

Lydia Lewis

Introduction

Feminist action has a long-established tradition in adult community learning (ACL). In the United Kingdom, the Workers' Educational Association (WEA), the largest third sector provider of adult education, has its foundations in the labour movement and has also historically been allied to the women's movement (WEA, 2013). In the radical tradition, 'serious, woman-centred education represents the intellectual dimension of the struggle for women's liberation. Its purpose is to raise consciousness, develop theories, clarify understanding and inform women's action for social change' (Lovett, 1997, p 69). It can also provide a vital source of support for women and a means of finding solidarity with others (Thompson, 1997; Coare and Johnston, 2003; Schuller and Watson, 2009).

In this chapter, I reflect on the ways in which ACL provision can be a constructive response to social injustice and its psychological consequences for women (Williams and Lindley, 1996; Sheppard, 2002), one of which may be 'alcohol misuse'. The chapter uses findings from a study of mental health ACL – provision that is targeted for mental health and often delivered in partnership with mental health agencies. It discusses alcohol problems among other imbricated consequences of the sociocultural contexts of women's everyday lives – domestic abuse, identity issues and depression (Staddon, 2011, 2013). The focus of the chapter is on the ways in which mental health ACL can provide a range of resources that can help engender agency freedom (Sen, 1999, 2010) for women in the context of social and mental health inequalities.

I begin by providing some background to inequalities and women's mental health before describing the study design. Findings are then set out. The conclusion summarises the findings and reflects on their implications for social policy and provisioning.

Women's mental health

Social determinants of health, and mental health more specifically, are driven by 'inequities in power, money and resources' (Marmot et al, 2010, p 10), by inequalities of capabilities (freedoms or opportunities that are a form of power; Sen, 1999, 2010) and of 'capitals', or resources (see also Schuller et al, 2004; Friedli, 2009; Schuller and Watson, 2009). As an organising principle and system of relations, gender suffuses social life and is of particular significance for mental health because 'while other social inequalities are also important, they are usually less central to our private lives and psychological functioning' (Williams, 2005, p 152). Social structural relations of gender are also central to the distribution of resources; globally, women remain economically disadvantaged to men in terms of earnings and property ownership (UNDPI, 2009; UNDESA, 2010), an imbalance that, as Thompson (1997, p 71) points out, is 'embedded in the historical development of patriarchy'.

Women's mental health is significantly impacted by gender power inequalities (see Krantz, 2002; Williams, 2005; Cotton and Lewis, 2011) and the cultural contexts of their lives (Stoppard, 2000; Laitinen and Ettorre, 2004), and by social injustice (Sheppard, 2002). Problems often relate to experiences of disempowerment (Williams, 2005) and 'experiences in families and personal relationships, identity issues, work and health' (Laitinen and Ettorre, 2004, p 204). Thus, the reasons women have poor mental health relate to their 'social legacy', being 'shaped by gendered experiences in both the public and private spheres of their lives … and embedded in patriarchal structures' (Laitinen and Ettorre, 2004, p 204).

The factors that impact women's mental health worldwide include disproportionate exposure to caring responsibilities, abuse, violence and unpaid domestic work, and unequal access to resources including high-reward educational opportunities, money, work, status and value (Krantz, 2002; Sheppard, 2002; Mancini Billson and Fluehr-Lobban, 2005; Williams, 2005; Deverill and King, 2009; see also UNDPI, 2009; UNDESA, 2010). Some of these factors are likely to explain the fact that the protective effects of marriage for health are less pronounced for women compared with men (Bates et al, 2013).

Research shows an association between domestic violence towards women and alcohol misuse (Rodriguez et al, 2001; Galvani and

Humphreys, 2007; Fuller et al, 2009), with social inequalities and their associated 'social injuries', such as status degradation and demoralisation, a causal factor in both cases (Rogers and Pilgrim, 2003; Friedli, 2009; Wilkinson and Pickett, 2009; Marmot et al, 2010). For women, the factors that make alcohol attractive 'commonly include previous experience of sexual abuse, domestic abuse, loneliness, depression and rage' (Staddon, 2013, p 113; see also Deverill and King, 2009; Fuller et al, 2009; Staddon, 2011). Poor mental health can, then, be both a cause and an effect of the misuse of drugs and alcohol (Friedli, 2009).

The consequences of unequal access to resources such as status and value for women's mental health are moderated by the interactive effects of other inequalities, including class, race, ethnicity, sexuality, disability and age (DH, 2002; Williams, 2005). For example, in England and Scotland, recent household surveys showed that while rates of reported 'common mental disorder' (anxiety and depression) were significantly higher among women than men overall, for both women and men levels were highest in the lowest income bracket (Deverill and King, 2009; Bromley et al, 2010; see also Sheppard, 2002). In Scotland, women in areas of high deprivation were also found to 'experience a higher burden of moderate to high severity depression and anxiety symptoms than men in similarly deprived areas' (Bromley et al, 2010, p 23). Education level has been found to be 'a significant predictor of wellbeing among women' (Rutherford et al, 2012, p 22), with increased levels of education linked to decreases in levels of depression (Sheppard, 2002; Ross and Mirowsky, 2006). In a recent review of health inequalities in England and Wales, although alcohol consumption was reported to have 'an inverse social gradient', those of lower socioeconomic status were reported to be more likely to experience alcohol dependence and hospital admission for alcohol-specific conditions (Marmot et al, 2010). Mental health is thus also a 'key pathway through which social inequality impacts on health' and other outcomes (Friedli, 2009, p 38).

Mental health inequalities affecting women are therefore variously defined by capitals comprising not only material assets but also those of a less tangible nature residing in the cultural or symbolic realm – the relational dimension of social justice (Gewirtz, 2001) encompassing matters of identity and social recognition (see Sheppard, 2002; Rogers and Pilgrim, 2003; Friedli, 2009; Marmot et al, 2010). Different forms of capital interact and convert into one another and their distribution is linked to inequalities of capabilities, which may be cumulative in their effects (Sen, 1999; Schuller et al, 2004; 2010; Lewis, 2012b). As such, poor mental health, or lack of 'mental capital' (GOS, 2008), can reinforce disadvantage; it is both an outcome and a determinant of capabilities in a range of life domains, including education (Friedli, 2009; Marmot et al, 2010). Social exclusion – a key factor relating to mental health (DH, 2002; SEU, 2004) – is most likely to be experienced by 'those with least access to capabilities, and consequently capital accumulation in the broad sense' (Schuller et al, 2004, p 6). Consequently, access to resources may be seen as interdependent with agency freedom – 'the capability to act purposefully to advance one's chosen goals and values as an element of a person's effective power' (Sen, 2010, pp 271, 289; Lewis, 2012a, p 528). The present study demonstrated a range of ways in which mental health ACL can help to build resources and to generate agency freedom, or 'empowerment', for women in the face of social, educational and mental health inequalities.

Study design

The study involved focus groups with adults attending targeted mental health ACL in England and tele-discussions with practitioners delivering the programmes. Five adult learner focus groups, each comprising between six and eight individuals, took place, two in the south-east and three in the north-west. The courses attended by participants included those themed according to 'mental health' as well as others. This chapter uses data from three of these focus groups (2, 4 and 5). In the last two of these, the adults were attending a 'self-help for life' course, the content of which was broad-ranging, encompassing techniques from positive and cognitive psychology, social support, relaxation, meditation and reiki, as well as broader philosophical, spiritual and social science elements (for example the exploration of knowledge and ideas from aboriginal cultures, metaphysics, politics and sociology). Some participants on the self-help courses had also attended other courses, including arts and creative writing. In focus group 2, participants had attended or were attending a range of courses including self-esteem/confidence building, assertiveness training, anxiety/stress/anger management and general 'personal development', as well as English, mathematics and computing.

The study aimed to explore the means through which ACL impacts mental health and to draw out implications for policy and practice.[1] Discussion group questions centred on why people had joined the courses and what this had enabled (or disenabled) them to do. A feminist interactive and reciprocal mode of facilitation was adopted (see Lather, 1995; Laitinen and Ettorre, 2004) and each focus group discussion lasted between 40 minutes and one and a half hours.

University ethical approval was gained and a process of informed consent followed. Data were anonymised and transcribing conventions were as follows:

- F for female respondent;
- M for male respondent;
- I for interviewer;
- (...) for missing speech, ... to indicate an ellipsis, // for an interruption, and square brackets showing added text or text changed for anonymity.

Focus groups 2, 4 and 5 comprised 19 participants (13 women and six men), with nearly two thirds of participants (12) aged between 41 and 60 years and the rest in the age brackets 18–30 and 61–70 years. In terms of ethnic classification, the majority of participants were White British, with one White Irish and one unspecified. Of the participants:

- two currently had no educational qualifications;
- one had achieved level 1 qualifications (foundation);
- four had achieved level 2 qualifications (GCSE or 'O' Levels);
- six had achieved level 3 qualifications ('A' Levels or BTEC diplomas);
- two specified other vocational qualifications (secretarial and computing skills);
- one had an Honours degree
- one had a Master's degree;
- two participants did not specify their educational attainment.

Participants' employment status was as follows:

- unemployed/in receipt of benefits (8);
- housewife/mother (4);
- retired/medically retired (4);
- volunteer (1);
- customer service (1);
- unspecified (1).

Developing resources

A framework of 'capitals' can help to identify the 'assets' that help to promote mental health (Friedli, 2009) and recovery from mental health problems (Tew, 2011a). In this section I discuss some of the forms of capital female participants identified as having been generated through their involvement in ACL and which were viewed as helpful to their mental health in the context of alcohol problems and other related issues. I begin with social and emotional capital and then consider cultural capital followed by identity capital.[2]

Social and emotional capital

Social capital refers to relationships that confer advantage (Bourdieu, 1986) and networks characterised by shared norms, values and trust that promote common goals and collective action (Field and Spence, 2000; Schuller and Watson, 2009). Its features can include informal interaction with friends or in neighbourhoods as well as more formal forms of participation (Preston, 2004). The relational or reciprocal aspects of social capital (Field and Spence, 2000) mean that it is linked to 'emotional capital' – the political economy of emotions and their management as socio-emotional resources that can enable or block access to other resources (Williams, 2000). These kinds of capital are important in relation to mental health, with 'social participation and social support [being] associated with reduced risk of common mental health problems and better self reported health' (Friedli, 2009, p 25); and social isolation, lack of social support and exclusion being key social determinants of poor mental health and subjective wellbeing (DH, 2002; SEU, 2004; Friedli, 2009; Marmot et al, 2010).

It was perhaps unsurprising, then, that in this research, social and emotional capital was the predominant form of capital discussed by participants. The provision through the groups of friendship and sociality was often mentioned as the most important, but unexpected, outcome of taking part in the adult education courses. For many these had become a significant, or even their only, source of social and emotional support. The continuity and support were described as helping participants to reconstruct their 'selves' in relation with others (Brison, 2002), often in the face of adverse or traumatic life experiences, which included abusive personal and family relationships, especially for female participants, and relationship break-ups leading to problems with alcohol use. This was described by two female participants on the 'self-help for life' courses as a 'journey' to a better place. This experience contrasted with that of mental health services where such continuity was described by some participants as lacking:

F4: 'I've found that seeing psychiatrists and psychotherapists, (...) when you went in each time, there'd be a different person, a different doctor.

All: 'Yeah, mm. That's right.'

F4: 'So really you were breaking your heart to tell them all what were the matter with you and then the following week or month later when you had to again, it was somebody else. They would say that they would see you next time, but you'd go in and it'd be a totally different person. Out it would come again and you think where is this going? There's no help. It's just some time, take these tablets, go away and that's it. (...) And there's so many things that's happened in my life, right from being a child that I always think of it as a set of dominoes stood up and every so often you know these dominoes will fall down and you, you manage to pick them all back up again but this particular time 10 years ago, which I thought it would be for the rest of my time (...), it [relationship] just fell apart and it just destroyed me, so (…) I wouldn't go anywhere but want to sort of be face to face with this person. A lot of it was put on weight through drinking so that made me self-conscious that I didn't want to see anyone as well and like I say sitting in the house week in, month in, year in and I'm still actually doing that at two o'clock in the afternoon. It's just the drink that I've tended to've hopefully conquered.'

I: 'Mm, mm, great. Yeah so you didn't find the help of the psychiatrist that beneficial 'cos there was lack of continuity but also it wasn't very therapeutic from what you're saying, so have you found coming to these groups more therapeutic in a sense?'

F4: 'It's like what you said, we all learn off one another. It becomes a more friendly feeling. I absolutely, I said it to [tutor] from day one, that when I first went with me support worker, balling me eyes out all the time because all [these] things were coming out, people's voices and all these emotions were coming out my head and tears and everything (...), it's just changed me; I just lived for Tuesday.'

M2: 'Yeah.'

F1: 'When the self-help group were on?'

F4: 'Yeah and then when the Wednesday one came up it were just, them two days of basically being my life 'cos the rest of it's zilch.'

I: 'It sounds as though its//'

F4: 'There's nothing.'

I: 'Sort of helped you get over a fear, you know a problem of being fearful as well about coming out and so on which is a big barrier to get over as well isn't it?'

F4: 'Yeah 'cos each morning I get up, I still do like on the weekends and like think, waken up and what am I going to do with myself today?' (Focus group 4)

This extract evidences the ways in which women's drinking often needs to be understood as 'an understandable reaction to the hardship, trauma and injustice in their lives' (Williams, 2005, p 156), which too often includes experiences of abuse (Staddon, 2009, 2013) and fear (Laitinen and Ettorre, 2004) which 'shrink women's "space for action"', or agency (Cotton and Lewis, 2011, p 4). It may also be a need and way of coping (Staddon, 2009, 2011, 2013), even a kind of resistance (Cotton and Lewis, 2011; Staddon, 2013), in an aftermath of violations, disappointments and loss (see also Tew, 2005, chapter 1). The above participant's account resonates with other research, which identifies relationship break-ups, social isolation and lack of support as key issues for women's mental health and the senses of powerlessness, emptiness, loneliness and despair that often accompany women's depression (see for example Laitenin and Ettorre, 2004). It conveys powerfully how, in the face of a range of capability deprivations, which may be multiple and reinforcing in their effects (Sen, 1999, 2010), community-based provision such as mental health ACL can help to meet the need for social spaces for help and support while also expanding educational capabilities (see also Williams and Watson, 1996; Fenner, 1999; Schuller et al, 2004; Morgan, 2007; Fullagar, 2008; Lewis, 2012b, 2014). Indeed, it is evident from the participant's testimony that the ACL classes could provide what was described as 'a lifeline' to those experiencing crises. The participant described how the adult learning provision had helped her overcome a fear of leaving the house as a crucial first step in a process of social reconnection and recovery – a recurring finding in the study (see also Hopper, 2007; Tew, 2011a, 2011b) – and was helping develop her agency freedom (see also Morgan, 2007; Cotton and Lewis, 2011). Her testimony also highlights the situated and relational nature of the social and emotional capital that the ACL provision helped to produce – that this existed within and through the relationships and community spaces it offered over a period of time, and the consequent need for ongoing provision if these personal resources for participants were to be sustained.

Cultural capital

The various kinds of knowledge and learning, or cultural capital, gained through the courses were also described by participants as being a valuable resource. Many attendees had been initially educationally disadvantaged and described how the adult learning had stimulated their cultural engagement, through reading and finding out about disciplines such as sociology, for example, and how this had helped with their motivation for life – their 'emotional capital'. Participants in the 'self-help for life' classes also recounted the importance of learning 'really useful knowledge' (Thompson, 1997) that could help with understanding the conditions of one's life and dealing with the consequences of these (Williams and Lindley, 1996). For example, one participant described how meeting informally with others with similar experiences through attending a 'personal development' course had helped her to contextualise experiences of abuse in social terms and how this had helped to challenge the aftermath of 'faulty thinking' characterised by personalisation and self-blame:

F4: 'Through doing the course I, I was in a mentally abusive relationship which to this day really affects me and through doing the courses I've come across other people who've been through what I've been through and had the same problems now because of what we've been through but there doesn't, I've not come across any courses that could help us challenge the faulty thinking as a result of ... It's just it was so refreshing when I went on a course to know that other people had been through what I'd been through and they felt like I felt. And it'd be nice if there was a course that could tackle the ..., specifically for that sort of scenario because it was reassuring to know I wasn't alone in feeling that way. (...)'

I: 'Yeah, (...) putting it more in a social perspective then because you realise other people are having similar experiences and it's to do with power (...).'

F4: 'Yeah and sort of realising.' (Focus group 2)

This discussion is illuminating because it demonstrates how valuable knowledge can be generated through the provision of opportunities for people to come together around a common purpose (Coare and Johnston, 2003; Thompson, 2007). Intriguingly, the above participant described how it was informal contact among adult learners that was most helpful here, how the courses provided an important 'chance to find shared realities' with others (Williams, 2005, p 156), which was not only a source of support but also helped her realisation of abuse towards women as a wider sociopolitical phenomenon (see Williams and Lindley, 1996; Williams and Watson, 1996; Thompson, 1997; Krantz, 2002; Cotton and Lewis, 2011). The extract therefore highlights the importance of responses to women's mental health needs across a range of settings being informed by feminist praxis – understanding in order to act (Lather, 1995; see, for example, Williams and Watson, 1996; Laitinen and Ettorre, 2004). It shows how, in the spirit of social purpose education, mental health ACL for women needs to be a 'reciprocally educative' process (Lather, 1995, p 295) for all in which participants are encouraged to find 'the point of connection between their direct concerns and wider social context and action' (Caldwell, 2013, pp 40–41).

The above findings and those in the previous section resonate with feminist calls for mental health services to find ways of enabling women 'to give voice to their experiences, and to find safe ways to express their anger and rage' (Williams, 2005, p 162). Participants described a sense of relief from being enabled through the groups to break silences surrounding socially taboo experiences, including suicide attempts, domestic violence and alcohol misuse, particularly in light of the further social harms of stigma and shame attached to these (see McKie, 2006). This breaking of silences was politically significant, not only in locating personal experiences in the wider social realm and, thereby, developing valuable knowledge from a politically engaged standpoint (see Thompson, 1997), but also in terms of taking a stand against injustice and coming to see oneself as agentic in the face of this – something that is integral to mental health (Lewis, 2012a) and a common theme in women's accounts of taking part in ACL (for example, Thompson, 1997; Morgan, 2007; Field, 2009). The following discussion, in the context of domestic violence, is illustrative here:

F2: 'But by, by telling people about it it's exposing him and it's, it's also because while, while women, 'cos they feel ashamed that, that they've allowed it happen as well I think but by talking about it, it's, it's almost erm, they can't get away with it as much, it's not acceptable.'

F1: 'Yeah it's not acceptable.' (Focus group 4)

The findings of the study therefore highlighted the important function of mental health ACL of bringing women together in a spirit of collectivity to challenge oppression (Thompson, 1997, 2007; see also Coare and Johnston, 2003). They illustrated the ways in which ACL can enable women 'to check their experience with each other and begin to name the feelings honestly which get in the way of growth and autonomy' (Thompson, 1997, p 37) and be used constructively to help women 'make links between their personal lives and social structure' (Laitinen and Ettorre, 2004, p 204). As previously indicated, then, the study highlighted the need for mental health ACL for women to be informed by a feminist praxis-oriented approach in which the development of emancipatory knowledge among women contributes towards transformative action (Lather, 1995) and democratic citizenship (Coare and Johnston, 2003).

Identity capital

Identity capital refers to the value and status we are afforded through the way others see us and the way we see ourselves. As well as social recognition, it encompasses such socially generated personal phenomena as self-esteem, self-efficacy and sense of purpose or direction in life (Schuller et al, 2004). Many of the ACL participants in this study had come to the programmes with damaged or compromised personal identities in some respects, which were the result of life experiences including poor schooling, abusive relationships, mental health crises and interactions with mental health services. Some participants had internalised pathologised identities such as being 'an alcoholic' or 'mentally ill' or constructions of themselves in opposition to 'normal' people, so that a question that remained in the research was the degree to which the targeted nature of the provision was helping participants to challenge rather than perpetuating marginalised and stigmatised identities (see Lewis, 2014, for further discussion; see also Lewis, 2009). There were also, however, clearly beneficial interactions between the social capital, cultural capital and identity capital generated through the adult learning provision; that is, the relationships and education involved were in many respects having a positive influence on people's self-identities (see Schuller et al, 2004). For some participants, the adult learning was allowing for some distancing from diminishing and stigmatising mental illness identities and here the holistic approach of the courses was described as helpful:

F1: 'You see yourself outside of the illness. I'm not just the illness. I'm a person as well and I, I'm more, and I'm more capable than I give myself credit for.'

F3: 'It's lost isn't it?'
F1: 'You get lost don't you?'
F3: 'Yeah and then you become a person again really don't you?' (Focus group 2)

The above extract conveys the impact of the holistic approach and humanistic environment of the ACL in terms of helping participants who had suffered mental health problems and been ascribed mental illness identities to reclaim their personhood, their sense of self and their agency (see also Hopper, 2007; Morgan, 2007; Tew, 2005, 2011a, 2011b; Lewis, 2009; Staddon, 2009, 2011). As indicated earlier, the ways in which the ACL was helping to counteract the effects of depersonalising experiences of mental health services through conferring full humanity was described by participants; one woman commented, for example: "in this they treat you as a human being; they, you know, get the stick" (focus group 2).

As previously illustrated, another key element of identity work described by participants was overcoming shame through breaking silences and connecting with others' experiences. The shame attached to identity constructions of being 'an alcoholic' was recounted by more than one participant, powerfully exposing the 'moral ingredient to the condition' (Staddon, 2013, p 106) and the further 'hidden injuries' this could cause (see McKie, 2006). In this context, talking about such issues in a non-judgemental and trusting atmosphere, being "able to talk freely however you're feeling without feeling that somebody's judging you", was seen by many participants as therapeutic and cathartic:

> 'One of the things that we were talking about earlier was shame and life is just covered with shame. (…) Shame does bring about a lot of depression (…) and with my own family, I think the shame is a big part of it, is a massive thing throughout your life. You carry it even if things are not your fault, but you can come to these groups and you're not judged and there is no shame.' (Focus group 5)

The speaking out that was made possible in the groups was important in facilitating the reconciliation of past experiences (a core theme of 'recovery work'; Hopper, 2007) and the tackling of problems such as alcohol misuse. The humanistic, non-judgemental environment of the ACL settings was a powerful antidote to the morality surrounding alcohol use and experiences of domestic abuse, which includes 'both blame and shame' (Ettorre, 1997, p 15; Cotton and Lewis, 2011), as well as traditional approaches to alcohol misuse as a 'disorder', which may cause 'additional pain, guilt and stigma' (Staddon, 2013, p 110; see also Staddon, 2009).

Several participants explained how the social support, mutual understanding and connection with others through participating in the groups had helped with lowered self-regard, which was also described in the context of unhappy or abusive relationships. For example, one participant commented:

F1: 'I think it enables you to see that in actual fact you are an ok person. (...) And I think that's really important actually, liking yourself.'

I: 'Mm, do you find that that has also come from the sort of group context, that//'

F1: 'Yeah, yeah (...) it comes from the group. We are quite a large group of people and several of us go to several different sort of [tutor-]led groups so we're in a, a sort of, quite a large supportive network and its very good. (...) I've been in sort of quite a dark place, you know mental health-wise, (...) and it's about that self-loathing and self-hating and actually bringing yourself away from that and that's what this has done for me.' (Focus group 5)

In the face of denials of 'recognition and respect' (Coare and Johnston, 2003, p 211), then, and experiences that could leave women with a punitive relation to the self (O'Grady, 2005; see also Fullagar and O'Brien, 2014) the humanistic environment of the ACL was described as affording participants acceptance, understanding and a sense of moral worth (see Hopper, 2007; Lewis, 2009, 2014). In this manner, the research evidenced the human rights-based social and symbolic 'characteristics that individuals and communities need to survive adversity: respect, dignity, self esteem, positive identity and connectedness' (Friedli, 2009, p 38) as well as the need for social approaches to distress and alcohol to enable people to 'feel OK about who they are' (Staddon, 2009, p 4; see Fenner, 1999; Tew, 2011a, 2011b). For many women, the learning was part of a life transformation, which sometimes involved realigning or leaving relationships. Chiming with other research (for example, Thompson, 1997; Laitinen and Ettorre, 2004; Morgan, 2007; Fullagar, 2008), this was often described in terms of overcoming invisibility in order to identify one's own needs and aspirations or "reclaiming who I was" (focus group 4). One participant described how the ACL had "changed my life completely. I've been able to escape a very abusive relationship; I heaved myself out of quite a severe depression (...) And [it's] given me strength to actually, and confidence to face up to those things" (focus group 5).

The findings therefore resonate with other studies that have described ACL as an 'agent of change' for women in the face of domestic abuse and its destructive effects (Morgan, 2007), helping to cultivate courage and a renewed sense of control and hope for the future (see for example Thompson, 1997). They illustrate how women's recovery from depression can involve a process of transformation with 'investments' in such social activities as ACL helping to 'maintain wellbeing and prevent relapse through supporting continuity and renewal of self' (Fullager, 2008, p 36). In alignment with other accounts (for example, Williams and Watson, 1996; Thompson, 1997; Fenner, 1999; Williams, 2005), and according with other research on the support needs of women experiencing alcohol issues (for example, Staddon, 2009, 2011, 2013) and depression (for example, Laitinen and Ettorre, 2004; Fullagar, 2008), the findings highlight how breaking isolation, finding social support and developing self-worth are integral to women's empowerment to deal with the consequences of social injustice in their everyday lives (see also Friedli, 2009; Marmot et al, 2010).

Conclusion

This chapter has evidenced the benefits of targeted ACL for women's mental health in the context of alcohol misuse and other related consequences of social harms (Rogers and Pilgrim, 2003; Friedli, 2009). It shows how such provision with a humanistic and liberatory ethos (see Lewis, 2014) can be 'a key resource in the broader struggle for social change' (Caldwell, 2013, p 40), helping to generate forms of capital and freedoms to address a range of issues relating to women's mental health, including social isolation, domestic violence and alcohol problems (see also Thompson, 1997; Morgan, 2007; Staddon, 2009, 2011, 2013; Lewis, 2014). The research evidences the significant value for community mental health and wellbeing of creating spaces for people to break silences and to speak about problems which are socially taboo in an environment of mutual support and trust. It shows the benefits of community-based mental health adult learning programmes that provide these opportunities, confer recognition and respect, and enable women to reframe personal experiences in critical social terms and challenge injustice. Such provision can be helpful to the reconciliation and identity work required in the face of damaging past experiences (Hopper, 2007) and to expanding the agency freedom, or 'space for action', that is integral to mental health (see Cotton and Lewis, 2011; Lewis, 2012a). In broader social policy terms, the research demonstrates the ways in which mental health ACL can play an important role in both responding to mental health problems and promoting democratic citizenship as inter-related and complementary aims (Lewis, 2014).

The study contributes towards a body of research on the wider benefits of learning (for example, Field, 2009; Schuller et al, 2004) as well as to literature on feminist responses to women's mental health needs (for example, Williams and Watson, 1996; Fenner, 1999; Laitinen and Ettorre, 2004; Williams, 2005) and social approaches to mental distress more generally (for example, Tew, 2005, 2011a, 2011b). Its implications for mental health services include the need to move away from a diagnosis and treatment-led system towards a community development approach in which feminist and other social perspectives are prominent (see Pilgrim et al, 2009; Carpenter and Raj, 2012). There is a need for gender-sensitive service responses (DH, 2002) that challenge oppression and 'deal constructively with the psychological consequences of social injustice and issues of power and powerlessness' for women (Williams and Lindley, 1996, p 4; see also Williams and Watson, 1996; Sheppard, 2002). For ACL policy, the findings demonstrate the importance of recognising the broad social contribution of the provision and its significant role in the equalities agenda (Schuller and Watson, 2009; Marmot et al, 2010) through addressing gender-based inequalities relating to women's capabilities, or freedoms, and human rights (Sen, 1999, 2010). They also highlight the need to balance ACL's generally dominant economic employment and skills agenda with its social justice agenda, with the two being inevitably interdependent. In the interests of women, they support a renewal of 'social purpose' ACL that is politically engaged, aiming towards social awareness and action as well as social connection (Coyne, 2011; Caldwell, 2013), and upholds 'the moral purpose at the heart of education – to be transformative' (Elliott, 2014).

Acknowledgements

I would like to thank all those who generously participated in this research and the adult learning charity staff for their assistance with it. Funding was from a University of Leicester College of Social Science Knowledge Exchange Post Doctoral Fellowship. Some of the focus group material in this chapter was originally cited in Lewis, L. (2014) 'Responding to the mental health and wellbeing agenda in adult community learning', *Research in Post-Compulsory Education*, © Further Education Research Association, reprinted with permission of Taylor & Francis Ltd, www.tandfonline.com, on behalf of The Further Education Research Association.

Notes

[1] For full findings, see Lewis (2012b, 2014).

[2] The study's full report (Lewis, 2012b) also includes discussion of 'spiritual capital' and 'human capital'.

References

Bates, L.M., Berkman, L.F. and Glymour, M.M. (2013) 'Socio-economic determinants of women's health: the changing landscape of education, work and marriage', in Goldman, M., Troisi, R. and Rexrode, K. (eds) *Women and health* (pp 671-682), London: Elsevier.

Bourdieu, P. (1986) 'The forms of capital', in Richardson, J.G. (ed) *Handbook of theory and research for the sociology of education* (pp 241-258), Westport, CT: Greenwood.

Brison, S. (2002) *Aftermath, violence and the remaking of the self*, Princeton, NJ: Princeton University Press.

Bromley, C., Given, L. and Ormston, R. (eds) (2010) *The Scottish Health Survey 2009. Volume 1: Main report*, Edinburgh: The Scottish Government, www.scotland.gov.uk

Caldwell, P. (2013) 'Recreating social purpose adult education', *Adults Learning*, vol 25, no 4, pp 39-41.

Carpenter, M. and Raj, T. (2012) 'Editorial introduction', mental health special issue, *Community Development Journal*, vol 47, no 4, pp 457-472.

Coare, P. and Johnston, R. (2003) *Adult learning, citizenship and community voices*, Leicester: NIACE.

Cotton, A. and Lewis, L. (2011) Proceedings of the British Sociological Association Mental Health Study Group symposium, *A difficult alliance? Making connections between mental health and domestic violence research and practice agendas*, Edgehill University, www.britsoc.co.uk/groups/medsocmharchive.aspx

Coyne, G. (2011) 'Developing a radical, action-learning oriented educational approach in the WEA to deal with old challenges in new times', working paper, http://blogs.erratum.org.uk/author/admin/

Deverill, C. and King, M. (2009) 'Common mental disorders', in McManus, S., Meltzer, H., Brugha, T., Bebbington, P. and Jenkins, R. (eds) *Adult psychiatric morbidity in England 2007: Results of a household survey* (pp 25-52), Leeds: Health and Social Care Information Centre.

DH (Department of Health) (2002) *Women's mental health: Into the mainstream*, London: DH.

Elliott, G. (2014) 'The new English post-compulsory education environment', paper presented to the University of Wolverhampton, CRADLE, Walsall, UK, 26 March.

Ettorre, E. (1997) *Women and alcohol: A private pleasure or a public problem?*, London: The Women's Press.

Fenner, J. (1999) 'Our way: Women's Action for Mental Health (Nottingham)', *Journal of Community and Applied Social Psychology*, vol 9, no 2, pp 79-91.

Field, J. (2009) 'Good for your soul? Adult learning and mental well-being', *International Journal of Lifelong Education*, vol 28, no 2, pp 175-91.

Field, J. and Spence, C. (2000) 'Social capital', in Coffield, E. (ed) *The necessity of informal learning*, Bristol: Policy Press, pp 32-42.

Friedli, L. (2009) *Mental health, resilience and inequalities*, Copenhagen: WHO Europe.

Fullagar, S. (2008) 'Leisure practices as counter-depressants: emotion-work and emotion play within women's recovery from depression', *Leisure Sciences*, vol 30, no 1, pp 35–52.

Fullagar, S. and O'Brien, W. (2014), 'Social recovery and the move beyond deficit models of depression: a feminist analysis of mid-life women's self-care practices', *Social Science and Medicine*, vol 117, pp 116-124.

Fuller, E., Jotangia, D. and Farrell, M. (2009) 'Alcohol misuse and dependence', in McManus, S., Meltzer, H., Brugha, T., Bebbington, T. and Jenkins, R. (eds) *Adult psychiatric morbidity in England 2007: Results of a household survey* (pp 151-174), Leeds: Health and Social Care Information Centre.

Galvani, S. and Humphreys, C. (2007) *The impact of violence and abuse on engagement and retention rates for women in substance use treatment*, London: NTA.

Gewirtz, S. (2001) 'Rethinking social justice: a conceptual analysis', in Demaine, J. (ed) *Sociology of education today* (pp 49-64), Basingstoke: Palgrave.

GOS (Government Office for Science) (2008) *Mental capital and wellbeing: Final project report*, http://tinyurl.com/ForesightReportMentalcapital

Hopper, K. (2007) 'Rethinking social recovery in schizophrenia: what a capabilities approach might offer', *Social Science and Medicine*, vol 65, no 5, pp 868-79.

Krantz, G. (2002) 'Violence against women: a global public health issue', *Journal of Epidemiology and Community Health*, vol 56, no 4, pp 242-243.

Laitinen, I. and Ettorre, E. (2004), 'The Women and Depression Project: feminist action research and guided self-help groups emerging from the Finnish women's movement', *Women's Studies International Forum*, vol 27, no 3, pp 203-221.

Lather, P. (1995) 'Feminist perspectives on empowering research methodologies', in Holland, J., Blair, M. with Sheldon, S. (eds) *Debates and issues in feminist research and pedagogy*, Clevedon: Multilingual Matters, pp 292-305.

Lewis, L. (2009) 'Politics of recognition: what can a human rights perspective contribute to understanding users' experiences of involvement in mental health services?', *Social Policy and Society*, vol 8, no 2, pp 257-74.

Lewis, L. (2012a) 'The capabilities approach, adult community learning and mental health', *Community Development Journal*, vol 47, no 4, pp 522-37.

Lewis, L. (2012b) *'You become a person again': Situated resilience through mental health adult community learning*, Research report, for the Workers' Educational Association.

Lewis, L. (2014) 'Responding to the mental health and well-being agenda in adult community learning', *Research in Post-Compulsory Education*, vol 19, no 4, pp 357-377.

Lovett, T. (1997) 'Adult education and the women's movement', in Thompson, J. (ed) *Words in edgeways: Radical learning for social change* (p 69), Leicester: NIACE,.

Mancini Billson, J. and Fluehr-Lobban, C. (2005) *Female well-being: Toward a global theory of social change*, New York, NY: Zed Books.

Marmot, M., Atkinson, T., Bell, J., Black, C., Broadfoot, P., Cumberlege, J., Diamond, I., Gilmore, I., Ham, C., Meacher, M. and Mulgan, G. (2010) *Fair society, healthy lives: The Marmot review: Strategic review of health inequalities in England 2010*, London: The Marmot Review.

McKie, L. (2006) 'The hidden injuries of everyday life: violations, care and health', *Medical Sociology Online*, vol 1, no 1, pp 61-72.

Morgan, A. (2007) '"You're nothing without me!": the positive role of education in regaining self-worth and "moving on" for survivors of domestic abuse', *Research in Post-Compulsory Education*, vol 12, no 2, pp 241-258.

O'Grady, H. (2005) *Woman's relationship with herself*, London: Routledge.

Pilgrim, D., Rogers, A. and Benthall, R. (2009) 'The centrality of personal relationships in the creation and amelioration of mental health problems: the current interdisciplinary case', *Health*, vol 13, no 2, pp 235-254.

Preston, J. (2004) '"A continuous effort of sociability": learning and social capital in adult life', in Schuller, T., Preston, J., Hammond, C., Brassett-Grundy, A. and Bynner, J., *The benefits of learning: The impact of education on health, family life and social capital*, London: RoutledgeFalmer, pp 119-36.

Rodriguez, E., Lasch, K., Chandra, P. and Lee, J. (2001) 'Family violence, employment status, welfare benefits, and alcohol drinking in the United States: what is the relation?', *Journal of Epidemiology and Community Health*, vol 55, no 3, pp 172-178.

Rogers, A. and Pilgrim, D. (2003) *Mental health and inequality*, Basingstoke: Palgrave Macmillan.

Ross, C. and Mirowsky, J. (2006) 'Sex differences in the effect of education on depression', *Social Science and Medicine*, vol 63, no 5, pp 1400-13.

Rutherford, L., Sharp, C. and Bromley, C. (eds) (2012) *The Scottish Health Survey, 2011. Volume 1: Adults*, Edinburgh: The Scottish Government.

Schuller, T. and Watson, D. (2009) *Learning through life: Inquiry into the future of lifelong learning*, London: NIACE (National Institute for Community Learning).

Schuller, T., Bynner, J. and Feinstein, L. (2004) *Capitals and capabilities*, London: Centre for Research on the Wider Benefits of Learning.

Schuller, T., Preston, J., Hammond, C., Brassett-Grundy, A. and Bynner, J. (2004) *The benefits of learning*, London: Routledge Falmer.

Sen, A. (1999) *Development as freedom*, Oxford: Oxford University Press.

Sen, A. (2010) *The idea of justice*, London: Penguin Books.

SEU (Social Exclusion Unit) (2004) *Mental health and social exclusion*, Wetherby: Office of the Deputy Prime Minister.

Sheppard, M. (2002) 'Mental health and social justice: gender, race and the psychological consequences of unfairness', *British Journal of Social Work*, vol 32, no 6, pp 779-97.

Staddon, P. (2009) 'Women, alcohol and mental health: achieving authenticity in a hostile environment', paper presented to the BSA/SRN seminar series, 'Researching in Mental Health: Sociological and Service User/Survivor Perspectives', The British Library, London, May 11, www.britsoc.co.uk/groups/medsocmharchive.aspx

Staddon, P. (2011) The bigger picture, *Mental Health Today*, February.

Staddon, P. (2013) 'Theorising a social model of "alcoholism": service users who misbehave', in Staddon, P. (ed) *Mental health service users in research: Critical sociological perspectives* (pp 105-120), Bristol: Policy Press.

Stoppard, J. (2000) *Understanding depression: Feminist social constructionist approaches*, New York, NY: Routledge.
Tew, J. (ed) (2005) *Social perspectives in mental health*, Philadelphia, PA: Jessica Kingsley Publishers.
Tew, J. (2011a) 'Recovery capital: what enables a sustainable recovery from mental health difficulties?', *European Journal of Social Work*, vol 16, no 3, pp 360-374.
Tew, J. (2011b) *Social approaches to mental distress*, Basingstoke: Palgrave Macmillan.
Thompson, J. (1997) *Words in edgeways: Radical learning for social change*, Leicester: NIACE.
Thompson, J. (2007) *More words in edgeways: Rediscovering adult education*, Leicester: NIACE.
UNDESA (United Nations Department of Economic and Social Affairs) (2010) *The world's women 2010: Trends and statistics*, New York: UN.
UNDPI (United Nations Department of Public Information) (2009) *Women's control over economic resources and access to financial resources*, World Survey on the Role of Women in Development Fact Sheet, www.un.org/womenwatch/
WEA (Workers' Educational Association) (2013) *A history of the Workers' Educational Association* [film], London: WEA, www.youtube.com/
Wilkinson, R. and Pickett, K. (2009) *The spirit level: Why more equal societies almost always do better*, London: Allen Lane.
Williams, J. (2005) 'Women's mental health: taking inequality into account', in Tew, J. (ed) *Social perspectives in mental health* (pp 151-167), Philadelphia, PA: Jessica Kingsley Publishers.
Williams, J. and Lindley, P. (1996) 'Working with mental health service users to change mental health services', *Journal of Community and Applied Social Psychology*, vol 6, no 1, pp 1-14.
Williams, J. and Watson, G. (1996) 'Mental health services that empower women', in Heller, T., Reynolds, J., Gomm, R., Muston, R. and Pattison, S. (eds) *Mental health matters: A reader* (pp 242-251). Basingstoke: Macmillan.
Williams, S.J. (2000) 'Reason, emotion and embodiment: is "mental" health a contradiction in terms?', in Busfield, J. (ed) *Rethinking the sociology of mental health* (pp 17-38), Oxford, Blackwell.

TWELVE

What alcohol support women say they need: evidence from service user-led research and practice

Patsy Staddon

Introduction

In this chapter I first explain the limitations of previous understanding of, and responses to, women's alcohol use. I also describe a piece of service user-controlled research, which indicates alternative ways in which women could receive help and support. Such support would better reflect the meaning of alcohol use for women and would be based on a 'social model' as described below. Finally, I reflect on the political dimensions of how women's alcohol use is seen and in consequence 'treated' and consider the extent to which human rights may be involved.

A social model of alcohol use, like a social model of mental health, is one that seeks to contextualise the need to use alcohol alongside such social factors as poverty, domestic abuse, loneliness, depression and anxiety (Staddon, 2009). It has been suggested in this book by Beresford (Chapter One) and by Staddon (Introduction) that a 'social model' may offer a more appropriate and effective approach for women with alcohol issues. Some of the ways in which society understands and attempts to deal with alcohol use may be based on misunderstandings as to its meaning for different groups.

Women's alcohol use and its treatment

Over the last decade there has been something of a shift in understandings of alcohol use, at least at an academic level, and to a certain extent at the treatment commissioning level. Although alcoholism may still be seen by some as a lifelong disease of the will, whereby, paradoxically, one is both immoral and ill (Willenbring, 2010; Perryman et al, 2011), it has now been shown that most people appear to recover without treatment, due to changes in the lifecourse (Penberthy, 2007; White, 2008; Willenbring, 2010), with full recovery from an addiction being well documented (Raistrick, 2005; Heather et al, 2006; White, 2008; Willenbring, 2010; Perryman et al, 2011). There is consequently a need to challenge traditional views of alcoholism, such as it being a chronic, lifelong condition. These views are, however, widely and generally held by the public (Ettorre, 2007; White, 2008) and in consequence may well affect the kinds of treatment chosen for funding by commissioners. Commissioners, including general practitioners (GPs), are naturally affected by the weight of what we call 'common knowledge'. They may not have updated or professional knowledge of research and practice in the area, particularly if their reading has failed to span findings in the fields of sociology and social policy, as well as health and medicine.

The research that is available also has often displayed shortcomings; for example, much of it is based on those in, or not long released from, treatment services. However, many social factors affect admission to the treatment system, and research based solely within it is grounded not in the experience of drinkers as a whole, but of those who have come forward for treatment. Recent figures indicate that only 6.4% people with alcohol problems approach treatment services, and of these less than half are women (Wolstenholme, 2012; Fernandez, Chapter Ten, this volume). There is now increasing recognition of the considerable differences between 'those who are seen "in treatment" and everyone who meets criteria for alcohol dependence in the general population' (Cunningham and McCambridge, 2012, p 8).

Gender has also not traditionally been seen as a significant factor in problematic alcohol use although it is becoming clear that there is a need to challenge this understanding. While it has been increasingly acknowledged academically that women's alcohol dependence might vary significantly from men's, in its causes, its patterns and how it needs to be treated (Thom, 1986, 1994; Ettorre, 1997; Plant, 1997; Angove and Fothergill, 2003; Niv and Hser, 2007; Tuchman, 2010; Staddon, 2011a), there is still little evidence of this knowledge consistently affecting approaches to treatment. Gender-specific treatment is now acknowledged to be helpful for women for a variety of reasons, not least their feelings of shame.

Women suffer disproportionately from shame when attempting to deal with alcohol issues (Linton et al, 2009), due to their failure to live up to accepted norms of femininity and to their iconic position as being central to family sustainability (Legault and Chasserio, 2003). Also, due to family commitments, women may find it harder to attend group sessions, counselling and social support outside the home (Small et al, 2010; Staddon, 2012). Research has indicated that women who have or who have had alcohol issues greatly value a non-judgemental approach and opportunities to develop an understanding of their alcohol use in a non-pressurised and women-only environment (Angove and Fothergill, 2003; Staddon, 2012). This would include availability of staff and of venues at weekends and evenings, which would improve access for women with jobs and family responsibilities.

It has been shown that for people who actually reach treatment services, whatever type of treatment is employed, their addiction tends to decrease for as long as they are provided with some form of attention (Project Match Research Group, 1997). For example, it is known that 'just talking' about alcohol and other problems with someone who has had similar issues is likely to help service users (Repper and Perkins, 2003; Tew, 2005). However, as pointed out above, only a tiny proportion of women with alcohol issues do approach GPs or treatment services, and when they do so, the frequent lack of understanding by staff as to the effects of gender issues, such as different responsibilities and feelings of shame, are serious stumbling blocks (Staddon, 2013a). Attitudes of healthcare staff may remain adversely affected by moral judgements, particularly their feelings about women with substance misuse issues (Hill, 2010).

Mixed-sex 'treatment groups' remain commonplace, and are said to be more economical to run (Staddon, 2009). Yet many researchers and writers have noted that women with alcohol issues do less well in such settings, often preferring women-only space (Thom, 1986, 1994; Ettorre, 1997; Plant, 1997; Angove and Fothergill, 2003; Niv and Hser, 2007). For example, in treatment, women's feelings of guilt and shame often multiply when they are expected to share information about humiliating and painful incidents in their lives, in the presence of males. Many, if not most, women with alcohol issues have experienced abuse in childhood and adult life, mostly from men, and they will be particularly reluctant to share these experiences when men are present. There are, however, very few women-only spaces, particularly for extended periods (Women's Resource Centre, 2007) and rarely on first entering treatment (Staddon, 2009).

It was in order to examine the evidence on the kinds of alcohol treatment and support available, their suitability to the needs of women dealing with alcohol issues and what kinds of alternative support would be most valued, that the following research projects were carried out in the southwest of England.

This chapter is based on two service user-led research projects, funded by Avon and Wiltshire Mental Health Trust, which took place between 2004 and 2007 in Bristol and the surrounding urban area (Staddon, 2009). The aim was to explore how other women felt about their alcohol use, other people's reaction to it and any treatment they had received. The projects, involving local women who had or had had alcohol issues, included 'Making a Start', which involved a series of in-depth interviews, followed by focus groups. Women who took part expressed distress about being made to feel that they had failed and that their only recourse was a lifetime of abstinence and attempted redress, meanwhile attending mixed-sex meetings that focused on their illness, while at the same time apparently seeing it as a form of moral failure. Such an approach, unthinkable in respect of physical illnesses such as cancer, or mental illnesses such as schizophrenia, frequently appeared to have impeded their recovery (Staddon, 2009, 2012). Their shame was causing them more distress than their substance use.

Women respondents in this research project seemed very pleased to be able to talk to a woman 'alcoholic' who had recovered, since the popular belief is that 'an alcoholic' is forever 'in recovery'. Subsequently, they were enthusiastic about creating a local women's social and support group, which emphasised understanding and lack of blame. This group, which came to be known as WIAS (Women's Independent Alcohol Support) offered telephone support as well as a face-to-face group, which gave women opportunities to socialise at times and in ways that suited their circumstances. Women in the group developed a number of strategies that made their lives more manageable and enjoyable, and either eliminated their alcohol use or helped them to take charge of that use.[1] The group ran for over four years, but attendance began to peter out, and the organisers felt they needed a break. We then restarted a few years later, this time registering as a charity.

A sizeable response to an article about my own recovery, published in *The Big Issue* (Staddon, 2011b), indicated that women (and many men) in other parts of the country also felt unhappy about the kind of support available for their alcohol issues, either from professional sources or from existing mutual aid organisations. And while the 'Making a Start' project had taken place in a predominantly urban area (Staddon, 2009, 2012), the response in *The Big Issue* (Staddon, 2011b) indicated that women in more rural areas might feel even greater isolation and lack of appropriate support.

'Improving support for women with alcohol issues'

To explore this possibility, I set up a new service user-controlled research project in September 2012 entitled 'Improving support for women with alcohol issues', with the support of Plymouth University, funded by Folk.us, a service user-controlled research unit based at the University of Exeter. I sought to establish how women in Devon and Cornwall felt about the alcohol services they had encountered, and what other support they might have liked, a suggested option being one following the lines of Bristol's WIAS group.

This was a research project firmly grounded in the practice of service user control and execution. The term 'service user' has been discussed and debated elsewhere (Beresford, 2005; McNicoll, 2012) but for the purposes of this chapter it refers to people who have sought, or who currently seek, some kind of help with alcohol issues. The project's advisory group included alcohol ex-service users Lynne Davies (who had been involved with me in previous research and in running support groups in Bristol) and myself, together with two Plymouth University academics, the sociologist Professor Gayle Letherby, and Angie Regan, the Practice Learning Manager in the School of Health Professions (Faculty of Health & Human Sciences) at Plymouth University.

The project was widely advertised, among a diverse range of communities, including Black, minority ethnic and refugees groups, lesbian, gay, bisexual and transgender groups, disabled people's groups, groups for mental health and substance use service users, church organisations and social services, as well as the general public. Platforms included websites, newsletters, local radio and numerous speaking opportunities, including the annual general meeting of Cornwall's Federation of Women's Institutes, and an event organised in Exeter by ROC (Redeeming our Communities). It was hoped that a number of women who might not have made contact with GPs or treatment services would respond, since their experiences might be very different from those who had done so (Ettorre, 1997). Despite this, it was a disappointment that in the end only 13 calls were received, even when the length of time had been extended from three to six months.

Participants were invited to ring a telephone number, to which only I responded. They were then invited to take part in a telephone interview, which, with their permission, was recorded. While the project was in operation, details were kept to hand of a variety of women's resources, both nationally and in Devon and Cornwall, in respect of mental health, domestic abuse and other sources of distress.

Sensitive topics and emotion work

Research studies such as this deal with 'sensitive topics' (Lee, 1993) and involve 'emotion work' (Letherby, 2003; Drake and Harvey, 2013), which may throw light in unexpected places but which may also present very particular challenges, both in the interviews themselves and in the analysis. Although I was the person receiving the calls, I was to be able to call Lynne to discuss any issues afterwards (without of course identifying callers, even if I had been able to do so). Sometimes I did have quite upsetting calls to deal with late at night but in practice I did not like to call on Lynne for support. On the other hand, my being available at such a time may have made it easier for the woman respondent to make the call, and it did seem that all the women who had made contact were very happy that they had done so.

The process of writing up and analysing the data could also be lonely and upsetting, since the content could be very painful and could be reminiscent of my own earlier experiences while still drinking. These might often include the withdrawal of friendship and support from the people we loved most, as well as the multiple difficulties being encountered in our everyday lives. The loneliness revealed by the women respondents, too, was caused largely because they had either lost their friends or were afraid that friends would find out about their drinking. I found that it was only possible to work for short periods before taking a break, because of the memories and feelings that were evoked. It made the process particularly time-consuming but the personal reflections involved were not only essential but also inevitable, so that the research process could be described as 'reflexive and self-reflexive, accessible to everyone and "not just to theoreticians as a special kind of person"' (Landman, 2006, p 430).

It was important to ensure that the respondent was allowed her own personhood, while using our own experiences to assist with the interpretation of the transcripts. There were many ways in which the respondents' lives paralleled mine. For example, Carol[2] would often use the third person to talk about the other 'alcoholics' to show she was not like them and this was one way in which I, too, had survived alienating treatment experiences by building a wall around my 'real self' to keep it safe. This relating of one's personal experiences to those of the respondents is a difficult and sometimes painful path to follow (Wilkins, 1993).

Some findings from the Devon and Cornwall research

Many of the women who did telephone talked for a long time. For example, Jane was on the telephone for well over an hour, in great distress. The women who made contact were all very grateful to have a chance to talk freely and in confidence about themselves:

> 'It does feel OK talking to you because you've been there and you know what it's like.' (Gina)

> 'I think something like this the chat with you is making me feel lots better already!' (Ester)

Three women saw their drinking as having begun as a pleasurable regular activity, before becoming a means of escape from the stress of their lives: "[A]s soon as the girls were in bed, it was 'Phew!' – open the bottle of wine and it'd be like, phew, that's the end of THAT day" (Ester). Frequently, the situation had developed over a number of years:

> "[M]y drinking crept up on me." (Beverley)

> "[O]ver the years it kind of spiralled out of control … I mean I'd always liked to drink…." (Helen)

Sometimes drinking escalated following a particular life crisis. Farah's husband had developed Alzheimer's disease, eventually being hospitalised in a locked ward: "I was up there every single day … and on coming home, I used to sit down and open a bottle of vodka. That was my life." Depression was cited by all respondents, pre-dating their drinking, but they still blamed themselves for what had happened: "Life was difficult … but it's still no excuse for some of the ways that I behaved … when I'd had too much to drink I was capable of anything" (Beverley). Women were also likely to accept the blame for a whole series of family crises and losses: "It's not been easy – but then I think you can't blame all these things it's you … just myself" (Delia).

I was aware of the considerable likelihood of domestic abuse in the respondents' lives (Holly and Horvath, 2012). In my earlier Avon research project, 'Making a Start', 12 out of 23 women reported domestic abuse. In this study, only three of the 13 women referred to it specifically. However, two women (out of three who did not want the conversation to be recorded) terminated the call hastily, sounding frightened, before we could read through the consent form. A fourth respondent, Irene, was hesitant about the term 'domestic abuse' itself, while referring to her mother as critical and distant and her husband as "quite nasty really".

Since the early 1990s, domestic abuse services have increasingly been raising awareness of the need to address domestic abuse and the substance use together (see Stella Project Toolkit, 2007). Despite this development, alcohol services are often unaware of this. For example, an alcohol worker who visited Beverley in her police cell was not interested in hearing about her very serious domestic abuse issues, insisting that the alcohol use must be dealt with first.

In this research project, comments about GPs were generally negative. Delia was fond of her GP but said she did not like to bother him with an issue like alcohol. Carol and Beverley avoided telling theirs for fear of having 'alcoholism' on their medical records. Five women did tell their GPs but "GPs don't know anything about [alcohol] at all" (Katy). Anne said that her GP had seemed bewildered:

> '[H]e didn't really understand. He was very much "well you need to stop drinking", and I said, "I know", and of course I didn't stop drinking. But he didn't know where to refer me to – and that isn't any criticism – he didn't understand where I could go to get help.' (Anne)

GPs, like other health professionals who deal with the public, sometimes adopt a moral stance in respect of certain sorts of illness, believing the patient to be responsible for their condition (Hill, 2010; van Boekel et al, 2013). GPs may also be wrong-footed when taken by surprise, as may have been the case with Anne's startled GP; he had not expected a respectable older woman, and a local church-goer, to have such a problem.

More than half of the women had tried going to meetings of Alcoholics Anonymous (AA). Anne, a Christian and a retired nurse, had felt at home there straight away: "I like to have some kind of discipline in my life – you can't run a ward or a district on a whim, can you?" AA was sometimes described as offering considerable kindness and support but several women disliked its religiosity: "it wasn't really my cup of tea" (Katy). Gina stated that the organisation had intimidated her and more than once had driven her to drink again. What it is like to be in an AA group will depend very much on which members are understood to have most 'seniority', and hence authority, at the time. Members may be rather controlling and expect newer people to behave in ways the group believes to be correct. It can be easy to say the 'wrong thing' and to be 'spoken to' about it after the meeting.

Similarly, some women in the study had been embarrassed by how their drinking behaviour was talked about in alcohol treatment, particularly by male staff, and in mixed-sex groups, making them feel belittled and shamed and more likely to return to the familiar comfort of the bottle. There appears sometimes to be an undercurrent of contempt and dislike here of women acting out of role (McCarthy, 2010). Some women's shame was increased by the behaviour and even the presence of men in treatment programmes, and other research has indicated that women generally prefer to speak to a female medical professional about intimate matters (Delgado et al, 2011). Shaming experiences would probably be included in this category.

Discussion

The attitude of the general public towards women's drinking 'to excess' exudes disapproval; women's iconic role, embracing both constructions of virginity and of maternity, is seen to be placed at risk by behaviour lacking dignity and self-possession (Ettorre, 1997). It was therefore not surprising that most respondents did blame themselves for having alcohol problems and were ashamed that they had failed to live up to such ideals. There appears to be a feeling of responsibility for the moral and physical wellbeing of everyone else. This has been noted by other researchers (Velleman and Templeton, 2007; Moore, 2008). Typically, women drinkers' families were described as having been relatively unsupportive, expecting respondents to 'pull themselves together' and get over it, or to fit into roles that were not appropriate for them.

The lack of understanding and sympathy from close friends and relatives that women in the present study experienced might be explained by numerous social factors, such as a discontinuity more generally of family and neighbourhood support (Beck, 1992), but essentially, these were women who had stepped outside the realms of behaviour expected of them, losing social status in the process and bringing shame on their families (Ettorre, 1992). This had led them to despair. Katy and Jane had histories of attempted suicide while Anne felt that her own daughter's suicide was a major cause of her beginning to drink heavily herself. Jane saw her alcohol issues as a consequence of poor treatment for mental health problems throughout her lifetime, a view that is supported by experts in the field (Guest and Holland, 2011).

Towards the end of each interview, I asked the respondent what she would have liked to have had available for general support with her alcohol issues, whether or not she had decided on, or had already had, treatment. A variety of possibilities were suggested, such as:

- a confidential non-medical helpline (similar to Saneline, for mental health issues);
- an interactive website, with forums for service users (similar to that of Women's Aid: www.womensaid.org.uk); and/or
- local face-to-face groups (like those that WIAS had run for four years in Bristol).

All but one of the respondents would ideally have had available a women's helpline as a first point of call: "It's the telephone support that was most helpful – the anonymity and being able to access it – I hear that from [people] all the time when [they] do feedback from consultations, they say that they want a telephone helpline" (Beverley).

Women like Katy, who felt positively about the alcohol treatment they had had, praised non-judgemental approaches and feeling safe to talk about these shaming experiences. One-to-one counselling was generally highly valued but often had to be paid for. Some women liked talking in single-sex groups, but all emphasised the importance of kindness and empathy, whatever kind of treatment was accessed. The attitude of staff and fellow patients was plainly what mattered most. The treatment and counselling already in place was satisfactory for some, but all would have valued greater availability of a wider range of confidential support, better information, and opportunities to talk and consult without fear of "it going on my record".

Conclusion

What had become clear as the research project progressed, was the overwhelming weight upon women with alcohol and mental health issues of the expectations of women's proper behaviour that they carried with them. The dual role as an icon of purity and respectability, crossed with sexual temptress and all-providing mother, affects all women (Fillmore, 1984; Ettorre, 1997; Raine, 2000; Letherby, 2002; Allen, 2003; Staddon, 2011a, 2012, 2013a, 2014) but causes particularly severe distress to those suffering from health issues or in destructive or impoverished circumstances. The impossibility of fulfilling such expectations can be crippling, with alcohol offering an immediate, if temporary, refuge.

Trying to block out unhappiness was a major reason for women's drinking. A range of social support might have helped with their problems, without recourse to alcohol treatment services. In nearly all cases, a sympathetic listener on the telephone would have been of great help and their preferred first point of contact, whether or not a treatment option might later be chosen – a woman with a similar life experience, and who would respond non-judgementally and without giving direct 'advice'. As well as the evidence shown above, there is ample evidence elsewhere that being able to talk freely on the telephone does help people with a wide spectrum of conditions (Phillips et al, 2008; Fukkink and Hermanns, 2009; Darbyshire et al, 2013).

Women-only groups (Blanch et al, 2012), and an interactive website, were also seen as desirable as a response to alcohol-associated needs. Their approach would be 'no blame, no shame' – a safe place for women to talk about their needs and their issues. There clearly remains a shortage of women-only help with alcohol issues and an even greater shortage of an approach that helps women to identify and to deal with causes as well as with consequences. Unfortunately, much conventional treatment does exacerbate shame (Linton et al, 2009) and perhaps the privacy of an interactive website might offer advantages to many women (Barak et al, 2008; Riper et al, 2009).

There is additionally a human rights issue here. Recognition politics draw attention to injustices that are part of the way that society's culture, by disadvantaging some sections in respect of others (whether involving poverty, race, disability or gender) multiplies these disadvantages in such a way as to violate their basic human rights (Fraser, 2007; Lewis, 2013). People are denied value and 'maligned or disparaged in everyday interactions or representations' (Lewis, 2013, p 88). In the case of the women I spoke to in the Folk.us and the Avon and Wiltshire Mental Health Trust research projects, their position as women had made their behaviour, itself a consequence of unrealistic cultural expectations attached to their gender, a symbol of their low worth and lifelong inferiority. What they sought was recognition of themselves as people worthy of respect (Lister, 1997).

Once alcohol use ceases to be someone's problem, the politics that once engendered its use become painfully clear. Inequality, social injustice, abuse, different ways of understanding the world, perhaps as a Black woman or a lesbian woman, are some of the issues that need to be addressed. The pain they have caused, and probably still cause, may literally drive women to drink. It is possible that other women's recognition and support may be a pathway to confronting unrealistic expectations, and working together it may be possible to make lasting social changes for all women. To achieve this, measures are required, similar to those mentioned by Moon and Staddon and by Lewis (Chapters Eight and Eleven, this volume) – opportunities for women to meet and empower themselves to address the issues of social disadvantage and abuse.

Despite the well-publicised, perceived phenomenon of young women drinking wildly, there is also a new wave of young feminists who are not afraid to address oppression, and whose confidence is inspiring. These include:

- the Everyday Sexism Project (www.everydaysexism.com);
- the F word blog (www.thefword.org.uk);
- the Vagenda blog (vagendamag.blogspot.co.uk);
- UK Feminista (ukfeminista.org.uk).

These are some of the new ways in which change could occur, so that women of the future are able to lead their lives with greater confidence, using or not using alcohol, but not needing it as a protective shield. Destructive alcohol use could cease to be a major issue for women of the future.

In this chapter I have emphasised the importance of approaching women's alcohol issues in a holistic way, addressing causes of distress, and assisting with a more helpful strategy for living. We need a social approach to alcohol issues, a contextualisation of the problem and a wide variety of kinds of support and encouragement for those women still in distress.

Notes

[1] This group has recently been set up again in Bristol, now as a registered charity (www.wiaswomen.org.uk).

[2] All respondents' names are pseudonyms.

References

Allen, V. (2003) 'The stereotypes of the male and female drunkard are the same as they've ever been: in a man alcohol is the harbinger of violence; in a woman, casual sex', *Sunday Herald Online*, 28 December.

Angove, R. and Fothergill, A. (2003) 'Women and alcohol: misrepresented and misunderstood', *Journal of Psychiatric and Mental Health Nursing*, vol 10, no 2, pp 213-219.

Barak, A., Boniel-Nissim, M. and Suler, J. (2008) 'Fostering empowerment in online support groups', *Computers in Human Behavior*, vol 24, no 5, pp 1867-1883.

Beck, U. (1992) *Risk society: Towards a new modernity*, translated by M.Ritter, London: Sage Publications, 1999.

Beresford, P. (2005) '"Service user": regressive or liberatory terminology?', *Disability & Society*, vol 22, no 4, pp 469-477.

Blanch, A., Filson, B. and Penney, D., with Cave, C. (2012) Engaging *women in trauma-informed peer support: A guidebook*, www.nasmhpd.org/docs/.../EngagingWomen/PEGFull_Document.pdf

Cunningham, J.A. and McCambridge, J. (2012) 'Is alcohol dependence best viewed as a chronic relapsing disorder?', *Addiction*, vol 107, no 1, pp 6-12, doi: 10.1111/j.1360-0443.2011.03583.x

Darbyshire, P., Cleghorn, A., Downes, M., Elford, J., Gannoni, A., Mccullagh, C. and Shute, R. (2013) 'Supporting bereaved parents: a phenomenological study of a telephone intervention programme in a paediatric oncology unit', *Journal of Clinical Nursing*, vol 22, no 3-4, pp 540-549.

Delgado, A., Andrés López-Fernández, L., de Dios Luna, J., Gil, N., Jiménez, M. and Puga, A. (2008) 'Patient expectations are not always the same', *Journal of Epidemiology and Community Health*, vol 62,no 5, pp 427-434, doi:10.1136/jech.2007.060095

Drake, D.H. and Harvey, J. (2013) 'Performing the role of ethnographer: processing and managing the emotional dimensions of prison research', *International Journal of Social Research Methodology*, doi: 10.1080/13645579.2013.769702

Ettorre, E. (1992) *Women and substance use*, New Brunswick, NJ: Rutgers University Press.

Ettorre, E. (1997) *Women and alcohol: A private pleasure or a public problem?*, London: The Women's Press.

Ettorre, E. (2007) *Revisioning women and drug use: Gender, power and the body*, Basingstoke: Palgrave Macmillan.

Fillmore, K.M. (1984) 'When angels fall: women's drinking as cultural preoccupation and as reality', in Wilsnack, S.C. and Beckman, L.J. (eds) *Alcohol problems in women*, New York, NY: Guilford Press.

Fraser, N. (2007) 'Reframing justice in a globalising world', in Lovell, T. (ed) *(Mis)recognition, social inequality and social justice: Nancy Fraser and Pierre Bourdieu*, London: Routledge.

Fukkink, R.G. and Hermanns, J.M.A. (2009) 'Children's experiences with chat support and telephone support', *Journal of Child Psychology and Psychiatry*, vol 50, no 6, pp 759-766.

Guest, C. and Holland, M. (2011) 'Co-existing mental health and substance use and alcohol difficulties---why do we persist with term "dual diagnosis" within mental health services?', *Advances in Dual Diagnosis*, vol 4, no 4, pp 162-172.

Heather, N., Raistrick, D. and Godfrey C. (2006) *Review of the effectiveness of treatment*, London: National Treatment Agency for Substance Misuse.

Hill, T.E. (2010) 'How clinicians make (or avoid) moral judgments of patients: implications of the evidence for relationships and research', *Philosophy, Ethics, and Humanities in Medicine*, vol 5, no 11, doi: 10.1186/1747-5341-5-11, http://www.peh-med.com/content/5/1/11

Holly, J. and Horvath, A.H. (2012) 'A question of commitment – improving practitioner responses to domestic and sexual violence, problematic substance use and mental ill-health', *Advances in Dual Diagnosis*, vol 5, no 2, pp 59-67.

Landman, M. (2006) 'Getting quality in qualitative research: a short introduction to feminist methodology and methods', *Proceedings of the Nutrition Society*, vol 65, pp 429-433.

Lee, R.M. (1993) *Doing research on sensitive topics*, London: Sage Publications.

Legault, M. and Chasserio, S. (2012) 'Women and addiction; the importance of gender issues in substance use treatment', *International Journal of Project Management*, vol 30, no 6, pp 697-707.

Legault, M. and Chasserio, S. (2003) 'Family obligations or cultural constraints? Obstacles in the path of professional women', *Journal of International Women's Studies*, vol 4, no 3, pp 108-25, http://vc.bridgew.edu/jiws/vol14/iss3/9 [Accessed 09/01/2014]

Letherby, G. (2002) 'Claims and disclaimers: knowledge, reflexivity and representation in feminist research', *Sociology Research Online*, vol 6 http://ideas.repec.org/a/sro/srosro/2001-19-2.html

Letherby, G. (2003) *Feminist research in theory and practice*, Philadelphia, PA: Open University Press.

Lewis, L. (2013) 'Recognition politics as a human rights perspective on service users' experiences of involvement in mental health services', in Staddon, P. (ed) *Mental health service users in research: A critical sociological perspective*, Bristol: Policy Press.

Linton, J.M., Flaim, M., Deuschle, C. and Larrier, Y. (2009) 'Women's experience in holistic chemical dependency treatment: an exploratory qualitative study', *Journal of Social Work Practice in the Addictions*, vol 9, no 3, pp 282-298.

Lister, R. (1997) *Citizenship: Feminist perspectives*, Basingstoke: Palgrave Macmillan.

McCarthy, D. (2010) 'Self-governance or professionalized paternalism?: The police, contractual injunctions and the differential management of deviant populations', *British Journal Criminology*, vol 50, no 5, pp 896-913, doi: 10.1093/bjc/azq026

McNicoll, A. (2012) '"Service user" or "client"? Social workers divided on best term', Mad World, *Community Care*, 30 July 2012, www.communitycare.co.uk/blogs/mental-health/2012/07/service-user-or-client-social-1/#sthash.tgORTK4U.dpuf. Accessed 21/04/2014

Moore, S.E.H. (2008) 'Gender and the "new paradigm" of health', *Sociology Compass*, vol 2, no 1, pp 268-280.

Niv, N. and Hser, Y. (2007) 'Women-only and mixed-sex treatment programmes: service needs, utilizations and outcomes', *Drug and Alcohol Dependence*, vol 87, nos.2-3, pp 194-201.

Penberthy, J.K., Ait-Daoud, N., Breton M. (2007) 'Evaluating readiness and treatment seeking effects in a pharmacotherapy trial for alcohol dependence', *Alcoholism: Clinical and Experimental Research*, vol 31, no 9, pp 1538-1544.

Perryman, K., Rose, A.K., Winfield, H., Jenner, J., Oyefeso, A., Phillips, T.S., Deluca, P., Heriot-Maitland, C., Galea, S., Cheeta, S., Saunders, V. and Drummond, C. (2011) 'The perceived challenges facing alcohol treatment services in England: a qualitative study of service providers', *Journal of Substance Use*, vol 16, no 1, pp 38-49, doi: 10.3109/14659891003706399

Phillips, J.L., Davidson, P.M., Newton, P.J. and DiGiacomo, M. (2008) 'Supporting patients and their caregivers after-hours at the end of life: the role of telephone support', *Journal of Pain and Symptom Management*, vol 36, no 1, pp 11-21.

Plant, M.L. (1997) *Women and alcohol: Contemporary and historical perspectives*, London: Free Association Books.

Project Match Research Group (1997) 'Matching alcoholism treatments to client heterogeneity: Project MATCH posttreatment drinking outcomes', *Journal of Studies on Alcohol*, vol 58, no 1, pp 7-29.

Raine, P. (2001) *Women's perspectives on drugs and alcohol: The vicious circle*, Aldershot: Ashgate.

Raistrick, D. (2005) 'The United Kingdom: alcohol today', *Addiction*, vol 100, no 9, pp 1212-1214.

Repper, J. and Perkins, R. (2003) *Social inclusion and recovery*, London: Bailliere Tindal.

Riper, H., Kramer, J., Conijn, B., Smit, F., Schippers, G. and Cuijpers, P. (2009) 'Translating effective web-based self-help for problem drinking into the real world', *Alcoholism: Clinical and Experimental Research*, vol 33, no 8, pp 1401-1408.

Small, J., Curran, G.M. and Booth, B. (2010) 'Barriers and facilitators for alcohol treatment for women: are there more or less for rural women?', *Journal of Substance Abuse Treatment*, vol 39, no 1, pp 1-13.

Staddon, P. (2009) 'Making whoopee'? An exploration of understandings and responses around women's alcohol use', PhD thesis, Plymouth University, http://hdl.handle.net/10026.1/415

Staddon, P. (2011a) 'Service user led research in the NHS: wasting our time?', in Barnes, M. and Cotterell, P. (eds) *Critical perspectives on user involvement*, Bristol: Policy Press.

Staddon, P. (2011b) 'Many roads to recovery', *The Big Issue*, 10 January.

Staddon, P. (2012) 'No blame, no shame: towards a social model of alcohol dependency – a story from emancipatory research', in Carr, S. and Beresford, P. (eds) *Social care, service users and user involvement: Building on research*, London: Jessica Kingsley Publishers.

Staddon, P. (2013a) 'Theorising a social model of "alcoholism": service users who misbehave', in Staddon, P. (ed) *Mental health service users in research: A critical sociological perspective*, Bristol: Policy Press.

Staddon, P. (2013b) *Improving support for women with alcohol issues*, report for Folk.us [Unpublished internal formal report submitted to the universities of Exeter and Plymouth and to Folk.us, who funded the research].

Staddon, P. (2014) 'Turning the tide', *Groupwork*, vol 24, no 1, pp 26-41.

Stella Project Toolkit (2007) *Domestic violence, drugs and alcohol: Good practice guidelines* (2nd edn), www.avaproject.org.uk-our- resources/goodpractice

Tew, J. (ed) (2005) *Social perspectives in mental health: Developing social models to understand and work with mental distress*, London: Jessica Kingsley Publishers.

Thom, B. (1986) 'Sex differences in help-seeking for alcohol problems-1: the barriers to help-seeking', *Addiction*, vol 81, no 6, pp 777-788.

Thom, B. (1994) 'Women and alcohol: the emergence of a risk group', in McDonald, M. (ed) *Gender, drink and drugs: Cross-cultural perspectives on women*, vol 10, London: Berg, 1997.

Tuchman, E. (2010) 'Women and addiction; the importance of gender issues in substance use treatment', *Journal of Addictive Diseases*, vol 29, no 2, pp 127-138.

van Boekel, L.C., Brouwers, E.P.M., van Weeghel, J. and Garretsen, H.F.L. (2013) 'Stigma among health professionals towards patients with substance use disorders and its consequences for healthcare delivery: systematic review', *Drug and Alcohol Dependence*, vol 131, no 1-2, pp 23-35.

Velleman, R. and Templeton, L. (2007) 'Understanding and modifying the impact of parents' substance misuse on children', *Advances in Psychiatric Treatment*, vol 13, pp 79-89.

White, W.L. (2008) *Recovery management and recovery-oriented systems of care: Scientific rationale and promising practices*, Northeast Addiction Technology Transfer Center, Great Lakes Addiction Technology Transfer Center, Philadelphia Department of Behavioral Health/ Mental Retardation Services.

Wilkins, R. (1993) 'Taking it personally: a note on emotion and autobiography', *Sociology*, vol 27, no 1, pp 93-100, doi: 10.1177/003803859302700109

Willenbring, M.D. (2010) 'The past and future of research on treatment of alcohol dependence', *Alcohol Research and Health*, Celebrating 40 Years of Alcohol Research, vol 33, nos 1 and 2, pp 55-63.

Wolstenholme, A., Drummond, C., Deluca, P. (2012) 'Chapter 9: Alcohol interventions and treatments in Europe', in AMPHORA *Alcohol policy In Europe: Evidence from AMPHORA*, http://alcoholreports.blogspot.co.uk/2012/10/alcohol-policy-in-europe-evidence-from.html

Women's Resource Centre (2007) *Why women-only? The value and benefits of by women, for women services*, London: Women's Resource Centre.

THIRTEEN

The social model in alcohol treatment services: the impact for women

Daisy Bogg, with Terry Bogg

Introduction

Alcohol treatment provision in the United Kingdom has undergone rapid change over the last 20 years, from something on the edges of substance misuse treatment, often treated in primary care, or by voluntary sector alcohol counselling services funded through charitable donations, to something that now features highly on the political agenda. This may in part be due to the economic impacts and variety of harms that alcohol creates in our communities.

The issue of gender, and, in particular, how services could or should respond to the needs of women accessing treatment, remains largely unexamined. For example, guidelines from the National Institute for Health and Care Excellence for the clinical treatment of alcohol use disorders (NICE, 2011) only mention women specifically in relation to accounting for differences in metabolic rates, and make no mention of other differences that need to be considered. While there are specific protocols for pregnant women and mothers – particularly in relation to risks such as foetal alcohol syndrome and child protection issues – there is scant acknowledgement of the wider impacts of alcohol misuse on women's social wellbeing. Services remain male-oriented in their approach, and the wider social context surrounding women's alcohol use is almost invariably not addressed.

For women experiencing difficulties as a result of hazardous, dependent or problematic alcohol use, there are some issues that need to be considered differently from those of men. These range from health considerations through to current and past domestic and sexual violence and abuse, issues of self-esteem, labelling, identity and the impact of role expectations. Those entering treatment services for the first time are likely to be presenting with high levels of anxiety and isolation, while those with wider experience of treatment services can often feel that they are just 'more of the same', with little hope on their own of delivering sustainable change in their lives.

What is particularly evident is that women are often poorly served by current service models (Staddon, 2012). This chapter considers the impact of alcohol treatment on women, and seeks to answer the question: What impact could a feminist perspective have on the development of a social model of treatment for women accessing services?

Feminism and alcohol use and misuse

How women are seen to use and misuse alcohol has changed dramatically since the early years of the 20th century.[1] The changing roles of women in our society, and the increasing focus on equality and equal rights, have created a situation where, for younger women in particular, alcohol has taken on a function similar to that which it previously had for men. In other words, at least for some women, excessive drinking has moved from being an unusual occurrence carried out in secret (if at all), to a regular activity that is not only socially acceptable, but also in some contexts expected.[2]

Women's patterns of alcohol use are an example of where shifting social perceptions and moves towards greater equality between the sexes have created a new set of problems. The emergence of the 'ladette culture' in the 1990s has sometimes been blamed on the effects of 24-hour drinking, perhaps encouraging an increase in binge drinking among young women (Whitehead, 2009). It may also be the case that the plethora of reality television shows, portraying young women as matching their male counterparts in terms of both consumption and behaviour, serves to normalise the excessive use of alcohol among women. However, the issues may be more complex.

Women's increased participation in the labour market, and an increase in the number of women in senior and executive roles, have also had their own impact. It is not just young women who are drinking differently, but professional women are showing a year-on-year increase in drinking (IAS, 2013). At the same time, the impact of economic pressures and the recession have been anecdotally reported to have resulted in an increase in women's drinking, with redundancy and financial pressures having a similar impact as had been the case for men in previous periods of economic decline.

It is not only young women and professional women who are affected. A poll in 2013 carried out by Netmums (an internet-based community service for mothers) surveyed 3,000 members and found that:

- half of mothers drank regularly at home and only 1.9% stated that they never drank;
- 22% were drinking more than the recommended limit and, of these, 83% cited winding down after a stressful day as being the main reason they reached for a glass of wine in the evenings; and
- 86% that felt they should drink less than they did (Netmums, 2013).

Whether looking at the media or just walking through any town centre on any night of the week, it is clear that women use alcohol as a social lubricant and as a means to relax, in ways very similar to its use by men [editor: but see Mackiewicz, Chapter Four, this volume]. However, while it is now often acceptable for women to match their male counterparts in terms of alcohol consumption, they may later find themselves isolated and judged if they behave in certain 'unladylike' ways as a result, or if they subsequently develop an alcohol 'problem'. When the issue moves beyond alcohol-fuelled nights out and becomes a maladaptive coping mechanism that gets the women through the day, or a comfort blanket used to manage stress, anxiety and the pressures and demands of life, the evidence suggests that women are often treated more harshly than men by the rest of society [editor: see Staddon, 2013; Blackman et al, Chapter Three, and Mackiewicz, Chapter Four, both this volume].

Women and alcohol dependence

It therefore appears that, despite the increased acceptability of women drinking to excess, and an increased incidence of drinking in both professional women (IAS, 2013) and mothers (Netmums, 2013), a clear social paradox has developed: it may be acceptable to get drunk on a Friday and Saturday night, or with colleagues in the pub on the way home every night, but it is not fine to reach for alcohol as a crutch when life becomes difficult.

Drinking is a social activity. Many women will be embroiled in a culture that encourages and embraces alcohol as a social lubricant, or where partners and friends routinely drink to hazardous levels. Moving out of this culture and into a life without alcohol is not just a matter of physiological readjustment, it also involves significant emotional and social upheaval, to which current services, with the ethos of brief intervention and detoxification, are not equipped to respond.

Alcohol is embedded in British culture; there is no getting away from it, but for women this creates a real dilemma – how can you be both a modern woman, who can compete with her male counterparts in alcohol consumption, while still being feminine and maintaining the roles, expectations and identities that current British society demands?

Since 2005 there has been a general reduction in average weekly alcohol consumption (IAS, 2013). However, at the same time there has been a significant proportion of women who would be deemed as drinking at hazardous levels (that is, at least once a week exceeding government recommended limits), and alcohol-related admissions to hospital over the same period for women has doubled (HSCIC, 2012; IAS, 2013). The number of new referrals to treatment services has also risen on an annual basis, from 23,484 in 2008/09 to 26,347 in 2011/12 (NTA, 2012). Within this, the proportion of women referred to, and accessing, treatment has remained relatively stable, at around 36%. This suggests that the increase in problematic alcohol consumption is not gender specific, and supports the view that women are now matching their male counterparts in terms of year-on-year increases in the incidence of alcohol-related difficulties. It seems that while fewer people are drinking (or are drinking less overall), at the same time larger numbers are becoming more aware of their need for support or treatment for alcohol issues.

When a woman's drinking becomes dependent, the aetiology becomes hugely complex, with biological, social and psychological factors all compounding the potentially catastrophic effect that problematic alcohol use can have on her health, wellbeing, relationships, physical safety, sexual behaviour and inhibitions, social roles and status, occupational aspirations, self-image and identity (Falkin and Strauss, 2003; Lyons and Willmott, 2008; La Flair et al, 2012). The literature cites a whole range of issues that are unique to women, ranging from greater physical damage due to physiological differences, through to emotional and relational impacts, with strong associations with domestic violence, sexual disinhibition, childhood abuse and sexual assault (La Flair et al, 2012; Tracy et al, 2012; Salter and Breckenbridge, 2014). Such issues are impossible to address without adopting a gender-specific social perspective.

The state of current treatment services

For anyone seeking help there are two main routes into services. The person's drinking behaviour may lead to criminal activity and to referral by the police and social services; or the woman herself may be concerned and seek help and advice. In the latter case, research has suggested that women are more likely to seek help via primary care or mental health services than directly from substance misuse services, as their male counterparts tend to do (Harvard Medical School, 2011).

It has been recognised that many barriers may exist for women entering treatment (Briggs and Pepperell, 2009; Best and Laudet, 2010; Greenfield et al, 2010; Liang and Long, 2013), such as:

- social labelling and stigma;
- fear of loss of access to children;
- difficulties in balancing family and work demands;
- complex mental health disorders;
- a scarcity of women-only programmes for women who have been the victims of abuse or who may have additional vulnerabilities in being exposed to male-dominated treatment groups (Greenfield et al, 2010; La Flair et al, 2012; IAS, 2013).

In addition, as discussed by Briggs and Pepperrell (2009, p 8), 'women's relational needs are often pathologised' and this can serve to alienate women from accessing and remaining in treatment. Women are more likely to become isolated, hide their difficulties and seek alternative sources of help than men with similar patterns of substance use or misuse (Briggs and Pepperell, 2009; Greenfield et al, 2010; Harvard Medical School, 2011).

While there is significant attention placed on equality and equal access within our health and social care provision, what seems to have happened is that substance misuse services have become gender blind, paying attention only to the additional health and parenting concerns. Women's issues are rarely a prioritised funding target, so that the service's hands are often tied when it comes to addressing some of the more complex social considerations that could make a real difference to achieving a positive treatment outcome.

Women in treatment

It seems that commissioners and service providers have not yet grasped and responded to women's alcohol issues, should these involve moving from the binge drinking of youth and into dependency and addiction. At this point, for these women, prescribed roles, such as the expectations of being 'a wife and a mother', and the social ideal of femininity, may suddenly become hard to maintain. The male-orientated services that are currently in place often fail to recognise and meet the many and varied social and psychological needs that may have led to their getting into difficulties with alcohol in the first place: '[T]he generalist "one size fits all" approach of many AOD [alcohol and other drug] services is not gender neutral but should be understood as implicitly gendered in that it neglects the specificity of women's needs in relation to abuse, mental illness and parenting' (Salter and Breckenridge, 2014, p 165).

What is clear is that there is a far greater focus on the health and medical issues associated with women's alcohol use, and far less focus on the social issues that have potentially devastating effects on a woman's life. Individuals, families, kinship networks and communities all have the potential both to support and to damage in terms of recovery from substance dependence (Falkin and Strauss, 2003; White, 2008). While some of the wider socioeconomic issues associated with alcohol dependence (such as employment, finance and housing) may now be considered gender neutral, women still have some specific needs, particularly in relation to abuse, vulnerability, mental health and parenting that current treatment services are unequipped to meet (Salter and Breckenbridge, 2014).

Effective treatment for women

There has been some research into what makes an effective treatment service for women with alcohol problems. Some examples include:

- *Women-only services:* services that address barriers such as childcare, and provide women-only groups, abuse counselling and pregnancy support, have all been shown to be important in achieving positive outcomes for women with both drug and alcohol issues (Copeland and Hall, 1992; Copeland et al, 1993; Greenfield et al, 2010).
- *Targeted interventions:* studies have shown that men and women respond to different treatment types (Sanchez-Craig et al, 1989, 1991; Copeland and Hall, 1992; Jarvis, 1992; Beckman, 1994; Liang and Long, 2013) and services should be tailored for gender as a result.
- *Individual and couple counselling:* research into whether women respond better to individual or couple counselling has been carried out. Many women's drinking behaviour is interlinked with that of their partners, and where this is the case, while women express a preference for individual counselling, couple counselling shows better outcomes in terms of days abstinent (McCrady et al, 2009, 2011). However, couple counselling should never be used where there is any suspicion of abuse or control within the relationship,

and individual assessments of each partner separately is essential prior to any proposal to offer joint counselling sessions (see Stella Project Toolkit, developed by AVA (Against Violence & Abuse): www.avaproject.org.uk/our-resources/good-practice-guidance--toolkits/complicated-matters-stella-project-toolkit-and-e-learning-(2013).aspx).

These examples start to create a picture in terms of effective treatment, which while far from comprehensive does suggest that women have very different treatment needs, which respond to different treatment modalities.

Medical aspects of alcohol dependence can be treated in a very short space of time, but this does not resolve the ongoing issue of recovery and re-establishing social capital following problems with alcohol use. In many ways, and with the exception of a few excellent projects targeting particular at-risk groups of women, such as the Stella Project, a 'one size fit all' scenario remains in evidence across our treatment services (Perryman et al, 2011). This is the case despite the government's own Alcohol Strategy (HM Government, 2012) explicitly stating that there is no such thing.

A recovery model

There has been extensive dialogue between research and treatment services in relation to 'recovery'. The definition of 'recovery' has been widely debated in drug, alcohol and mental health services, and it remains a term that has very personal meanings to many service users. What is clear is that recovery is seen as a journey rather than an outcome, and each individual goes through their own process.

One definition that has been influential within the field is that set out by Anthony (1993, p 17), who stated that recovery is 'a deeply personal, unique process of changing one's attitudes, values, feelings, goals, skills and/or roles. It is a way of living a satisfying, hopeful, and contributing life.... Recovery involves the development of new meaning and purpose in one's life.'

While this definition was originally applied to mental health settings, it is highly applicable here, capturing the individual nature of women's struggle and recovery from alcohol dependence.

Understanding recovery capital

There is a current focus on increased social capital as a treatment outcome in both alcohol and drugs services and across mental health (Granfield and Cloud, 2001; Ferlander, 2007; Cloud and Granfield, 2008; Laudet and White, 2008; Shepherd et al, 2008). To date this has neglected to consider the different needs of women in terms of delivery. While the discourse includes a more holistic view of people, treatment services remain focused around medication and pay less attention to the relational needs that a woman may have, and which are often intertwined with her use of alcohol. An example is that women in need of treatment are often outnumbered in peer and recovery support groups, which may not be conducive to engagement. This is particularly so where the women has experienced a history of abusive relationships with men, which may have led to her current levels of drinking. In addition, social anxiety is common, and issues of guilt and shame prevalent, with alcohol misuse having a direct impact on how a woman sees herself, how others perceive her and the social roles and capital available to her (Staddon, 2012).

The concept of 'recovery', and more specifically the role of treatment services in supporting individuals to develop 'recovery capital', has received significant attention over recent years (Granfield and Cloud, 1999). It may be that the experience of women is improving as a result, but the gender blindness noted earlier in this chapter continues to act as a barrier towards achieving this for many women experiencing problems with alcohol.

Recovery capital has been defined as 'the breadth and depth of internal and external resources that can be drawn upon to initiate and sustain recovery from AOD [alcohol and other drug] problems'(Granfield and Cloud, 1999, p 154).

In this context, recovery is seen as a process rather than an end in and of itself. The concept of 'recovery capital' is fundamentally a socially orientated approach, focusing on building strengths and resources in four key areas

Social capital

Social capital is the sum of resources that is ascribed to each person as a result of their relationships, and includes both support from and obligations to groups to which they belong; for example, family membership provides supports but will also demand commitments and obligations to the other family members.

A woman's relationships with family, friends and her community are often inextricably linked with the way she perceives herself. Society places a range of expectations and conflicting demands on women that are different from those experienced by their male counterparts. Women now have access to employment, vocation and recreation in ways that approach that of men (although there is still some way to go to achieve complete equality). What has not been removed is the maternal and caring roles and expectations that women have placed on them as a condition of their social capital. These role conflicts create a high degree of stress in many women: those who maintain both roles will undertake a delicate balancing act on a daily basis, and those who have chosen careers over families find themselves judged (by other women as well as men) in terms of their female identity. Yet those who have chosen families over careers may find themselves socially isolated – particularly in a society in which fewer women choose this option – as well as almost certainly financially dependent on either a partner (usually male) or the state. Each of these positions can have devastating effects on a woman's self-image and identity, giving rise to emotional conflicts and stress, and may often provide the ideal conditions for developing a problem with alcohol.

Physical capital

Physical capital consists of tangible assets such as property and money that may increase recovery options (for example, being willing or able to move away from existing partners, friends or networks).

Those women who have opted for a career and competing with men in the marketplace are likely to have access to physical capital in ways approaching those of their male counterparts, although women's earnings are still effectively less than those of men (Peacock, 2012). In these instances, the resources available to them might include the ability to move into a different job, home and so on. However, where a woman is balancing roles or is dependent on a partner there is an additional complexity to be considered.

A significant proportion of women experiencing alcohol problems may have a history of abusive relationships, domestic violence and childhood abuse, and for these groups the choices available can become extremely limited, and physical capital may not be available, or will be markedly reduced. Issues such as low self-esteem, limited access to resources and both emotional and financial dependency all combine to maintain both the alcohol problem as a coping mechanism and the continued lack of physical capital available to the woman, and in some cases, the abusive partner may seek to control her by the use of alcohol (Galvani and Humphreys, 2007).

Human capital

Human capital includes skills, positive health, aspirations and hopes. Personal resources and resilience are essential ingredients of recovery to enable people to make desired changes to their lives and situations.

Alcohol use has been shown to have a direct impact on women's self-esteem and identity (Lyons and Willmott, 2008; Shinebourne and Smith, 2009) and many women entering services present with additional vulnerabilities (Burman, 1994; La Flair et al, 2012; Tracy et al, 2012). In this context it is likely that while the woman may have retained skills, positive health, aspirations and hopes, she may not recognise them as such, and may have limited personal resources available to her. Building resilience and resources will be a key task and may require a great deal of support. Women's networks and support groups will have a key role to play along with in-depth therapeutic intervention and support. This area may include medical treatment and detoxification and mutual aid groups.

Cultural capital

Cultural capital includes the values, beliefs and attitudes that link to social conformity and the ability to fit into dominant social behaviours (Cloud and Granfield, 2008).

The complex and conflicting social messages, already discussed, place women in a unique cultural position. Each subgroup has its own values, beliefs and attitudes and the ability to fit into dominant social behaviours may include excessive alcohol use while simultaneously creating judgement and self-judgement that serve to sustain hazardous drinking patterns. For recovery to be sustainable this will need to be disentangled and strategies developed to enable women to re-establish cultural capital that supports non-drinking or moderated drinking behaviour.

This type of approach has the potential to improve both the outcomes and experience of women in treatment services. However, in order to achieve this, services will need to develop an explicit acknowledgement of, and response to, the specific needs and contexts of women and the roles they play in communities, and families.

Towards a social approach for women

For treatment services both to attract women and to be effective, the notion of recovery and social capital will need to be considered as it specifically applies to them. It is unlikely that a male-orientated approach will be successful in treating the complexities of female drinking behaviour as it does not acknowledge the myriad of losses that a woman may experience in both physical and practical terms, and the resulting risks that she may face. A gender-neutral approach may not be appropriate to support a woman to become alcohol-free, if indeed this is the goal, and the trend for women to access other sources of support and employ 'natural' recovery strategies would support this view.

In order to achieve a truly inclusive social approach to alcohol treatment that is able to respond to the uniqueness and diversity of female experience, it will be necessary to remove the gender blinkers and explicitly state that men and women are different and have different needs. The model may be the same, but the elements within it need to be specific to women's experiences in order to increase women's engagement with and retention in alcohol treatment. Figure 13.1 illustrates this type of approach.

Our current treatment services offer a limited provision within this model: medication, brief interventions and cognitive behavioural therapy are the common components of current alcohol treatment services. While these can be helpful for some women for some problems, the wider social context of female drinking behaviour needs to be explored within our treatment services in order to support women to develop recovery capital that is specific to their needs, and which ultimately leads to more sustained and meaningful recovery experiences. This may include the development of more women-only services, as has been the case in some mental health services, or may be the development of current delivery models to expand the service response to encompass more of these issues as part of the treatment pathways.

Figure 13.1: A social model of treatment for women

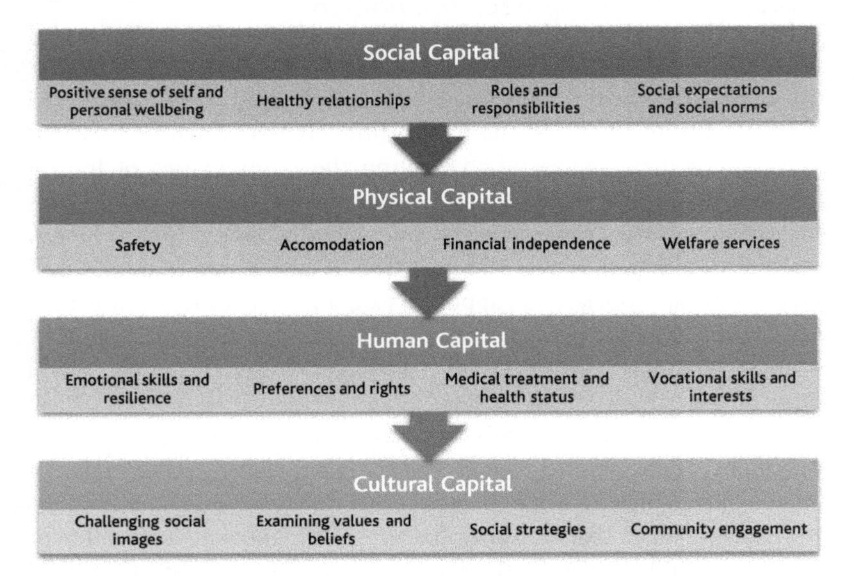

Conclusion

While treatment research and policy espouse the social approach, it appears that many of our treatment services have some way to go before they achieve this. Many services are moving towards recovery orientation; however, the emphasis on gender equality has actually resulted in a gender blindness in some of our health and care services, which means that women's specific needs in many cases are neither acknowledged nor responded to. Commissioners have a specific responsibility and duty of care to ensure that services can respond in a gender-specific way and appropriate attention is given to the needs of women in their local area.

While some women-only services have been developed, these remain scarce, and – while necessary – in and of themselves are not the sole solution, any more than medication and detoxification are. For a social- and recovery-orientated approach to be successful, women need to be responded to as the diverse group that they are, with different views, needs, preferences and beliefs. Role conflicts and complex social relations must be recognised and addressed. There is now a focus on increased social capital as a treatment outcome in both alcohol and drugs services and across mental health (Granfield and Cloud, 2001; Ferlander, 2007; Cloud and Granville, 2008; Laudet and White, 2008; Shepherd et al, 2008). To date this has neglected to consider the different needs of women in terms of delivery and while the discourse includes a more holistic view of people, treatment services remain focused around medication and pay less attention to the relational needs that a woman may have, and which are often intertwined with her use of alcohol. The woman may have experienced a history of abusive relationships with men, leading to her current levels of drinking; social anxiety is common, and issues of guilt and shame prevalent, with alcohol misuse having a direct impact on how a woman sees herself, how others perceive her and the social roles and capital available to her (Staddon, 2012).

The current model of recovery capital needs to take account of the differences that are due to gender, and draw on the evidence relating to women's varying roles in society, in order to ensure that recovery-orientated treatment is able to respond to the complex aetiology of female alcohol use.

What we are effectively striving for is cultural competence, taking gender fully into account. Equality does not mean being the same; it means that services should work with diversity and recognise the value of difference in a way that is currently not evident in many services.

Notes

[1] Editor: but also see McErlain, Chapter Two, this volume – there is some debate about this.

[2] Editor: see also Blackman et al, Chapter Three, this volume.

References

Anthony, W.A. (1993) 'Recovery from mental illness: the guiding vision of the mental health service system in the 1990's', *Psychosocial Rehabilitation Journal*, vol 16, no 4, pp 11-23.

Beckman, L. (1994) 'Treatment needs of women with alcohol problems', *Alcohol Health and Research World*, vol 18, no 3, pp 206-211.

Best, D. and Laudet, A.B. (2010) *The potential of recovery capital*, London: RSA, www.uniad.org.br/desenvolvimento/images/stories/arquivos/The_potential_of_recovery_capital_-_2010.pdf

Briggs, C.A. and Pepperell, L. (2009) *Women, girls and addiction: Celebrating the feminine in counselling treatment and recovery*, New York, NY and Hove: Routledge.

Burman, S. (1994) 'The disease concept of alcoholism: its impact on women's treatment', *Journal of Substance Abuse Treatment*, vol 11, no 2, pp 121-126.

Cloud, W. and Granfield, W. (2008) 'Conceptualising recovery capital: expansion of a theoretical construct', *Substance Use and Misuse*, vol 42, no 12/13, pp 1971-1986.

Copeland, J. and Hall, W. (1992) 'A comparison of women seeking drug and alcohol treatment in a specialist women's and two traditional mixed-sex treatment services', *British Journal of Addictions*, vol 87, no 9, pp 1293- 1302.

Copeland, J., Hall, W., Didcott, P. and Biggs, V (1993) 'A comparison of a specialist women's alcohol and other drug treatment service with two traditional mixed sex services: client characteristics and treatment outcome', *Drug and Alcohol Dependence*, vol 32, no 1, pp 81-92.

Falkin, G.P. and Strauss, S.M. (2003) 'Social supporters and drug use enablers: a dilemma for women in recovery', *Addictive Behaviours*, vol 28, no 1, pp 141-155.

Ferlander, S. (2007) 'The importance of different forms of social capital for health', *Acta Sociologica*, vol 50, no 2, pp 115-128.

Galvani, S. and Humphreys, C. (2007) *The impact of violence and abuse on engagement and retention rates for women in substance use treatment*, London: National Treatment Agency for Substance Misuse.

Granfield, R. and Cloud, W. (1999) *Coming clean: Overcoming addiction without treatment*, New York, NY: NYU Press.

Granfield, R. and Cloud, W. (2001) 'Social context and "natural recovery": the role of social capital in the resolution of drug-associated problems', *Substance Use and Misuse*, vol 36, no 11, pp 1543-1570.

Greenfield, S.F., Back, S.E., Lawson, K. and Brady, K.T. (2010) 'Substance abuse in women', *Psychiatric Clinics of North America*, vol 33, no 2, pp 339-355.

Harvard Medical School (2011) *Alcohol use and abuse: Special report*, Cambridge, MA: Harvard University Press.

HM Government (2012) *The government's alcohol strategy*, Cm 8336, London: The Stationery Office, https://www.gov.uk/government/uploads/system/uploads/attachment_data/file/224075/alcohol-strategy.pdf

HSCIC (Health and Social Care Information Centre) (2013) *Statistics on alcohol, 2012*, www.hscic.gov.uk/pubs/alcohol12IAS

Institute for Alcohol Studies) (2013) *Women and alcohol: Factsheet*, London: IAS, www.ias.org.uk/uploads/pdf/Factsheets/Women%20and%20alcohol%20factsheet%20May%202013.pdf

Jarvis, T.J. (1992) 'Implications of gender for alcohol treatment research: a quantitative and qualitative review', *British Journal of Addiction*, vol 87, no 9, pp 1249-1261.

La Flair, L.N., Bradshaw, C.P., Storr, C.L., Green, K.M., Alvanzo, A.A.H. and Crum, R.M. (2012) 'Intimate partner violence and patterns of alcohol abuse and dependence criteria among women: a latent class analysis', *Journal of Studies on Alcohol and Drugs*, vol 73, no 3, pp 351-360.

Laudet, A.B. and White, W.L. (2008) 'Recovery capital as prospective predictor of sustained recovery, life satisfaction, and stress among former poly-substance users', *Substance Use and Misuse*, vol 43, no 1, pp 27-54.

Liang, B. and Long, M.A. (2013) 'Testing the gender effect in drug and alcohol treatment: women's participation in Tulsa county drug and DUI programs', *Journal of Drug Issues*, vol 43, no 3, pp 270-288.

Lyons, A.C. and Willmott, S. (2008) 'Alcohol consumption, gender identities and women's changing social positions', *Sex Roles*, vol 59, no 9-10, pp 694-712.

McCrady, B.S., Epstein, E.E., Cook, S., Jenson, N. and Hildebrandt, T. (2009) 'A randomized trial of individual and couple behavioural alcohol treatment for women', *Journal of Consulting and clinical Psychology*, vol 77, no 2, pp 243-256.

McCrady, B.S., Epstein, E., Cook, S., Jenson, N.K. and Ladd, B.O. (2011) 'What do women want? Alcohol treatment choices, treatment entry and retention', *Psychology of Addictive Behaviours*, vol 25, no 3, pp 521-529.

Netmums (2013) *Netmums and alcohol: Full survey results*, www.netmums.com/woman/fitness-diet/mums-and-drinking/netmums-and-alcohol-the-full-results/netmums-alcohol-full-survey-results

NICE (2011) *Alcohol-use disorders: diagnosis, assessment and management of harmful drinking and alcohol dependence*, CG115, London: NICE. Available at - http://www.nice.org.uk/guidance/cg115 (accessed 14/09/14)

NTA (National Treatment Agency for Substance Misuse) (October 2012) 'Alcohol statistics from the National Drug Treatment Monitoring System (NDTMS)', *The Telegraph*, 1 March, p 20, table 5.2.1.

Peacock, L. (2012) 'Women earn £500,000 less than men over working lives', *The Telegraph*, 7 November, www.telegraph.co.uk/finance/jobs/9659232/Women-earn-500000-less-than-men-over-working-lives.html

Perryman, K., Rose, A.K., Winfield, H., Jenner, J., Oyefeso, A., Phillips, T.S., Deluca, P., Heriot-Maitland, C., Galea, S., Cheeta, S., Saunders, V. and Drummond, C. (2011) 'The perceived challenges facing alcohol treatment services in England: a qualitative study of service providers', *Journal of Substance Use*, vol 16, no 1, pp 38-49, doi:10.3109/14659891003706399

Salter, M. and Breckenbridge, J. (2014) 'Women, trauma and substance abuse: understanding the experience of female survivors of childhood abuse in alcohol and drug treatment', *International Journal of Social Welfare*, vol 23, pp 165-173, www.academia.edu/3539934/Women_trauma_and_substance_abuse_Understanding_the_experiences_of_female_survivors_of_childhood_abuse_in_alcohol_and_drug_treatment

Sanchez-Craig, M., Leigh, G., Spivak, K. and Lei, H. (1989) 'Superior outcome of females over males after brief treatment for the reduction of heavy drinking', *British Journal of Addiction*, vol 84, no 4, pp 395-404.

Sanchez-Craig, M., Spivak, K. and Davila, R. (1991) 'Superior outcome of females over males after brief treatment for the reduction of heavy drinking: replication and report of therapist effects', *British Journal of Addiction*, vol 86, no 7, pp 867-876.

Shepherd, G., Boardman, J. and Slade, M. (2008) *Making recovery a reality*, London: Sainsbury Centre for Mental Health, www.recoverydevon.co.uk/download/Making_recovery_a_reality.pdf

Shinebourne, P. and Smith, J.A. (2009) 'Alcohol and the self: an interpretative phenomenological analysis of the experience of addiction and its impact on the sense of self and identity', *Addiction Research and Theory*, vol 17, no 2, pp 152-167.

Staddon, P. (2012) 'No blame, no shame: towards a social model of alcohol dependency – a story from emancipatory research', in (eds) *Social care, service users and user involvement: Building on research*, London: Jessica Kingsley Publishers.

Staddon, P. (2013) 'Theorising a social model of "alcoholism": service users who misbehave', in Staddon, P. (ed) *Mental health service users in research: A critical sociological perspective*, Bristol: Policy Press.

Tracy, E.M., Laudet, A.B., Min, M.O., Brown, S., Jun, M.K. and Singer, L. (2012) 'Prospective patterns and correlates of quality of life among women in substance abuse treatment', *Drug and Alcohol Dependence*, vol 124, no 3, pp 242-249.

White, W.L. (2008) 'The mobilization of community resources to support long-term addiction recovery', *Journal of Substance Abuse Treatment*, vol 36, no 2, pp 146-158.

Whitehead, T. (2009) 'Rise of "ladette" culture as 241 women arrested each day for violence', *The Telegraph*, 1 May, www.telegraph.co.uk/news/uknews/law-and-order/5251042/Rise-of-ladette-culture-as-241-women-arrested-each-day-for-violence.html

Conclusion

Patsy Staddon

In the book's Introduction, I stated that the issues regarding alcohol 'misuse' could only be understood with reference to social and environmental factors. In the book, we have seen this perspective develop, through a questioning and refining of terms, and through reference to alternative understandings of the meaning of alcohol use, to suggested policies for addressing women's alcohol use that are consistent with political and feminist understandings. The perspective is tellingly phrased in Chapter Five by Galvani with Toft: 'The job of the professionals is to work to ensure an approach that avoids further victimising and blaming while at the same time provides an empowering, empathic and informed response with safety at its core.'

Support with alcohol issues is seen ideally to be provided outside current treatment services, using women-only peer support (Barnes and Ward, Chapter Six; Staddon, Chapter Twelve) and alternative spaces for minority groups (Serrant, Chapter Seven; Moon and Staddon, Chapter Eight). A women-only, survivor-led helpline is strongly recommended (Staddon, Chapter Twelve). Women's groups within an adult community learning framework (Lewis, Chapter Eleven) and a local 'special space' for women to be helped with alcohol abstention (Fernandez, Chapter Ten) are also suggested, as is a shift within NHS treatment services, whereby women's alcohol use is understood and treated separately (Bogg with Bogg, Chapter Thirteen).

However, the book is not just about recovery; it is also about the meaning of women's alcohol use to the women themselves and about how public reaction to it has shaped conventional treatment. This public reaction is seen to have an historical dimension, whereby shaming has been used as a device to assist in the social control of women (McErlain, Chapter Two). There are additionally misunderstandings, confusion and misrepresentation as regards both the meaning and the extent of young women's drinking (Blackman et al, Chapter Three; Mackiewicz, Chapter Four) and that of older women (Barnes and Ward, Chapter Six). We have also heard how great the damage and significance of domestic abuse are and its considerable relevance to women's drinking (Galvani, Chapter Five). The misunderstandings that have frequently informed alcohol treatment are particularly illustrated in the way that they affect Black Caribbean women (Serrant, Chapter Seven) and lesbian women (Moon and Staddon, Chapter Eight). The consequent anguish and despair, offering however a gleam of hope, are expressed in the auto-ethnographic account by Moon (Chapter Nine).

This background of shame and misrepresentation, still qualified by the hope of better understandings and a more helpful public response, is of immense significance, going far to explain the lack of public sympathy, the deficiencies of the treatment services, and the confusion in laws and government recommendations around alcohol use. Behind them all lies the belief that those who 'misuse' alcohol are 'other', are not like us (Becker, 1963), and need strict control, if not compulsory residential 'treatment' for their own good. This belief is most unfortunately supported by the best-known mutual aid organisation, Alcoholics Anonymous (AA). Far from encouraging problem drinkers to seek explanations and ways of coping with their alcohol use (see Moon, Chapter Nine), AA states that 'we [are] powerless over alcohol' with 'defects of character' that require humility, 'a spiritual awakening' and attempts to '[m]ake direct amends' (Alcoholics Anonymous, 1939). This book's chapters have demonstrated that powerlessness and making amends are frequently not only inappropriate and damaging, but also dangerous (Galvani, Chapter Five). Women need to reclaim their power, not relinquish it. The book suggests that this reclaiming of power over our own lives requires a broader understanding of the meaning of alcohol in different women's lives. As Serrant suggests, and Moon and Staddon acknowledge, different cultures use alcohol differently and a better knowledge of those cultures may transform alcohol knowledge more generally.

Within the book is contained acknowledgement of the important role that alcohol may play in women's lives. Even when problems occur, abstinence is not necessarily the best or the first solution for everyone. Social networks are important to wellbeing and should not be limited to weekly recovery groups. Rather, they need to be developed and extended, and women need to learn ways of negotiating social spaces without detriment to their lives. We see in the book that both younger and older women are putting this into practice, and it is the editor's hope that a day may come when no newcomer to an alcohol treatment centre is advised to cross the road rather than walk past a pub.

References

Alcoholics Anonymous (1939) *The little book*, 2001, New York, NY: Alcoholics Anonymous, reprinted with permission of A.A. World Service, Inc.

Becker, H.S. (1963) *Outsiders: Studies in the sociology of deviance*, New York, NY: The Free Press, 1966.

Subject index

Author index